ARTPOLITIK

Social Anarchist Aesthetics in an
Age of Fragmentation

NEALA SCHLEUNING

Minor Compositions 2013

Artpolitik: Social Anarchist Aesthetics in an Age of
Fragmentation
Neala Schleuning

ISBN 978-1-57027-248-6

Cover design by Haduhi Szukis
Cover image by bildwechsel
Interior design by Margaret Killjoy

Released by Minor Compositions 2013
Wivenhoe / New York / Port Watson

Minor Compositions is a series of interventions & provocations drawing from autonomous politics, avant-garde
aesthetics, and the revolutions of everyday life.

Minor Compositions is an imprint of Autonomedia
www.minorcompositions.info | minorcompositions@
gmail.com

Distributed by Autonomedia
PO Box 568 Williamsburgh Station
Brooklyn, NY 11211

www.autonomedia.org
info@autonomedia.org

CONTENTS

ACKNOWLEDGEMENTS

Thanks to: Nancy Luomala who came up with the title (including a backward K which can't be reproduced typographically), Fred Whitehead, Wayne Nealis, Jeanette Daines, Penelope Rosemont, Maggie Petersen, Jesse Cohn, and other anonymous reviewers for their careful and thoughtful review. A special thank you to Stevphen Shukaitis at Minor Compositions for his interest in and support for this project. Finally, a big thanks to my sister, Carol Radkiewicz, who caught most of my embarrassing grammatical and mechanical errors.

PERMISSIONS

THEODOR ADORNO, *AESTHETIC Theory*, edited by Gretel Adorno and Rolf Tiedemann, newly translated and edited by Robert Hullot-Kentor (English edition published by University of Minnesota Press, 1997, Regents of the University of Minnesota). Original, German-language edition copyright 1970 by Suhrkamp Verlag.

Bob Black, "The Realization and Supression of Situationism."

Guy Debord, *Society of the Spectacle* (1977) (anti-copyright)

Martin Espada, *Poetry Like Bread*, Curbstone, 1994. Lines of poetry from: Martin Espada, "Federico's Ghost;" Ernesto Cardinal, "PeasantWoman from Cua;" Otto Castillo, Untitled;

Margaret Randall, "Immigration Law;" and Claribel Alegria, "From the Bridge."

Ken Knabb, ed. and trans., *Situationist International Anthology* (anti-copyright)

Jude Nutter, *I Wish I had a Heart like Yours*, Walt Whitman University of Notre Dame Press

Raoul Vaneigem, *The Cavalier History of Surrealism*, Donald Nicholson-Smith, translator.

Some of the ideas in this book have been previously explored in review essays published in the journal *Social Anarchism*.

ABOUT THE COVER

COVER IMAGE BY: bildwechsel, a graphic design studio in Berlin, dedicated to cultural, social and political graphic and communication design, print, and other media: image-shift.net.

The cover image was initially designed as a poster for the campaign against the 2001 German residential law. "Free movement is our right," the poster proclaims.

This law, like the former apartheid "Pass laws" in South Africa, was passed in 1982. The law forbids refugees to move freely about in Germany. They are not allowed to leave the local districts where they are confined to living in places in isolated buildings, often in the woods and isolated city areas under permanent surveillance. They must apply for permission to travel from the Foreign Office, which forbid the movement of refugees. They have to pay administration fees for an application for traveling permission. They have to pay these fees from their meager monthly social allowances of 80 deutschmark. The fees are not refunded even in the case of a rejection of permission. This situation pushes them to cross their district borders "illegally," resulting in greater police control, criminalization and illegality. The last consequence of illegality is the deportation of refugees through isolation and confinement in deportation prisons.

CHAPTER 1

INTRODUCTION: **THE NATURE OF ART**

> *Art is not cozy and it is not mocked. Art tells the*
> *only truth that ultimately matters. It is the light*
> *by which human things can be mended. And after*
> *Art there is, let me assure you all, nothing.1*

INTRODUCTION

THIS STUDY BEGINS AT THE END OF THE NINETEENTH CENTURY
with the rise of a sweeping aesthetic movement called
Modernism. It focuses on the relationship between visual
art and politics over the course of the twentieth century
as articulated by several key radical aesthetic movements.
During the same time period, the capitalist mode of unbridled production and consumption achieved ascendency.
Capitalist production, in turn, was augmented by the growing impact of mass communication media which fueled its
ethos of over-consumption. Art was quickly appropriated
and put in service to the capitalist economy. It was de-my-
thologized and stripped of meaning, and the re-constructed
image moved out of the museums and the cathedrals into the
daily lives of people via mass communication media – into
movie theatres, onto the streets, into people's living rooms.

---

1   Iris Murdoch, *The Black Prince* (London: Penguin, 1975), 416.

This study focuses on the representational visual arts as opposed to other art forms such as literature, music, and performance. There are several reasons for privileging the visual. First, vision is our most important sense. It is how we initially apprehend the world. To make sense of our visual environment, we collectively create symbolic constructions of meaning. These representations have a powerful social function, bringing people together in a meaningful social reality. Packed into these representations are layers of meaning, feelings, affects, hopes, and dreams. Second, representational visual art has had the most powerful impact in the contemporary world. As the twentieth century progressed, the world was awash in visual imagery, and the images took on an increasingly significant role in shaping the reality in which we all live. In such an environment, it becomes even more important to understand the nature of imagery, of its impact on our lives, and of how we might play a greater role in controlling and countering the images that surround us. It is in the world of visual representation that the battle for the hearts and minds of people must be fought and won. This emphasis on the visual arts, however, does not preclude considerations of other art forms. The aesthetic concepts discussed in these pages are applicable to many different art forms, and all artists will benefit from the subsequent discussions.

We live in a visually artful world. Our fascination with form, shape, color, light, and visual texture begins at birth. As we grow, the external world takes on increasingly subtle distinctions. A small child discovers a flower and may try to eat it; the adult appreciates its beauty. We buy a new car, and it pleases our senses. We see our first mountain, and something happens that has never happened before. We sit for hours and contemplate the Sistine Chapel ceiling. I see the face of my beloved and call it exquisite. Can we call all of these experiences aesthetic? What is art? How do we know?

We also live with others in a political world. We work together to shape the world around us – for ourselves and for others. We gather and make decisions in our neighborhoods, in our places of work, in our nation, in the world. We decide to help one another or to allow competition to determine our relationships. We spend our money on war or on health care. We debate intensely; or we are indifferent, allowing others to think for us. We vote. Or, we don't.

Historically, works of art expressed broad social interests and concerns, presumed a social function, and interacted with a wide audience. The making of art was a social activity, involving both the individual artist and the larger community. An icon, for example, was not just a religious picture. It carried in its representation hopes, dreams, and prayers; messages of actions to be taken; the lives and histories of individuals and communities; psychological states of feeling; and the experience of past and future affective states. In medieval Russia, for example, icons were carried into battle to ensure victory with their power. Art had a social task; that was its power. To create a work of art is to represent existing and potential social realities, to realize collective acts and dreams.

Art can also energize action in the political arena. Traditionally, representational art invested the material world with meaning. Throughout history works of art represented a variety of political messages: heroic bronze statues of mounted soldiers in full armor, early photographs of captains of industry standing astride railroad tracks with factory smokestacks in the background, and paintings of great battles celebrating military victories. Dorothea Lange's stark photographic images brought home the realities of poverty. Rolling up her sleeves, Rosie the Riveter mobilized the home front in the United States during World War II, along with similar images in German and Russian propaganda. In Germany films were used to fuel anti-Semitic feelings; in America they offered an escape from the realities of the Great Depression. In the 1960's the symbol of a raised fist signaled a call to rebellion around the world. Since the 1960s, the raised fist has inspired and motivated generations of political activists.

The desire to shape external reality in meaningful ways is a basic human impulse. It is how we make our lived experience concrete and give it meaning.[2] This meaning is often materialized in objects including works of art. Creating meaning is how we bring order out of the chaos of images and impressions assaulting our senses. It is how we make sense of the material world; comprehend and organize past, present, and future time; and understand the world around us. Art gives us a way to *place* meaning, to bring things, places, and ideas to life. Art is a kind of naming: naming something creates a symbol which can incorporate many levels of individual and collective expression. Symbols are rich packets of information that distill dense contexts of experience. Through this process of symbolic created meaning we communicate with one another and find common ground, a collective sense of community, a shared meaning.

Similarly, politics is a mechanism for sharing symbols and affirming collective meaning. Art and politics are two of the most powerful mechanisms for visioning, for inventing our future. Together, they hold the key to determining what kind of world we will create. In the following pages I will explore how politics can – or should – inform art; and, similarly, in what ways art can – or should – inform politics. I will examine such questions as: How do we convey political messages visually? How do we put imagination, desire, and determination to work to enable the realization of symbolic messages of freedom and future hopes and dreams? What role will art play in addressing the critical challenges of the twenty-first century?

2   For an excellent discussion of the creation of visual meaning see Sut Jhally, *The Codes of Advertising: Fetishism and the Political Economy of Meaning in the Consumer Society* (New York, NY: St. Martin's Press, 1987).

REASONS FOR WRITING THIS BOOK

I LOVE ART, but I am not an artist; I am not an art critic. But, the visual has always fascinated me. I love the play of stories, images, and techniques as they work together to make visual art. And so, I began this effort to understand art and why it "worked" on my senses, on my mind, on my heart. I am also a student of politics. For the past forty years, I have studied the history of politics and political philosophy; and I have explored a range of visions about how we live politically. These philosophies were written visions; and while these word images were compelling, a picture, it is said, is worth a thousand words. Over many years I have come to believe that art and politics have much to inform each other and that they have a mutual agenda: to make our lives and our world a fit place to live for all people. We accomplish these goals through developing and implementing effective artistic and political mechanisms for social change.

To further narrow the focus, this book will explore a particular type of political activity – the theories that inspired the radical, progressive political movements and built upon socialist, communist, and anarchist political agendas. The study is not exhaustive. It does not explore specific works of art; it does not claim to be a definitive history of art. Instead, it focuses on the most influential political and aesthetic ideas that inspired the art that energized social change and the creation of new worlds through protest: Dada, Surrealism, Socialist Realism, the Situationist International (SI), and certain strains of postmodern aesthetics. I also wanted to understand how political activists in various times chose particular artistic tools and aesthetic elements to convey their political agendas and to shape public opinion. To my mind it was not a question of whether a particular approach to art is an artistic movement or a political movement but of how the two inform one another – whether we think of a political aesthetic and/or an aesthetic politics. Does art, in the final analysis, "matter" in the political context? And if it does matter, why and how does it "work" to effectively convey a political message? How, then, is vision put to the service of our desires?

In the beginning there is vision – our most powerful sense and our primary way of knowing the world. But, the visual environment is chaotic; the world around us is a restless sea of movement. What captures (a word I consciously use) our visual attention is movement; what holds our attention is interesting movement. We watch for movement and then focus our attention. One can define art by this capacity to gain and to hold our attention.

Imagery and images are shaped by the world around us, and these images have power. Further, I believe that our culture is in the midst of a profound transition from a print to a richer visual mode of communication. Currently, the control of mass distribution of images is in the hands of very few media corporations, and these media serve non-progressive forces worldwide. This situation is a political problem. These highly controlled images are designed in a calculated way to move us, to manipulate our emotions, to get us to think a certain way, to buy certain "stuff," and to come to certain political conclusions. Understanding the construction and the use of images in politics should be a central mission in the radical community.

The making of art is a special, consciously constructed kind of social activity. Art can change the world. It can change minds, hearts, and perspectives and it can create new values, new social realities. Only through a deep understanding of how imagery and images affect us can we sort out and then create an alternative, more humane, and nourishing reality.

In the early twentieth century there were many actors competing to shape the political landscape by corralling the powers of art and artistic representation. The Industrial Workers of the World (IWW) used popular music, posters, and flyers to challenge corporate and state power over workers' lives; posters encouraging United States involvement in World War I were publicly displayed; and newspapers and magazines published political cartoons. Beginning in the 1920's the expanding mass media made the ability to communicate to and manipulate people on a broad scale much easier. The German National Socialist Workers' Party (Nationalsozialistische Deutsche Arbeiterpartei – Nazi) movement created gigantic spectacles and used the radio and newsreels to spread its propaganda; the Soviet government dictated Socialist Realism; and capitalism developed a highly sophisticated advertising aesthetic to promote endless cycles of consumerism.[3] Propaganda works and art works, but everyone interested in social change should understand how the aesthetic and narrative techniques make them effective. This is not to say that political actors should "use" art only to convey a pre-packaged message (which is what Socialist Realism did and what advertising does); they should also recognize the pivotal role that individual artists play, bringing their own special visions to analyzing the old culture and imagining the new. The viewer has an active role, too. Communication through art is an interactive process. In true art the visions of artists are social visions bringing together the skills and personal perspectives of the artist and

---

3   In an essay entitled "The Engineering of Consent," Edward L. Bernays (often referred to as the father of public relations) discussed the relationship between what he determined was the Constitutional right of persuasion and the emerging mass media which "provide open doors to the public mind." ... A certain naivety can be recognized in his works. "The engineering of consent is the very essence of the democratic process, the freedom to persuade and suggest. ... The engineer must be wary of subversion of the process, however: "He must apply his energies to mastering the operational know-how of consent engineering, and to out-maneuvering his opponents in the public interest." Edward L. Bernays, The Engineering of Consent, *The Annals of the American Academy of Political and Social Science* 250, 1947, 113, 114, 115.

the aspirations and dreams of the people. How will the viewer perceive the work of art, the political message?

A necessary attribute of both politics and art is adaptability: to cultures, to time periods, to specific political settings, to specific communities. Thus, the responses of the Bolsheviks in 1917, the surrealists in 1924, and the communists in the 1930s are different from the response of the Situationist International in 1968. But, the same impulse – imagining a better world – guided them all. The sense of excitement, the creativity of "newness," and visionary responsiveness are the source of political change and of art as well.

Finally, I hope to encourage readers to engage in dialogue about political aesthetics. We cannot simply default to the fantasies of the surrealists, the party line of the socialist realists, the clever challenges to advertising by the situationists, or the despair and meaninglessness of most postmodern aesthetics. An ongoing discussion of the synergy between art and politics is crucial.

FROM A WRITTEN TO A VISUAL CULTURE

READING AND WRITING are relatively new means of communication. Until the invention of printing, the skills of reading and writing were largely confined to a small elite class of writers, philosophers, and theologians. Prior to the spread of universal written communication, oral transmission of knowledge was the predominant form of communication. Epic narratives were memorized and transmitted from one individual to another in a long tradition of collective memory. Since the early part of the twentieth century, the United States (and much of the developed world) has been gradually shifting from a written to a visual culture. Historian and social critic Morris Berman noted in *The Twilight of American Culture*, that today "of the 158 countries in the United Nations, the United States ranks forty-ninth in literacy. Roughly 60 percent of the adult population has never read a book of any kind; and only 6 percent reads as much as one book a year, where book is defined to include Harlequin romances and self-help manuals. Something like 120 million adults are illiterate or read at no better than a fifth-grade level."[4] If we are, indeed, shifting to a visual culture, the future challenge for political art will be how to communicate and incorporate feelings, emotions and imaginations that express the complexity, subtlety, and nuances of political ideas. Compounding these challenges is the shortening of attention spans as new technologies stream endless amounts of information. The sheer volume of visual media and its omnipresence in contemporary culture present major problems for the organization of ideas, for making sense of the visual world around us and for interpreting complex ideas.

Among the many studies of the transition toward a more visual culture, an essay entitled, "Twilight of the Books: What Will Life Be Like if People Stop Reading?" merits attention. Author Caleb Crain's thesis warrants careful examination because of its bleak conclusions. Crain began with some sobering data: in 1955, reading consumed 21 percent of people's time; by 1995 that number had dropped to nine percent.[5] Crain's essay outlined the theories of Walter J. Ong who "speculated that television and similar media are taking us into an era of 'secondary orality,' akin to the primary orality that existed before the emergence of text."[6] The transmission of information orally had significant shortcomings, according to Crain. He examined Eric A. Havelock's contention that cultures where memorization is the primary means to preserve and to perpetuate a culture's idea set may have come at

4   Morris Berman, *The Twilight of American Culture: Ideas of Creativity in Western Culture* (New York, NY: W.W. Norton, 2000), 26.

5   Caleb Crain, "Twilight of the Books: What Will Life Be Like if People Stop Reading?", *The New Yorker*, December 24 & 31, 2007, 135.

6   Crain, 137.

a significant price: "Enormous powers of poetic memorization could be purchased only at the cost of total loss of objectivity." Havelock speculated that this contention may have been why Plato was suspicious of poets because they were subject to emotional rather than rational ways of knowing.[7] Crain concluded that information is processed differently in written and oral cultures: "Whereas literates can rotate concepts in their minds abstractly, orals embed their thoughts in stories." According to Ong, "in an oral culture, 'cliché and stereotype are valued as accumulations of wisdom, and analysis is frowned upon for putting those accumulations at risk.'"[8]

If Ong is correct in assuming that careful, rational analysis will be secondary to simplistic, formulaic communication of ideas, political discourse will be profoundly compromised. Crain warned that instead of a personal engagement with ideas themselves, politics will increasingly focus on the person communicating the ideas.

> Streaming media give actual pictures and sounds instead of mere descriptions of them. ... Moving and talking images are much richer in information about a performer's appearance, manner, and tone of voice. ... The viewer may not catch all the details of a candidate's health-care plan, but he has a much more definite sense of her as a personality, and his response to her is therefore likely to be more full of emotion. ... Emotional responsiveness to streaming media harks back to the world of primary orality, and, as in Plato's day, the solidarity amounts almost to a mutual possession. ... And so in a culture of secondary orality, we may be less likely to spend time with ideas we disagree with.

---

7   Eric A. Havelock, in Crain, 137.
8   Crain, 138.

Self-doubt, therefore, becomes less likely. In fact, doubt of any kind is rarer.[9]

In *The Gutenberg Elegies: The Fate of Reading in an Electronic Age*, Sven Birkerts argued that as we move into the ever-more sophisticated electronic multimedia age (which is, by and large, a visual experience), there are losses and gains to ways of knowing. Deficiencies included the loss of depth, duration, attention span (what he calls "a fragmented sense of time"); the fragmentation of meaning resulting in "a shattered faith in institutions and in the explanatory narratives that formerly gave shape to subjective experience;" the loss of a sense of history, a disconnection from community and a sense of place; and perhaps most significant, "an absence of any strong vision of a personal or collective future."[10] Despite his concerns about the contemporary world, Birkerts acknowledged important positive features our electronic world brings to our understanding. These features include "an increased awareness of the 'big picture,' a global perspective that admits the extraordinary complexity of interrelations, ... an expanded neural capacity, an ability to accommodate a broad range of stimuli simultaneously," a greater sense of tolerance, and a "willingness to try new situations."[11]

Since I first began thinking about how the transition from writing to visual means of communication might change the communication of political ideas, many books and articles have raised similar concerns about how all learning will change to respond to the new medium of communication. Web designer Andreas Viklund shared these concerns: "Obviously we are still a writing culture, but ... It seems to me that writing has started to be more and more affixed to images, as opposed to the other way

9   Crain, 139.
10 Sven Birkerts, *The Gutenberg Elegies: The Fate of Reading in an Electronic Age* (New York, NY: Fawcett Columbine, 1994), 27.
11 Birkerts, 27.

around, and that this is a step in the direction of an imag-
istic culture."[12]

The implications of this shift will certainly have a profound effect on the national discourse, according to Crain.

> But if, over time, many people choose tele-
> vision over books, then a nation's conversa-
> tion with itself is likely to change. A reader
> learns about the world and imagines it differ-
> ently from the way a viewer does; according to
> some experimental psychologists, a reader and
> a viewer even think differently. If the eclipse
> of reading continues, the alteration is likely to
> matter in ways that aren't foreseeable.[13]

Obviously, there are important implications for the future of politics and for the future of communication of political ideas.

CLASSICAL AESTHETICS: THE CASE FOR MEANING

THE QUESTIONS RAISED in this book are not new. The role
of art in culture and the relationship of art to politics have
been persistent themes in western philosophy across millennia, beginning with the Greeks. Although classical
ideas about aesthetics, art, and beauty have been largely
ignored and even rejected by contemporary philosophers,
I will briefly explore the classical tradition to re-consider
some of the dropped threads of classical aesthetic arguments. In particular, the importance of meaning in aesthetics has changed profoundly in the modern world.

Art, in the classical tradition, had a specific purpose
and outcome. It meant something beyond the art itself.
Aesthetics and philosophy were deeply entwined. It is important to point this linkage out because in the modern

---

12 Andreas Viklund, "Adorno, Barthes, and Benjamin." http://andyw.
    wordpress.com/2007/03/28/adorno-barthes-and-benjamin/
13 Crain, 135.

era, aesthetics has consciously been separated from larger questions of collective meaning and purpose. In the modern era, art speaks for itself; it is its own category of knowledge and makes its own rules. It claims no intrinsic meaning beyond itself. Most pre-modern aesthetics, on the other hand, was grounded in a coherent metaphysics that served as a standard for evaluating the relative merits of art and the aesthetic experience. Art was to have a specific purpose: to focus on some determined end and to reflect collective meaning.

For centuries the concept of beauty dominated the philosophical and aesthetic dialogue in western culture. The idea of beauty was linked to other larger truths such as the good and the true. From the classical philosophers of Plato, Aristotle, and Plotinus, through the Christian era, and to a lesser extent into the modern era via the Hegelian philosophers, the discussion focused on what the purpose of art was vis a vis beauty and how we were to recognize beauty in art. The task of the artist was in many ways predetermined; art was to reflect some agreed-upon standard and objective, and artists were called to place their talents at the service of a metaphysical or theological ideal. However, beginning with the Renaissance, through the romantic era, and into the modern era, the roles of art and the artist changed. The inspiration for art and beauty was increasingly attributed to the private visions of individual artists, and by the late nineteenth century the importance of these personal visions came to dominate the aesthetic dialogue.[14]

In Plato's philosophy the good, the true, and the beautiful existed in fixed and timeless ideas called the Forms. The Forms were perfect patterns of ideal states which were permanent and immutable. The real world was a less-than-perfect copy of the Forms. For Plato, art had one purpose – to articulate the Form of the beautiful. Through the contemplation of art, the soul could approach the ideal Form

---

14 See Emmanuel Kant's writings on aesthetics.

of beauty. According to contemporary critic Jackson
Lears, idealists like Plato sought to find the metaphysical
ultimate in beauty: "Like seekers of religious experience,
worshipers at the shrine of beauty aimed to reconnect
body and soul, self and world, by turning a particular form
of experience into a stand-in for the whole – or at least a
path to wholeness."[15]

There is an erotic aspect of beauty in Plato's philosophy that borders on an almost passionate religious love of
the Forms: "The fourth and last kind of madness, which is
imputed to him who, when he sees the beautiful of earth,
is transported with the recollection of the true beauty; ...
And I have shown this of all inspirations to be the noblest
and highest and the offspring of the highest to him who
has or shares in it, and that he who loves the beautiful is
called a lover because he partakes of it."[16] This *eros* is the
desire to participate in the Form of beauty. Plato's dialogue
Symposium includes a long exchange with Diotima (his
professed teacher) about the source of the love of beauty.
The dialogue moves from a discussion of the desire to possess beauty, to the desire to procreate, to finally come to
know the ideal of beauty: "But what if man had eyes to see
the true beauty – the divine beauty, I mean, pure and clear
and unalloyed, not clogged with the pollutions of mortal-
ity and all the colors and vanities of human life – thither
looking, and holding converse with the true beauty simple
and divine?"[17]

Plato was more interested in the idea of beauty as a
search for metaphysical meaning than he was in the material manifestations and products of art. He was skeptical

15 Jackson Lears, "Keeping It Real," rev. of *Songs of Experience: Modern
American and European Variations on a Universal Theme* by Martin Jay,
The Nation, June 12, 2006, 28.

16 Plato, *Phaedrus*, para 249, in *Philosophies of Art and Beauty: Selected
Readings in Aesthetics from Plato to Heidegger*, eds. Albert Hofstadter
and Richard Kuhns (New York, NY: Modern Library, 1964), 60.

17 Plato, *Symposium*, para 211, in *Philosophies of Art and Beauty*, 77.

of art for a variety of reasons: art paid attention to appearances rather than the ideal of the Forms; art distracted people from adoring the ideal; and it appealed to uncontrollable passions. In the *Ion* he observed, "[A]ll good poets, epic as well as lyric, compose their beautiful poems not by art, but because they are inspired and possessed."[18] The political implications of Plato's position are obvious; unruly passions that artists set free can disrupt an orderly society and must be closely controlled.

Plato was so wary of the power of art that in his treatise outlining an ideal society, *The Republic*, he outlawed poets and poetry because poetry stirred the passions in a negative way. In Book II he called for outright censorship of the arts: "Then the first thing will be to establish a censorship of the writers of fiction, and let the censors receive any tale of fiction which is good, and reject the bad; and we will desire mothers and nurses to tell their children the authorized ones only. ... [M]ost of those which are now in use must be discarded."[19] In Book III, he argued that art was merely imitative of the Forms and, as such, was inferior. Art, therefore, must be banned: "Poetry and mythology are, in some cases, wholly imitative. ... And therefore when any one of these pantomimic gentlemen, who are so clever that they can imitate anything, come to us, and make a proposal to exhibit himself and his poetry, we will fall down and worship him as a sweet and holy and wonderful being; but we must also inform him that in our State such as he are not permitted to exist; the law will not allow them."[20] In Book X he shared similar concerns about the visual artists.

Following in Plato's footsteps, Aristotle moved away from Plato's transcendent idealism toward a more balanced relationship between the ideal and the real worlds,

---

18 Plato, *Ion*, para 533 in *Philosophies of Art and Beauty*, 54.

19 Plato, *The Republic*, Book II. http://ww.classics.mit.edu/Plato/republich.html

20 Plato, *The Republic*, Book III. http://ww.classics.mit.edu/Plato/republich.html

between the idea of beauty and the products of art. The idea of balance he called the Mean: "We often say of good works of art that it is not possible either to take away or to add anything, implying that excess and defect destroy the goodness of works of art, while the Mean preserves it."[21] For Aristotle, beauty was not laid up in the abstract Forms but was found in the work of art itself. Like Plato, Aristotle believed that art was imitative but that imitation was a natural human trait: "This is why people enjoy looking at pictures: one consequence of their looking is that they learn and realize what each thing is, e.g., 'this is so-and-so.' If a person has not previously seen the original, his pleasure will not be caused by the imitation, but will be because of the execution of the color or some such reason."[22]

Unlike Plato, Aristotle was far more accepting of the passions, believing that art could be used to teach valuable moral lessons. For example, works of art could be designed to instill pity or fear in order to purge excess passions by a process he called *katharsis*. In the *Poetics*, Aristotle outlined the elements of an ideal tragedy that would induce catharsis. He emphasized the need for a coherent narrative plot and a focus on action by well-developed characters: "Plot is the imitation of the action. ... [T]he point and purpose of the story is a particular kind of action, not a quality. ... Plot, then, is the starting point, the soul as it were, of tragedy; and character comes next. A similar situation exists in painting: a confused mess of the most attractive colors will not give as much pleasure as a likeness in black and white."[23] The narrative should be both complex and compelling, such that it will be remembered as a whole.

Neo-Platonist philosopher Plotinus developed a metaphysic of art that had a strong influence on subsequent

---

21 Aristotle, *Nicomachean Ethics*, 1106:10, in *Philosophies of Art and Beauty*, 83.

22 Aristotle, *Poetics*, Part IV, http://classics.mit.edu//Aristotle/poetics.html

23 Aristotle, *Poetics*, Part VI.

Christian religious art and on later idealist philosophers. Like Plato, Plotinus posited ideal Forms: "We hold that all the loveliness of this world comes by communion in Ideal-Form. ... And Beauty, this Beauty which is also The Good, must be posed as The First: directly deriving from this First is the Intellectual-Principle which is pre-eminently the manifestation of Beauty."[24] For Plotinus, beauty required a quality of wholeness that was "symmetrical and patterned. ... Only a compound can be beautiful, never anything devoid of parts; and only a whole; the several parts will have beauty, not in themselves, but only as working together to give a comely total."[25]

Representational art conveying higher meaning and transcendent purpose continued to be the dominant aesthetic for thousands of years. Christian church art was enshrined in every cathedral and small church. Images told the stories of the Christian message and Biblical truths in highly realistic styles. In some sects three dimensional art took up the same message; in others like the Russian Orthodox Church, religious symbolism was primarily two dimensional. Religious images played an extremely powerful role in communicating ideas to the general public. In recognition of the power of Catholic imagery, one of the first things Reformation sects did was reject that iconography, adopting plain architecture and direct oral communication.

The importance of meaning in art persisted into the modern era. Nearly two millennia later, German philosopher George Wilhelm Friedrich Hegel continued the philosophical tradition linking art to idealism, bringing to the discussion his own ideas about the ongoing relationship between idea and matter as the spirit moves toward what he called the Absolute Idea. Art was the sensuous manifestation of this Absolute. While Hegel technically is

---

24 Plotinus, *Ennead I*, Sixth Tractate, "Beauty," para 6, in *Philosophies of Art and Beauty*, 143 and 147.

25 Plotinus, *Ennead I*, Sixth Tractate, "Beauty," 1, 141, 142.

a "modern" thinker, his ideas harkened back to Platonic idealism. He wrote: "The philosophical idea of the beautiful ... must combine ... metaphysical universality with the determinate content of real particularity."[26]

> Fine art is not art ... until it is also thus free, and its *highest* function is only then satisfied when it has established itself in a sphere where it shares with religion and philosophy. ... [F]ine art supplies a key of interpretation to the wisdom and religion of peoples. ... This is an attribute which art shares in common with religion and philosophy.[27]

ART, POLITICS, AND AESTHETICS IN THE MODERN ERA

THE TRANSITION TO the modern era had profound implications for aesthetics. The cultural shifts in philosophy, industrialization processes, science, new modes of mass communication, and rapid urbanization were manifested in modernist artistic practice and theory. Traditional aesthetic theories came under increasing criticism and fell out of favor. Idealist philosophies were swept aside in the path of materialist and pragmatic ways of knowing. The concept of beauty (or any other absolutist idea) along with the expectation of meaning in art was summarily rejected. Increasingly, art was defined as autonomous, freed up from the constraints of specific meaning or larger purposes that metaphysics or theology proscribed. Instead, modern art proposed its own standard – art for art's sake. Human psychology and personality played a central role in the modernist vision and the inner world of the individual artist increasingly took precedence over socially engaged art. Style, technique, and subject

---

26 George *Wilhelm* Friedrich Hegel, "The Philosophy of Fine Art," Introduction, II, in *Philosophies of Art and Beauty*, 395.
27 George Wilhelm Friedrich Hegel, "The Philosophy of Fine Art," Introduction, I, in *Philosophies of Art and Beauty*, 388.

matter were left undefined and constant exploration and experimentation were embraced. All of these tendencies defined the emerging aesthetic of what came to be known as Modernism.

Politics, too, underwent dramatic changes in the transition to the modern era. The ideologies of progressivism, communism, and anarchism all clashed with traditional and conservative views of power and authority, with the abuses of capitalist production, and with the persisting hegemony of the church. In all of the aesthetic movements to be examined in this study, a series of political issues had to be resolved: (1) the role of ideology and propaganda in works of art, (2) the internal conflicts between competing ideologies and agendas – in particular anarchism and communism, (3) the fragmentation of postmodern politics and aesthetics; and (4) the role of the state in shaping and controlling aesthetics.

While the transition from classical to modern aesthetics and politics was a profound shift, even more significant was the transformation in the relationship *between* art and politics. The battle shifted to competing modernisms as one experimental model after another sought its particular aesthetic niche and promoted its unique voice. In the absence of any dominant aesthetic in Modernism, artists were left to seek the elusive relationship between art and politics on their own. At the center of the story of twentieth century political aesthetics was the struggle between an emerging capitalist consumer aesthetic and the various political and aesthetic rebellions against that hegemony. A succession of self-conscious radical aesthetic movements emerged, all of which have had a lasting impact on radical political aesthetics: Dada, Surrealism, Socialist Realism, Lettrism, the Situationist International, and most recently, neo-Dada and postmodern critical theory. Each was central to shaping the twentieth century response to traditional aesthetics and capitalist aesthetics and each attempted to carve out a self-conscious political role for art. Each, in turn, was shaped by its predecessors and developed its own response to the issues raised by its unique cultural and political milieu.

Dada and Surrealism were the first modernist movements to challenge classical aesthetics and to explicitly raise the question of the relation of art to politics. Dada called into question the entire role of art as representation, and rejected an ideological articulation of the movement's aesthetic approach. In many ways, the Dada artists prepared the foundation for later postmodernist anarchist aesthetics. They challenged not only the content and making of art, but the meaning of art itself and its relationship to the political world. They redefined the role of art to demand personal artistic autonomy; to insist upon autonomy for art itself as a precondition for a politicized art; and to actively engage the artist in the task of bringing art into everyday life. According to Gavin Grindon, "For the Dadaists, the artist-organizer was replaced by the artist-agitator, whose symbolic assault on culture also had precedents in social movement practices, most recently in suffragette attacks on art during 1914."[28]

Surrealist ideas presented a template for a more conservative, ideological approach to politics and art. Like the Dadaists, they made a case for the preeminence of the individual artist's vision, rejecting the bourgeois aesthetic of the mainstream art community. They highlighted the role of imagination in political change; they challenged traditional techniques and styles, and they consciously rejected realism, calling instead for a sur-realism.

Socialist Realism revived the argument for the importance of realism and the personal narrative in art and reasserted the centrality of community in shaping aesthetic style and meaning. The socialist realists celebrated the connection of art to people's real lives, and they were the

28 Gavin Grindon, "Surrealism, Dada, and the Refusal of Work: Autonomy, Activism, and Social Participation in the Radical Avant-Garde," *Oxford Art Journal* 34, 1, 90.

first to consciously apply defined aesthetic techniques and styles in political propaganda efforts aimed at a mass market and using modern mass communication media.

The Situationist International (SI) narrowed and sharpened the focus of art's political role by developing an incisive critique of capitalist consumer aesthetics and the impact of these images on shaping the culture as whole. They developed the central concept of the spectacle to explain the hegemony of political and aesthetic control undergirding contemporary society. Where Socialist Realism focused its political message on the political power structures, the SI focused on the cultural mechanisms of control through mass communication media.

Postmodern anarchist aesthetics privileges the performative through the seamlessly merger of art and politics, to create new, living realities, and to emphasize the shared making of art and political change. Performative art is also consistent with anarchist principles of direct action and autonomous expression. Further, performance is proposed as a way to remain free of the hegemony of the structures of global power, and the control of representation by the mass media.

Less clear is the impact of the ever-shifting contributions of more recent critical theory in responding to the challenges of the contemporary era. Postmodernist aesthetics is, in many ways a continuation of the early Dada modernist agenda and is often referred to as neo-Dadaism. It rejects the notion of a fixed ideological mission for art; it is committed to art as action, and it is deeply committed to autonomy for the individual artist. More than Dada, it emphasizes participatory activities. It does not appear to have a coherent theory or a consistent, predictable practice, celebrating, instead, the fragmentation of the postmodern word. It also lacks a commitment to a concise political meaning. In many ways it can be interpreted as a warmed-over Modernism, in that it seeks only to reconstitute the fragments of the existing reality. Its contributions to the spirit of exploration cannot be minimized, however, as postmodern art is continually moving into new arenas of communication.

All of these aesthetic movements struggled with multiple conflicting challenges in questions of style, content, and meaning. Each had to resolve the dialectical[29] tensions between past and present, old and new, traditional and avant-garde. These tensions included the following themes – each of which will be examined in the context of the radical aesthetic movements under study: (1) the relationship between the expectations of traditional aesthetics and the desire for dramatic change, including making decisions about techniques, subject matter and purpose, and the unresolved debate over the role of meaning in art; (2) the relationship between art and community, including resolving questions of the artist's role in community and the relationship between individual artistic freedom and socially responsive art; (3) the influence of the emergence of multiple mass communication techniques on the dissemination of art; and (4) the role of capital in influencing aesthetic design and intent.

These debates over the nature of art and politics did not take place in a linear fashion; they took place sometimes simultaneously, sometimes serendipitously. The various approaches were neither discrete nor conclusive. The questions raised by these movements persist into our own era. Each incorporates in its own way the modernist commitment to change and rebellion. Each then took different paths. Each movement and its critics will be examined closely with an eye to evaluating the strengths and weaknesses of each and building on those strengths. While all of these movements focused on different concerns, they informed one another in many significant ways; and

---

29 The term "dialectical" is used here, and throughout, in the sense of interactivity and even clashing of ideas to spark new directions. It is not used in the Hegelian sense of dialectically moving to the realization of a higher order of idealist authority..

collectively they have continued the tradition of bringing art and politics into a meaningful dialogue to change the course of the modern world. Together these radical aesthetic movements also provided the background for an emerging social anarchist aesthetic.

The book concludes with an examination of contemporary social anarchist aesthetic ideas. It offers ways to re-conceptualize the aesthetic/political debate and calls for a dynamic realism that builds on the strengths of twentieth century political and aesthetic movements. Questions to be explored include:

1. The political role of art: Whether art should be political; and if so, in what way? Should art convey a conscious political message to educate, to shape, to manipulate, to inspire? In what ways should art be political?

2. The source of inspiration for art: Should art reflect the social experience of the people or the visions of the individual artist?

3. The role of the artist: Is the artist a visionary of the future, and should we entrust the artist with this role? Does the artist have a social responsibility to reflect the culture as a whole, or should the artist's private vision determine the role of the artist?

4. The content and techniques of political art: Which styles and techniques are the most effective in communicating complex political ideas?

5. Art and politics: What are the most effective political means for confronting the forces of power in the modern world? What elements of the visual image might serve to empower people to challenge the oppression in their lives? What is there about

the making of art that might inform the making of politics? Is politics in the service of art, or is art in the service of politics?

For those seeking certainty, this book does not provide a definitive answer. Instead, it explores a series of illuminations followed by even more questions. The making of the future is ever thus. Art is ever contentious, always moving, and restless in its need to shake off old frameworks of thinking and representation. In this ongoing dialectical process, art continues its relentless pursuit of redefining purpose and meaning.

This study is also driven by a certain urgency. The search for meaningful artistic expression has become imperative as new, more global challenges have emerged: the hegemony of capitalist aesthetics, the centralization of political and corporate power, the fragmentation of the aesthetic by postmodern discourses, and the now obvious threat to global natural environments. All of these challenges require a fresh, twenty-first century reconsideration of the role of art in the political process. At the nexus of all of these cultural, aesthetic, and political cross currents is the struggle for the soul of the modern world. The options have never been quite so clear – whether an art and a politics of capitalist consumption will dominate our society or whether an alternative art and a politics of freedom and justice will prevail.

CHAPTER 2

MODERNISM: **ART AS REBELLION**

The mutilation of symbol, value, history and even of self was crucial to the Modernist urge. The moderns wanted to be new, fast. ... Modernism was all about destroying restraint, pushing to the edge, living life dangerously. Modernism was an extremism of the soul in an age of extremes.[1]

INTRODUCTION

THIS STORY BEGINS WITH MODERNISM – THE NEXUS AROUND which the question of art and politics continues to swirl in contemporary culture. Modernism was, and is, a child of the modern age; and, as such, it is a work still unfolding. Toward the end of the nineteenth century, Modernism emerged as the new avant-garde – a restless force that sought to move ideas, politics, and art in new directions more compatible with the fast-paced and variable spirit of modern industrial society. Modernism was characterized by a rebellion against tradition and the rejection of aesthetic formalisms of the symbolist and romantic movements. It celebrated artistic liberation, openness, and

---

1 Modris Eksteins, "Drowned in *Eau de Vie*," rev. of *Modernism: The Lure of Heresy from Baudelaire to Beckett and Beyond*, by Peter Gay, *London Review of Books*, 30, 4 (February 21, 2008). Lrb.co.uk/v30/n04.

experimentation. This new art was independent of any standards, freed of any external expectations. It insisted on creating its own value and evaluating its own merits and reinforcing the philosophy of art for art's sake.

From the beginning, Modernism celebrated the individual artist as the source of all inspiration, the creator of new worlds and new visions. Modernism was edgy; the artists took great pride in their alienation from traditional art and the society. The role of the modernist artist was to be outraged and outrageous: "Art has transcended reason, didacticism, and a moral purpose: art has become provocation and event," observed historian Modris Eksteins. [2] In the spirit of bohemia, rebellious artists embodied the ideas of alienation, experimentation, and artistic freedom; and they were self-conscious of their own efforts to be continually new and different. Eksteins saw the Russian impresario Serge Diaghilev as the preeminent orchestrator of the Modernist drama. Diaghilev was renowned for acting out the essence of the rebellious modernist artist. He was a master at creating sensational events in music and art – most famously, as impresario of the *Ballet Russes*. He is best remembered for staging the supreme iconic modernist event – the Paris premier in 1913 of Igor Stravinsky's ballet *The Rite of Spring*. A raucous rebellion by the audience who shouted, applauded, and even fought with one another accompanied the performance throughout. Diaghilev was a master of technique according to Eksteins:

> He conceived of art as a means of deliverance and regeneration ... deliverance from the social constraints of morality and convention [and] ... the recovery of a spontaneous emotional life. ... Art, in this outlook, is a life force; it has the invigorating power of religion; it acts through the individual but in the

2   Eksteins, 15.

end is greater than that individual; it is in fact
a surrogate religion.[3]

The romantic idea of the individual artist mirrored a culture increasingly preoccupied with a fascination with the self in the new field of psychology, the emerging idea of the individual as consumer, and the linkages between freedom and individual self-expression. Modernist art plumbed the depths of the individual artist's inner world of the unconscious for its inspiration. As cultural critic Daniel Bell observed, "The individual and his or her self-realization is the new ideal and imago of life, and one can remake one's self and remake society in the effort to achieve those individual goals."[4]

Modernism also found a welcoming home in the emerging world of mass communication. This new art had a message of change that had to be communicated. The rebel needed a platform, a stage from which to thumb his nose at the modern world. There was a sense of posturing, a need for advertising one's self and conveying a message to society through art. In one sense, Modernism could be interpreted as both a shaper and a victim of the age of commodification: the artist marketing the self, the artworks selling a new vision as product, but all subject to the vagaries of the marketplace.

AESTHETIC ELEMENTS OF MODERNISM

THERE ARE NO clearly defined modernist aesthetic styles. Styles of modernist art were constantly changing and this diversity was gathered under the gargantuan modernist tent: Impressionism, Constructivism, Cubism, twelve-tone music, the Bauhaus, as well as the explicitly political aesthetic movements of Dada, Surrealism, Lettrism, and later, the Situationist International. The even more varied

---

3   Eksteins, 30.
4   Daniel Bell, "Modernism Mummified," *American Quarterly* 39, 1
    (1987): 123.

permutations of postmodern art represented by abstract expressionism, minimalism, and the likes of Andy Warhol and Robert Mapplethorpe stand side by side in the modernist tradition with commercial advertising, Picasso, and Nazi propaganda posters.

In rejecting tradition, many modernist artists sought to distance themselves from formal academic painting techniques and content. They consciously disregarded the skills and conventions that preceded them; and every effort was made to use novel and untried techniques, many of which were designed to produce shock in the viewer. Images were altered impressionistically; geometric abstraction was embraced; collages reorganized pieces of reality; artists poured, dripped, splashed, and squirted paint on canvases; urinals were submitted to art exhibitions as statements of irreverence and rebellion; images were abstracted beyond recognition; and photographic images were manipulated. New technologies were incorporated into works of modern art, and others were adopted to aid in the mass distribution of images and ideas. Representational images were discarded in favor of the deconstructed images of Cubism, Dada, and Lettrism; the phantasmagorical inner visions of Surrealism, and the minimalist abstractions of the Supremicists. Rejection of "tradition" often meant rejecting representation in favor of stylistic experimentation. Representational art persisted, of course, but was assigned an inferior place in the new eclecticism of experimentation and rebellion. Realism came to be identified with aesthetic rigidity, the demand for political conformity, and the popular art of consumer advertising, Socialist Realism, and political propaganda.

CRITICISM OF MODERNISM

CRITIQUES OF MODERNISM abound, and many focus on the underlying motivations driving Modernism. Some traditionalists mourned the rejection of a standardized aesthetic because individual expression and rebellion for its own sake replaced quality, value, and aesthetic standards. Other traditionalists mourned the impact of modernization, technology, the ascendency of capitalist aesthetics, and the demise of "fine" art. Two philosophers working in the Marxist tradition, Walter Benjamin and Theodor Adorno, were instrumental in framing the early and subsequent criticisms of Modernism. They were also outspoken critics of what I will call capitalist aesthetics and are important figures in the late twentieth century postmodernist movement.

Modernist art was potentially political at its core, and the questions of whose politics and what messages art would convey were critical. However, some of the most vocal criticisms of Modernism came from the political left. The Marxist Left argued that Modernism was the embodiment of bourgeois capitalism, that it was tainted as art, that it was flawed because it placed itself outside of the political realities, and that it destroyed community. All factions of the left were deeply involved in communicating the political messages of rebellion, hope, and change; and they expected art to play a major role in the effort to shape political realities. More recently several theorists have argued the opposite – that Modernism was itself politics, the politics of individualist anarchism – political activism as art.

In an effort to keep Modernism above the political fray, other critics argued that Modernism was merely the latest step, the cutting edge or avant-garde of a long line of fine art recreating itself for each historic era. For true art to exist, it could not be beholden to either culture or politics: it must remain aloof. Some modernists themselves argued that Modernism wasn't political because it didn't want to be political: it was, by choice, alienated from traditional politics and the life of the community.

In the sections that follow, I have selected individual critics to outline a variety of critiques.

Aesthetic value and the idea of quality

In his critique of Modernism, art critic Clement Greenberg grounded his ideas in traditional aesthetics and in a belief in the need for a standard of quality. The emergence of mass consumer culture and its leveling affect on all art, including fine art, deeply concerned Greenberg. He believed that the role of Modernism was to hold back the commonplace, such that he defined Modernism as "a kind of holding operation against the leveling and relaxing tendencies of middlebrow taste."[5] Given his desire to see Modernism as the continuation of traditional fine art aesthetics, one can understand why Greenberg found support for that effort in several key modernist aesthetic elements. He endorsed the idea of art for art's sake, believing that the work of art itself is where we should make the judgment about its quality – what he saw as the "simple aspiration to quality, to aesthetic value and excellence for its own sake, as end in itself."[6] He even put the idea of rebellion into a traditional context. Modernist art had to be rebellious but only to defend aesthetic quality: "If rebellion and revolt have truly belonged to Modernism, it's been only when felt to be necessary in the interests of aesthetic value, not for political ends." From Greenberg's perspective, "saving art" was the primary challenge of Modernism:

> What singles Modernism out and gives it its place and identity more than anything else is its response to a heightened sense of threats to aesthetic value: threats from the social and material ambience, from the temper of the times, all conveyed through the demands of a new and open cultural market, middlebrow

---

5   Clement Greenberg. "Modern and Postmodern." William Dobell Memorial Lecture, Sydney, Australia, October 31, 1979, *Arts* 54, 6 (February 1980). http://www.sharecom.ca/greenberg/

6   Greenberg, "Modern and Postmodern."

demands. Modernism dates from the time, in the mid-nineteenth century, when that market became not only established – it had been there long before – but entrenched and dominant, without significant competition.[7]

Technology and the mechanization of art

Walter Benjamin was one of the first theorists to fully articulate the impact of technology and modernization on the creation of art. His analysis focused on aesthetics; but in a larger sense, it foreshadowed an insightful critique of the worldview we have come to call the "modern." In his seminal essay entitled, "The World of Art in the Age of Mechanical Reproduction," modernist aesthetics is characterized as the child of technology and the modern capitalistic industrial process. Benjamin argued that the omnipresence and power of technology shaped all aspects of art in the modern era. By its very nature, advances in technology have politicized art by controlling and shaping the mass marketing of aesthetic representations.[8]

Prior to the modern era, art was seen as the embodiment of essences or the "aura," Benjamin argued. A work of art with an aura had symbolic meaning that was situated in a particular cultural context, connected with an objective reality that reflected some larger truth accessible by the viewer. In his essay Benjamin declared the "death" of art as it had been known for millennia. In an era of reproducible images, the uniqueness of the aura disappeared.

Benjamin also believed that "The uniqueness of a work of art is inseparable from its being imbedded in the fabric of tradition."[9] His essay argued that mechanical reproduction

---

7   Greenberg, "Modern and Postmodern."

8   Walter Benjamin, "The Work of Art in the Age of Mechanical Reproduction," in *Illuminations*, trans. Harry Zohn, ed. and intro. Hannah Arendt, 217-251 (New York, NY: Schocken, 1969).

9   Benjamin, "Work of Art," 223.

resulted in a break with tradition, leaving art rudderless and unfocused, without depth and meaning.

> [F]or the first time in history, mechanical reproduction emancipates the work of art from its parasitical dependence on ritual. *To an ever greater degree the work of art reproduced becomes the work of art designed for reproducibility.* ... But the instant the criterion of authenticity ceases to be applicable to artistic production, the total function of art is reversed. Instead of being based on ritual, it begins to be based on another practice – politics.[10]

Benjamin was ambiguous about the loss of the aura. Art divorced from symbolic meaning created two conflicting outcomes. On the one hand, it set society adrift from history and context (the upside of which was freedom from the bondage of custom and control); and on the other, it cast society into a new context – the manufactured community of mass culture, mass marketing, and mass advertising which built upon the incessant reproduction of images and control of their distribution. The loss of traditional art that reflected inherent symbolic meaning, according to Benjamin, is yet to be completely understood.

At the same time that he mourned the loss of the aura of a work of art, Walter Benjamin embraced the mass production and distribution of art as a political tool for creating revolutionary change. According to Adam Kirsch, "Surprisingly, Benjamin welcomed the idea of art without aura. He reasoned that aura was a kind of aristocratic mystery and that its disappearance should herald a new, more democratic art."[11] Technology profoundly affects both the creation and the distribution of art and the shaping of the

---

10 Benjamin, "Work of Art," 224, my italics.

11 Adam Kirsch, "The Philosopher Stoned," *The New Yorker,* August 21, 2006, 81.

collective, social context. According to John Roberts, a contemporary critic of postmodern aesthetics, art continues to move in this direction. "Artists in the late seventies and early eighties ... had fallen under the sway of Walter Benjamin, and were convinced, in their respective ways, that the dissolution of the category of Art into the forms of modern technology and everyday life was a good thing."[12] Art could, theoretically, become more democratic as it became reproducible as a result of access to the vast networks of mass media.

Benjamin was especially interested in the democratic potential of the emerging technology of photography. According to Rajeev Patke,

> Benjamin takes the history of photography to embody the political potential of Surrealism in at least four ways. (1) Photography renovates representation by emancipating it from degenerate conventions and debased social functions. (2) Benjamin replaces the notion of *"photography as an art"* with the idea of *"art as photography."* The reorientation foregrounds the social relevance of art. ... (3) Photography offers to consciousness modes of reality that would remain in the unconscious without its action. ... [and] (4) finally, photography is magical in a special way.[13]

---

12 John Roberts, "After Adorno: Art, Autonomy, and Critique." Paper presented at apexart, London, March 8, 2000. http://www.apexart. org/residency/roberts.htm

13 Rajeev S. Patke, "Walter Benjamin, Surrealism, and Photography," paper presented at Workshop on 'Literature as Revolt in twentieth Century Europe', 17 August 1998, The University of Haifa, Israel (6the ISSEI Conference). www.sunwalked.wordpress. com/2009/12/17/interesting-paper-on-walter-benjamin-surrealism- and-photography-by-rajeev-s-patke

But, is mechanically reproduced art really libratory and democratic? In the rush to embrace the wonders of technology, what is often elided is the centralization required to maintain complex technological systems and the implications of that centralization on politics generally. Anarchists, more than other critics of capitalism on the Left have historically been wary of the implications of technology for politics, in part, because they understand that technology is the handmaiden of capitalism. In contrast, Karl Marx embraced centralized industrialization and the age of the machine which would free workers from hard labor. The anarchist critique of technology is based on the argument that technology leads inexorably to centralization of control. When technologies introduced the practice of the division of labor, this was seen as threatening freedom of expression (work as art). The anarchists were not of one mind about the merits of technology, however. Adopting a Luddite argument, William Morris, for example, decried all technology. Other early anarchists such as William Godwin and Peter Kropotkin supported the uses of emerging technologies but insisted on their local control.

Other anarchist voices weighed in after the First World War when the centralization of control of technological and communication forces became apparent. Lewis Mumford, who did not identify himself as an anarchist, nevertheless developed one of the most trenchant arguments for a decentralized and democratically controlled technology in *The Myth of the Machine* and *Technics and Civilization*.[14] Mumford, in turn, influenced a whole generation of thinkers such as Paul and Percival Goodman (*Communitas*), Jacques Ellul (*The Technological Society*), the Back to the Land movement in the 1960s, and contemporary ideas of environmental sustainability.

Walter Benjamin, too, recognized the dark side of technology: its power to distract and its potential for

---

14 See also Lewis Mumford, *The Pentagon of Power*.

manipulation. The shift from the artist shaping the aesthetic to the technology dictating the aesthetic was a profound one. It was a function of the automation effect of technological processes. Comparing the traditional role of art with the new, more democratic and technological art, Benjamin concluded, "Distraction and concentration form polar opposites which may be stated as follows: A man who concentrates before a work of art is absorbed by it. ... In contrast, the distracted mass absorbs the work of art."[15] The engaged viewer becomes the passive spectator.

Benjamin was an early critic of mass visual communication, exploring how the mass production of art affected both art and modern politics. He seemed to imply that the use of technology may leave human beings more open to manipulation. He used the example of film to describe the potential for the manipulation by new technologies *as technologies* to shape social context and define social meaning: "The painting invites the spectator to contemplation; before it the spectator can abandon himself to his associations. Before the movie frame he cannot do so. No sooner has his eye grasped a scene than it is already changed. It cannot be arrested."[16] The techniques of film move imagery quickly, denying the viewer an opportunity for reflection. His meaning is clear: technology takes on a life of its own and has its own effects, regardless of the particular images and the messages communicated.

In the visual arts, the mass media have had pervasive control over both the medium and the message since the second decade of the twentieth century. However, it is not just a question of who might have control of the technology; technology itself can be a tool of control and manipulation to shape the political agenda and even the entire culture by means of mechanical reproduction and mass distribution. Marxist theoretician Herbert Marcuse argued that technology ultimately created what he called a "one-dimensional

---

15 Benjamin, "Work of Art," 239.
16 Benjamin, "Work of Art," 238.

mind." Furthermore, technology reinforces a tendency toward standardization at the expense of the unique and the abstraction of the real into the technical – ideas developed by Mumford as well in *Art and Technics*. The result is a loss of diversity in message and form. The essence of a work of art is not only its aura but also its uniqueness. In a technological world, the fascination with the new runs up against the resistance to the new, and the unique loses out to the mundane and duplicative. Contemporary anarchist primitivist John Zerzan concluded that "The meaning of a universal, homogenizing technology ... is not only unquestioned but is embraced. The connection between the imperialism of technology and the loss of meaning in society never dawns on the postmodernists."[17] Technology is especially effective in undermining democratic political processes, Jean Baudrillard noted, "*All* the media and *all* information cut both ways: while appearing to augment the social, in reality, they neutralize social relations and the social itself at a profound level."[18]

Art as meaning and purpose

Theodor Adorno was less enamored with technology than Benjamin was and did not fully embrace the new, mechanistic foundations of aesthetics. However, he certainly recognized the dominance of technologically reproduced art in the modern era. Like Benjamin, Adorno was wary of the power of the new medium of film in the service of political propaganda. Benjamin's critique focused on the technology itself, but Adorno was more interested in the corporate and political forces controlling the technology, warning of the power of the "culture industry"

---

17 John Zerzan, *Twilight of the Machines* (Port Townsend, WA: Feral House, 2008), 66. http://www.feralhouse.com

18 Jean Baudrillard, "The Implosion of Meaning in the Media and the Implosion of the Social in the Masses," in *Questioning Technology: A Critical Anthology*, by John Zerzan and Alice Carnes (London: Freedom Press, 1988), 158.

to shape collective consciousness. He was especially concerned about the potential for the co-optation of art by the capitalist mass media. According to Austin Harrington, Adorno "famously argues that contemporary artworks must negate their immediate sensuous tendencies in order to hold out the prospect of a utopia that resists pandering to the 'system of illusions' of capitalist consumerism and lapsing into premature reconciliation with the status quo."[19]

Adorno was deeply committed to the idea that art must convey meaning. He developed a complex aesthetic theory to bring Hegel's idealism (with its recognition of the importance of meaning in art) and Marx's materialism (with its focus on the production of art) into a new kind of interaction, one which I would characterize as a more complex dialectic of interrelationship. In *Aesthetic Theory*, Adorno called for artists to reject the modernist fragmented aesthetic which "cultivates art as a natural reserve for irrationalism from which thought is to be excluded" and rethink and reconsider classical aesthetics with its search for a coherent meaning. He stated unequivocally, "No theory, aesthetic theory included, can dispense with the element of universality."[20] Because Modernism had succumbed to the irrational impulses of capitalist aesthetics, the classical linkages with philosophy had to be reestablished; art had to become reflective. But, Adorno did not call for a return to a purely idealist position: "Art does not stand in need of an aesthetics that will prescribe norms where it finds itself in difficulty but rather an aesthetics that will provide the capacity for reflection which art on its own is hardly able

---

19 Austin Harrington, "New German Aesthetic Theory: Martin Seel's art of diremption," *Radical Philosophy* (September/October 2001). http://www.radicalphilosophy.com

20 Theodor W. Adorno, "Draft Introduction," in *Aesthetic Theory*, edited by Gretel Adorno and Rolf Tiedemann, and introduction by Robert Hullot-Kentor, trans., (Minneapolis: University of Minnesota Press,1997), 336 and 339.

to achieve. ... The truth content of an artwork requires philosophy."[21]

Adorno was critical of Hegel's extreme idealism and argued that art is not reflective of the absolute spirit but of the dialectic itself and is the manifestation of the tension within the dialectic. "Every artwork, even if it presents itself as a work of perfect harmony, is, in itself, the nexus of a problem. As such it participates in history and, thus, oversteps its own uniqueness."[22] He called for a "dialectical aesthetics" where each element was mutually dependent and mutually reinforced the other. In his theory, art "lives" in the tension between the cognitive understanding and the materiality of art, between the objective and the subjective, between the history of aesthetics and the contemporary individual artist. But, understanding is not reducible to a simplistic formula of adopting either a conceptual analysis or analyzing only the artworks themselves against some empirical standards. Art must stand dialectically in relation to the immanent reality. He believed that this is the foundation upon which art must develop its theory. "Not experience alone but only thought that is fully saturated with experience is equal to the phenomenon. ... Consciousness of the antagonism between interior and exterior is requisite to the experience of art. ... What is required is experience of works rather than thoughts simply applied to the matter."[23] Meaning is a process of becoming. This is the underlying dynamic of Adorno's dialectic as it seeks to know the truth content of the work of art: "The knowledge of art means to render objectified spirit once again fluid through the medium of reflection."[24]

The social context of art was an important element in Adorno's aesthetic. He was always attentive to the potential political import of art. Art cannot be reduced to a simplistic

---

21 Adorno, "Draft Introduction," 341.
22 Adorno, "Draft Introduction," 358.
23 Adorno, "Draft Introduction," 347.
24 Adorno, "Draft Introduction," 357.

categorization or meaning, Adorno observed: "Today the nomenclature of formalism and Socialist Realism is used, with great consequence, to distinguish between the autonomous and the social essence of art. ... This dichotomization is false because it presents the two dynamically related elements as simple alternatives." [25] While Adorno endorsed the idea of the autonomy of the artist, he also stated that both the art and the artist should not be isolated and outside of culture but live within the context of culture. According to Roberts, "What distinguishes Adorno's theory of autonomy ... is that art is seen simultaneously as socially determined and autonomous. Or rather, the autonomy of the art object is something which is produced out of the social relations which constitute the institution of art itself."[26] Adorno did not separate art from the social base but insisted that it be reflective of that social base. Roberts noted, "rather, autonomy is the name given to the process of formal and cognitive self-criticism which art must undergo in order to constitute the conditions of its very possibility and emergence."[27]

Avoiding both the rock of idealism and the hard place of rigid materialism yet embracing both perspectives, Adorno argued that "Artworks are ... objective as well as ... spiritual; otherwise they would be in principle indistinguishable from eating and drinking," and, "Art is to be dialectically construed insofar as spirit inheres in it, without art's possessing it or giving surety of it as something absolute."[28] An art based upon subjective, individual motivations cannot approach truth; and similarly, an idealized art cannot reflect the real and material social context of its roots. The artist had to maintain a sense of autonomy and at the same moment reflect the social reality.

---

25 Adorno, *Aesthetic Theory*, 256.

26 Roberts, "After Adorno."

27 Roberts, "After Adorno."

28 Adorno, "Draft Introduction," 344.

The critique from the left: the alienation of art from community

From the end of the nineteenth century through the first half of the twentieth, Marxists, Socialists, anarchists, and others on the left developed strong critiques of Modernism and its link to capitalism. In recent years, historian Modris Eksteins, sociologist Daniel Bell, art critic Clement Greenberg, consumer society critic Jackson Lears, and some postmodernists have also weighed in on the meaning of Modernism and found it wanting.

Art and work. While Karl Marx did not specifically address Modernism or the consumer society, he did develop a well-known critique of the emerging capitalist economy and anticipated many of the subsequent arguments critiquing consumer aesthetics. While he did not develop a separate aesthetic treatise, several core ideas in his writings have guided much of the Marxist criticism of contemporary culture. In particular, his theory of the "fetishization of the commodity," first presented in *Das Kapital,* has had a profound impact on aesthetics.

Marx built his materialist aesthetic by linking labor and art. Like labor, art was a shared, social exercise. Like labor, art addressed a basic human need. Both were grounded in the real social world of human and economic relationships. Marx drew a distinction between goods made for "use" value that were essentially a sharing of mutual work between known people in a community and goods made for "exchange" where the value was determined by the market. In the emerging capitalist economy based on exchange value, the products of labor were "alienated" into an abstract marketplace where they took on a life of their own. Later theorists developed a sophisticated version of this idea of the fetishization of the commodity. They argued that the products in the consumer economy had similarly taken on a life of their own and, indeed, were now shaping the social reality.

The Marxist understanding of art-as-made-object was a refinement of this labor theory of use value. It, thus, was embedded in economic and social relationships; and the artist had a responsibility to reflect these values of social relationships. Spanish philosopher of aesthetics Adolfo Sánchez Vázquez summarized Marx's position as follows:

> Labor is thus not only the creation of useful objects that satisfy specific human needs, but also the art of objectifying or molding human goals, ideas, or feelings in and through material, concrete-sensuous objects. In this capacity to realize the human essence – resides the human potential to create objects, such as works of art, that elevate the capacity for expression and confirmation that is already present in the products of labor.[29]

Alienated art. French socialist-anarchist-mutualist Pierre Proudhon was an early critic of the modernist impulse. His principle aesthetics work, *Du Principe de l'art et de sa destination sociale,* written in 1865, outlines his anarchist aesthetic principles.[30] He made the case for a political art grounded in a social context in contrast to the romanticist and idealist representations in traditional visual art of the era.

Proudhon's history of art traced the metamorphosis of traditional art from art that was situated within community and which articulated the meaning of community to the emerging modernist art that celebrated individual, alienated art. Proudhon's critique included a criticism of Renaissance and romantic art according to Ali Nematollahy: "For Proudhon, the Renaissance is not merely a regression from the Middle Ages but a permanent tendency in art. ... It is *decadent.* It turns its

---

29 Adolpho Sánchez Vázquez, *Art and Society: Essays in Marxist Aesthetics* (New York, NY and London: Monthly Review Press, 1973), 63.

30 Pierre Proudhon, *Du Principe de l'art et de sa destination sociale* (Paris: Garnier Frères, 1865).

back on reality and everyday life. It idolizes form and sensuality."[31]

Proudhon's critique of Modernism had historical antecedents. In a related article, *La Pornocratie, ou les femmes dans les temps moderns*, he is especially concerned about the ascendency of art that appealed to the passions, echoing Plato's distrust of poetry. According to Nematollahy,

> For Proudhon, art for art's sake is not so much a historical and literary movement as a permanent tendency of art: the appreciation of beauty for its own sake. "Art, inasmuch as it has as its aim the awakening of the ideal, especially that of form, is therefore a stimulation leading to pleasure. If the passion that it rouses is love, it is a pornocratic[32] agent, the most dangerous of all."[33] ... [A]rt for art's sake, [is] an art that privileges the sensual over the moral: "The supremacy granted to the aesthetic principle over the juridical and the moral is the true pornocratic ferment. It is in this way that many people slip into the prostitution of their conscience, to the abandonment of right, and to the philosophy of Epicures."[34]

This perspective seems curiously antiquated to the contemporary anarchist ear: why would an anarchist seem to critique pleasure and argue for the repression of the

31 Ali Nematollahy, "Proudhon, from aesthetics to politics," *Anarchist Studies* 13, 1(2005), 50-51.

32 Definition of pornocratic: "A corrupt democracy often focusing on phallic desires and instant gratification of those desires. Emphasis on physical needs and attributes over morals, ethics, and education." Urban Dictionary

33 Nematollahy, quoting Proudhon, *Du Principe*, 255.

34 Nematollahy, quoting Proudhon, *La Pornocratie, ou les femmes dans les temps modernes* (Paris: A Lacroix, 1875), 228-229.

passions and appeal instead to the ascendency of morality and justice? One explanation might simply be that nineteenth century philosophy was still operating in the idealist and religious traditions, and the language and rhetoric are colored by that context. While that may be true and the language may seem archaic, the answer lies in the manner in which Proudhon defined these terms in his political (and aesthetic) philosophies. Justice in his mutualist formulation was not an absolute, but a manifestation of individual action within reciprocal social relationships.[35] Justice had two aspects: the right to be respected by others, and the obligation to respect others. Rejecting any objective standards, Proudhon finds morality and justice to be functions of the individual-in-society. But at the same time, he was skeptical of the passions driving the individual which warred against the realization of this perception of justice. Thus, throughout his philosophy, he warns against passions getting out of control, and argues for an incremental approach to achieving his anarchist society. His criticism above, then, warns of the seductions in art to turn the individual away from true revolutionary morality and justice. Art, in his formulation, is another absolute warranting skepticism.

Proudhon was also concerned about the alienation of the individual artist from community, Nematollahy observed: "Not only is the artist cut off from the people, he systematically cultivates his detachment and autonomy. The isolation of the artist, the solitude, and his lack of principles have in turn generated an art that is merely made for its own sake, the school of 'art for art's sake.'"[36] The artist had a critical role to play, Proudhon believed, in changing the social reality; and he saw Modernism as abandoning that mission.[37]

---

35 See Pierre Proudhon, *De la Justice*. An excellent analysis of Proudhon's concept of justice can be found in Robert L. Hoffman's *Revolutionary Justice: The Social and Political Theory of P.-J. Proudhon* (Urbana and others: University of Illinois Press, 1972.

36 Nematollahy, 51, quoting Proudhon, *Du Principe*, 9.

37 Proudhon, *Du Principe*, 199.

In many ways Proudhon laid out the theoretical foundations of a social anarchist aesthetic that insisted upon linking art to the need for social change. This position was not without its problems. The historical example of Socialist Realism is a warning for Proudhon's position. His concern about alienation from community bears careful consideration, however.

Modernism as bourgeois art. Christopher (St. John Sprigg) Caudwell was a Marxist aesthetician writing in the first third of the twentieth century. He critiqued the modernist movement as a manifestation of capitalism and an exemplification of Marx's concept of commodity fetishism. Commodities became imbued with power of their own, in a quasi-religious sense, and became fetishized. As Frederich Engels concluded in *Anti-Dühring,* "the product dominates the producers."[38] The result is the alienation of art and the substitution of objects that previously represented the social and economic relationships in an exchange between people, with the commodity which is designed merely for exchange, having no connection to the community. Art becomes fetishized when it enters the market and becomes merely another commodity for sale. It has no higher purpose; it is merely an exchangeable object.

For Caudwell, aesthetics had to be grounded in collective social relations, and Modernism failed as true art primarily because it rejected the pre-eminence of social relations in favor of the individual as free agent. More recently, Glen Close offered a similar critique: "Cultural Modernism opened an attack, often an unyielding rage, against the social order; became concerned with the self, often to a narcissistic extent; denied art the function of representation; and became unusually absorbed with the materials alone – textures and sounds – which it used for expressiveness."[39]

38 Friedrich Engels, quoted in Christopher Caudwell, *Illusion and Reality* (New York, NY: International Publishers, 1937, 1977), 117.
39 Glen S. Close, "Literature and politics in early twentieth-century Argentina: The anarchist modernism of Roberto Arlt," *Anarchist*

Caudwell was also critical of Modernism because he viewed the rebellious modernist artist as a manifestation of bourgeois capitalism – as a part of the problem, not the solution. The modernist artist was an individualist who was "the final bourgeois revolutionary ... so disgusted with the development of bourgeois society that he asserts the bourgeois creed in the most essential way: complete 'personal' freedom, complete destruction of all social relations." Caudwell did offer an endorsement of the anarchist artist despite his fear that even the anarchist artist would eventually be co-opted: "The anarchist is yet revolutionary because he represents the destructive element and the complete negation of all bourgeois society ... but he cannot really pass beyond bourgeois society because he remains caught in its toils."[40]

The dark side of Modernism. In *Fascist Modernism: Aesthetics, Politics, and the Avant-Garde,* Andrew Hewitt undertook a wide-ranging and complex analysis of the relationship between Modernism and fascism. He explored in painstaking steps the many strands of aesthetic theory linking these two seemingly unrelated forces in contemporary society. His point of departure is the avant-garde and its relationship to the gathering forces of fascism as he seeks to identify parallelisms that inform each movement. Although he does not argue for a causal relationship, he suggests linkages and analogous relationships that suggest the two are fellow travelers in some key ways. Like Modernism's open embrace of contention, action, and disruption as necessary for change, fascism exhibited a predilection for political agitation in the futurist "aesthetics of struggle." Art, according to Hewitt, "is expected to create a realm of acceptable rebellion."[41] Both Modernism and Fascism are underscored

Studies 12, 2 (2004), 123.

40 Christopher Caudwell, *Illusion and Reality* (New York, NY: International Publishers, 1937, 1977), 127-128.

41 Andrew Hewitt, *Fascist Modernism: Aesthetics, Politics, and the Avant-Garde* (Stanford, CA: Stanford University Press, 1993), 135.

by preferencing subjective individualism; the desire for self-expression which was manifested as the autonomous performing avant-garde artist and as an anonymous singularity within the mass of the fascist "regimented spectacle"; and the rejection of nineteenth century absolutist aesthetics.

To focus his study, Hewitt explored the writings of Italian futurist poet Filippo Marinetti. He summarized the main elements of Martinetti's 1905 Futurist Manifesto as "the loathing of nostalgia, the celebration of an androcentric machine culture over the Symbolist 'soliloquizing vegetation' and 'botanical sentimentality,' and above all the rejection of 'a passion for eternal things, a desire for immortal, imperishable masterworks.'"[42] Like the avant-garde modernists, Marinetti rejected the aesthetic traditions that preceded him.

One of the central features of futurist aesthetics was the unabashed praise of mechanization through technological and industrial advances. Hewitt labeled this tendency as a "perverted form of organicism."[43] The metaphor of the machine played a powerful role in fascist art and politics, according to Hewitt:

> With the supposed fusion of life and art in the avant-garde it is no longer a question, within the affirmative aesthetic of futurism, of art *compensating* for life, but rather of art offering another way of living life. It is the same machine that operates in each "realm." Art ceases to be life's affirmative "other" and offers instead the possibility of affirming the totalizing negativity of the social machine itself.[44]

The idealization of technological social engineering was a key element in the Technocracy Movement – initially

---

42 Hewitt, 108.
43 Hewitt, 143.
44 Hewitt, 137-145; 137.

developed in the United States in the 1920s and spread across Europe. It was in part, a response to the failures of capitalism preceding the Great Depression.

Hewitt concludes (tentatively), that although there is no causal relationship between the avant-garde and fascism, both "Both take root among marginalized groups otherwise disenfranchised politically or culturally, by the rationalization of economic production and social reproduction. ... The argument at least bears examination that the same process of centralization – of capital and of culture – potentializes both the fascist and the avant-garde impulses."[45]

Similarly, historian Modris Eksteins made a compelling but troubling case for linking Modernism in art to fascism in politics. In the introduction to *Rites of Spring* he outlines his thesis:

> Avant-garde has for us a positive ring: storm troops have a frightening connotation. This book suggests that there may be a sibling relationship between these two terms that extends beyond their military origins. Introspection, primitivism, abstraction, and myth making in the arts, and introspection, primitivism, abstraction and myth making in politics, may be related manifestations.[46]

Eksteins identified the following key elements of German Nazism that can also be found in Modernism: a celebration of the individual with an emphasis on the subjective self and one's feelings; a preference for revolt and action over reflection; the creation of grand spectacles and ritual to create a sense of community and belonging; and racism, narcissism, and the use of modern mass technologies and

---

45 Hewitt,189.
46 Modris Eksteins, *Rites of Spring: The Great War and the Birth of the Modern Age* (New York, NY and others: Doubleday, 1989), xvi.

proscribed propaganda to reach people.[47] Sophisticated use of propaganda and mass communication media were central to Adolf Hitler's rise to power in Germany and to his continued hold over the culture: "Propaganda was to Hitler not just a necessary evil, a question of justifiable lies, of warranted exaggeration. Propaganda was to him an art."[48] Eksteins concluded that the heart of the problem was the fascination with individual expression: "Nazi faith had no real direction or definition other than its vulgar affirmation of self. That faith was pointed at the 'nation,' but its locus was the individual."[49] Eksteins attributed the source of this individualism to a Modernism inspired by individualist anarchism. At the turn of the century, there had been a revival of interest in Max Stirner's radical individualism. Stirner wrote the archetypal model of the central image in Modernism: the rebellious, alienated artist taking on the world.[50]

According to Eksteins, the parallels between Nazism and Modernism are obvious. They share the fascination with the individual, the imagination, and an emphasis on dreams and passions; the idealization of revolt against the status quo, and the insistence that art be an active political agent in society. "If there has been a single principal theme in our century's aesthetics, it is that the life of imagination and the life of action are one and the same," Eksteins concluded.[51] Ultimately Nazism was a realization of the modernist agenda, including the fascination with technology: "Nazism was a popular variant of many of the impulses of the avant-garde. It expressed on a more popular level

---

47 Eksteins, 311, 312, 313, 318.

48 Eksteins, 321.

49 Eksteins, 318.

50 Stirner's ideas will be explore in depth in the next section. He developed his philosophy in Max Stirner, *The Ego and His Own: The Case of the Individual Against Authority*, Trans. Steven T. Byington (New York, NY: Dover, 1973).

51 Eksteins, 4.

many of the same tendencies and posited many of the same solutions. ... Above all, it, like the moderns it claimed to despise, tried to marry subjectivism and technicism."[52]

Writer Susan Sontag expanded on a definition of fascist aesthetics – a definition similar to that proposed by Modris Eksteins. Fascist art was preoccupied

> with situations of control, submissive be-
> havior, and extravagant behavior. ... The rela-
> tions of domination and enslavement take the
> form of a characteristic pageantry: the mass-
> ing of groups of people; the turning of people
> into things; ... an all-powerful hypnotic leader
> figure or force. ... The fascist ideal is to trans-
> form sexual energy into a "spiritual" force, for
> the benefit of the community. [53]

All fascist aesthetics is built on the underlying principle that art and politics are a seamless experience.[54]

In the essay "Stalinism as Aesthetic Phenomenon," crit-ic Boris Groys developed a similar but more provocative analysis, linking Nazism and Russian Socialist Realism with the idea of totalitarian art as a cult of personality. He argued that Stalinist totalitarianism was

> the organic continuation of the avant-garde
> but also its culmination and in some sense its
> completion. ... [I]n Stalinist Russia (as well
> as in Nazi Germany) the project of the avant-
> garde passed into its final phase: ... The po-
> litical leadership of the totalitarian countries

---

52 Eksteins, 311.

53 Susan Sontag, "Fascinating Fascism," rev. of *The Last of the Nuba* by Leni Reifenthal and *SS Regalia* by Jack Pia, *The New York Review of Books*, February 6, 1975. www.nybooks.com/articles/archives/1975/feb/06/fascinating-fascism/

54 Sontag.

accepted the challenge of the avant-garde. The avant-garde artist, however, did not receive political power. Instead the political leader found aesthetic power. In essence, Stalin was the only artist of the Stalin era. ... Socialist Realism is, therefore, the aesthetics of Stalin's politics, which placed aesthetic goals first, even before itself.[55]

Walter Benjamin was also concerned about the potential for manipulation of art by fascist propagandists. He noted that the shift to a mass-produced mechanical art could easily result in art becoming a political tool of control. He alluded to the complexities of the relationship between mechanically reproduced art, the politics of capitalism, and the implicit dangers of political manipulation as he watched the emerging fascist state in Germany. Absent any central meaning, transcendent purpose, and social cohesion, art falls to the level of the personal and the subjective and individual but, an individual as a member of a mass, not as unique: "Fascism attempts to organize the newly created proletarian masses without affecting the property structure which the masses strive to eliminate. Fascism sees its salvation in giving these masses not their right but, instead, a chance to express themselves. ... The logical result of Fascism is the introduction of aesthetics into political life."[56]

Modernism and advertising. In a compelling analysis, cultural critic Jackson Lears explored the relationship between Modernism and advertising art, arguing that advertising is the aesthetic of capitalism and that the parallels between the two are too obvious to ignore. In "Uneasy

---

55 Boris Groys, "Stalinism as Aesthetic Phenomenon," in *Textura: Russian Essays on Visual Culture*, ed. and trans. by Alla Efimova and Lev Manovich, Forward by Stephen Bann (Chicago and London: University of Chicago Press, 1993), 120, 121 and 123.

56 Benjamin, "Work of Art," 241.

Courtship: Modern Art and Modern Advertising," Lears began his analysis of Modernism by exploring the role of the artist in traditional and modernist art. What he found was ambivalence on the part of modernist artists – they were caught between "a thirst for artistic novelty and experimentation, combined with longings for a sense of spiritual authenticity that seemed absent amid the everyday business of modern life."[57]

Lears also argued that there were similarities between traditional art and advertising. Ironically, advertising does serve the traditional role of art to reflect community goals and aspirations. He concluded, however, that advertising did not reflect or embody the living culture but, instead, created a false culture, a new synthetic reality dedicated to disseminating the intentionally constructed culture of capitalism.[58] Advertising only approximated the real world. Lears referred to this deception with Northrup Frye's term, "stupid realism," which was a term "meant to apply to corporate advertising and political propaganda – 'official' discourses that legitimate existing structures of power."[59] He went on to point out that "the problem with stupid realism is not that it is tacky – it can often be technically superb – but that it strips realism of its nineteenth-century rationale: the attempt to tell the truth (or at least *a* truth) even when it is sordid or disturbing."[60]

One of the goals of Modernism was to rebel against the status quo, to articulate a revolt against the existing cultural reality. Here, too, advertising failed to provoke rebellion: "The advertising artist ... locates commodities in a given symbolic universe decreed by current fashion. Rather than challenging the status quo, his work reinforces it, makes it seem natural, inevitable, inescapable. Rather

---

57 Jackson Lears, "Uneasy Courtship: Modern Art and Modern Advertising," *American Quarterly* 39, 1 (1987), 134.
58 Lears, "Uneasy Courtship," 138-139.
59 Lears, "Uneasy Courtship," 136.
60 Lears, "Uneasy Courtship," 142.

than exalting the ignoble or grotesque, the process reaffirms existing hierarchies of economic power and cultural meaning."[61]

Against the prevailing critics of the time who argued that Modernism had been entirely co-opted by advertising, Lears made an effort to retain some distinction between Modernism and advertising, concluding that some modernist artists were able to resist the allures of advertising and to maintain their aesthetic integrity. His examples were few: while some surrealists remained independent, others adapted quite easily to the world of advertising. The surrealist art that was easily accommodated by advertising art was "more representational and illusionistic."[62]

Lears was also concerned about the freedom of the individual artist to create – one of the primary aesthetic goals of Modernism. He believed that there was no room in advertising art for personal vision: "instead it demands that one perform one's craft smoothly enough to fit into the larger package prepared to please the corporate client."[63] Lears concluded, finally, that advertising art failed as art because its goal was to perpetuate an economic system, not to fulfill the traditional role of art as the vehicle for human inspiration and aspiration.

> Advertising art … can never nurture a truly disinterested aesthetic involvement; it always pulls up short at the point of sale. Nor can advertising ever sustain a transcendent vision of life, beyond the performance principle of advanced capitalism; it is fated to serve as the iconography of mass production and the corporate system.[64]

---

61 Lears, "Uneasy Courtship," 145.
62 Lears, "Uneasy Courtship," 146.
63 Lears, "Uneasy Courtship," 138.
64 Lears, "Uneasy Courtship," 141.

Edward L. Bernays, often referred to as the father of modern public relations, did not see advertising in this light, however. He saw it as an opportunity to communicate with vast audiences and move them in certain directions. According to Bernays, the effectiveness of propaganda had become apparent during the First World War: "It was only natural after the war ended, that intelligent persons should ask themselves whether it was not possible to apply a similar technique to the problems of peace." One of the challenges of peacetime was how to expand the promotion and sale of mass produced goods. Propaganda was the answer and there were effective techniques that could be applied: it "serves to focus and realize the desires of the masses," and these tools should be widely adopted. [65] An important tool of advertising was the application of the new insights of psychology: "The group mind does not think. ... In place of thoughts it has impulses, habits, and emotions." Communication to mass audiences could be successful by "means of clichés, pat words or images which stand for a whole group of ideas or experiences."[66]

Bernays believed he was operating with the loftiest intentions. In "The Engineering of Consent" he argued that advertising was simply another manifestation of U.S. Constitutional rights:

> Freedom of speech and its democratic corollary, a free press, have tacitly expanded our Bill of Rights to include the right of persuasion. ... All these [mass] media provide open doors to the public mind. Any one of us through these media may influence the attitudes and actions of our fellow citizens. ... We must recognize the significance of modern communications not only as a highly organized

---

65 Edward L. Bernays, *Propaganda* (NY: Horace Liveright, 1928), 27, 28, 30-31.

66 Bernays, 50.

mechanical web but as a potential force for social good or possible evil.[67]

He further observed that "The engineering of consent
will always be needed as an adjunct to, or a partner of,
the educational process."[68] There is a certain naivety reading Bernays across the decades. He believed that access to
the media was available to anyone, that engineered consent was a social good, and that influencing public opinion
was necessary to enhance political dialogue and preserve
democratic values (although he did warn that demagogues
could subvert the lofty goals).

Nevertheless, advertising was, in the end, only a cover
for an economy of exploitation and manipulation, Lears
believed. He concluded that advertising was a warped and
thwarted dream of transcendence that could never rise to
the level of true art: "The admaker's social functions resemble those of a Soviet party hack: both serve as cogs in
a vast cultural apparatus that justifies and celebrates the
existing economic system."[69]

MODERNISM, ANARCHISM, AND AESTHETICS IN THE UNITED STATES

ANARCHISM WAS ONE of many radical responses to the
profound dislocations in society created by the Industrial
Revolution, the rise of the nation state, and the burgeoning of capitalism. Urban industrialization had broken up
traditional village communities, and radicals of all persua-
sions were proposing political alternative models to bring
people together in urban and industrial environments.

In general, anarchism calls for a close relationship
between means and ends; it is concerned with both the

---

67 Edward L Bernays, "The Engineering of Consent," *The Annals of the*
    American Academy of Political and Social Science 250 (1947), 113. See
    also Edward L. Bernays, *Propaganda* (NY: Horace Liveright, 1928).

68 Bernays, 115.

69 Lears, "Uneasy Courtship," 151.

political and the cultural; and it advocates decentralization but not fragmentation; organization, not chaos. The anarchists' commitment to a decentralized political organizational model sets anarchism apart from other statist theories. This resulted in the initial ideological split between the Bolsheviks and the anarchists at the meeting of the First International in 1872. The Bolsheviks argued for a centrally-controlled state power structure, while the anarchists maintained that political power needed to be decentralized into a federation of democratically-governed collectives and cooperatives.

There are two broad strains of anarchist theory in the classical tradition: individualist anarchism and a variety of collectivist strains or social anarchism. These strains are not mutually exclusive; each strain informs the other, but they do have distinct philosophical roots. Individualist anarchism emphasizes the empowerment of the unique individual over and against society. It rejects any social or cultural constraints on individual action, emphasizing individual freedoms over collective claims. It spans a spectrum of individual libertarian thought from William Godwin to Ayn Rand, but its principle theoretical basis is the radical, almost solipsistic individualism of Max Stirner. Prominent American individualist anarchists include Josiah Warren, Benjamin Tucker (who translated Stirner into English), and the abolitionist lawyer, Lysander Spooner.

Social anarchism, on the other hand, called for the creation of an environment of freedom for everyone living together in community; it advocated for social justice for all; it was concerned with the process and practice of living everyday life. Beginning about 1850, European immigrants fleeing conscription and the Peasant Wars being waged across the continent came to the United States bringing with them their political experiences with various forms of European socialisms. Social anarchists included Peter Kropotkin, Michael Bakunin, Fourier utopian socialists, Christian anarchists like Lev Tolstoy, the Proudhonian mutualists, and the anarcho-syndicalists. Social anarchists inspired the American Industrial Workers of the World (IWW), and more broadly the Midwestern cooperative movement. Until well into the twentieth century, these anarcho-communist-socialist philosophies dominated anarchist theory and practice in both the United States and Europe. Most political activities were concentrated among workers – in particular, the worldwide anarcho-syndicalist workers' movements.

In the United States the anarchist movement was based in the large urban centers and their burgeoning immigrant communities. Alexander Berkman and Emma Goldman were two of the most important intellectual voices in these immigrant communities, tirelessly organizing workers, participating in strikes, speaking out on behalf of women, defending free-speech, organizing against conscription and war, defending the rights of prisoners, and relentlessly criticizing the rampant abuses of industrial capitalism. Of the two, Berkman was more committed to socialist and communist anarchist theories. Goldman was closer in spirit to the avant-garde bohemian individualist community. She was also a keen critic of capitalism and advocated for the collective rights of working people. In her introduction to *Red Emma Speaks*, Alix Kates Shulman described Goldman as an accomplished orator in both Russian and English, her second language. She crisscrossed Europe and the United States speaking out on the major political issues of the era at massive public demonstrations and in hundreds of smaller venues. Shulman noted that on a nationwide tour in 1910, Goldman reported "speaking 120 times in thirty-seven cities in twenty-five states to 25,000 paying and even more non-paying listeners."[70] Other American anarchist activists included such diverse groups as the free-spirited Wobblies (Industrial Workers

---

70 Alix Kates Shulman, ed., *Red Emma Speaks: Selected Writings and Speeches by Emma Goldman* (New York, NY: Vintage Books, 1972), 15.

of the World – IWW) whose primary spokesman was "Big Bill" Haywood, the Anti-Conscription League, the Francisco Ferrer Modern School movement (named after the Spanish anarchist and designer of new models for education), Dorothy Day's Catholic Worker movement, and the Free Speech League, to name only a few.

In *Beyond the Martyrs: A Social History of Chicago's Anarchists, 1870-1900*, Bruce Nelson provided a rich and detailed assessment of the size and influence of a working class anarchist community in one large American city – Chicago. Anarchists played a major role in the city's left wing political movements for decades.[71] Nelson's research found that in Chicago alone there were tens of thousands of active anarchists who sustained a vital alternative culture. Anarchist political actions were primarily organized around the labor unions of the International Working People's Association (IWPA). Estimates of the size of the IWPA ranged from an initial 1,000 members up to 3,000 members. Their political constituency and cultural impact were much larger, however.[72] At the end of 1885, for example, the anarchist journal *The Alarm* reported that over a ten-month period, "387,537 books, pamphlets, and circulars had been distributed by the organization;" and the "IWPA's seven papers enjoyed a total circulation of 30,880 in 1886."[73]

Early twentieth century anarchist aesthetics

In *Anarchist Modernism: Art, Politics, and the First American Avant-Garde*, Allan Antliff made the case that American Modernism was grounded in the philosophies of Friedrich Nietzsche, Michael Bakunin, and Max

---

71 Bruce C. Nelson, *Beyond the Martyrs: A Social History of Chicago's Anarchists, 1870-1900* (New Brunswick NJ: Rutgers University Press, 1988).

72 Nelson, 80.

73 Nelson, 121 and 123.

Stirner, all of which had a distinct individualist bent. [74]
Antliff argued that it was Max Stirner's radical egoism in
particular that resonated with Modernism. Stirner is the
acknowledged seminal theorist of individualist anarchism,
and most theoreticians from both the left and the right of
the political spectrum agree that while he is always pre-
cious (he's good at sound bites), he can be theoretically
problematic. In *The Ego and Its Own*, Stirner outlined a bold
critique of Hegelian philosophy and its followers. Stirner
postulated a nihilist radical individualism that rejected any
and all objective standards other than those upon which
the individual chose to act. He rejected all manifestations
of external authority – of a state, of a religion, or even of
democracy. His book alarmed Friedrich Engels and Karl
Marx so much that two years later they published the six-
hundred-page *The German Ideology* to refute Stirner's arguments – a sure sign that his ideas were deeply threatening
to Marxism. [75] Freed of any external standards or principles, Stirner's philosophy articulated the perfect relativistic reality.

The "core project" of Modernism, according to Antliff,
is individual "artistic liberation."[76] He proposed that
Modernism's conscious break with the authority of artistic "academism" and its formalized stylistic elements in
favor of freedom of individual artist's expression and the
open experimentation with form and content were key elements in Modernist aesthetics.[77] Underlying all elements
of Modernism, he argued, is the anarchistic impulse for
revolution and rebellion against authority.[78] Antliff char-

---

74 Allan Antliff, *Anarchist Modernism: Art, Politics, and the First American
    Avant-Garde* (Chicago and London: The University of Chicago
    Press, 2001), 52.

75 Karl Marx and Frederich Engels, *The German Ideology* (Moscow:
    Progress Publishers, 1964).

76 Antliff, 73.

77 Antliff, 34, 47.

78 Antliff, 43.

acterized political art as a personal revolt against anything that inhibited individual expression.

Antliff identified Robert Henri, one of the Ashcan School of American painters, as a key figure linking Modernist aesthetics to the theory of anarchism in the American art scene. In 1908 Henri organized an exhibition of nonacademic artists as a challenge to the academic art establishment. He consciously linked the exhibit "to the cause of artistic individualism and freedom of expression."[79] According to Antliff, while Henri "did not tout the show as an 'anarchist' event, … nonetheless, what he set in motion in 1908 was an attempt to establish a counter community in the arts whose defining features – individualism, freedom of expression, contemporary subject matter, and egalitarianism in art schools and exhibition spaces – owed much to the anarchist movement."[80]

Antliff credited two other individuals with forging the theoretical links between the anarchist and artist communities in the United States: Hutchin Hapgood and Hippolyte Havel, both of whom had solid anarchist credentials. Hapgood, a journalist and art critic, was a well-known spokesperson for anarchism and an active participant in two anarchist cultural venues: the Modern School Ferrer Center and photographer Alfred Steiglitz's studio 291. It was in studio 291 that Hapgood met the likes of Alexander Berkman, Emma Goldman, and Stieglitz himself, who openly endorsed the philosophy of anarchism.[81] According to Antliff, "In a polemic suffused with the anarchist values of individualism and unconstrained freedom of expression, Hapgood argued such art would break with all rules and regulations in a quest to return to 'the primitive, to the simple, to the direct material, to crude contact with nature' as expressed by the personality of the artist."[82]

---

79 Antliff, 43.

80 Antliff, 17.

81 Antliff, 31-34.

82 Antliff, 43.

Hippolyte Havel met Emma Goldman in London in 1899 and became her lover. He joined her in New York in 1900 where he became her "right-hand man" at *Mother Earth*, a mainstay at the Modern School Ferrer Center and a friend of Hapgood and Stieglitz. Havel also founded three journals – *Social War*, *The Revolutionary Almanac*, and *The Revolt* which served as important venues for modernist art with a political bent.[83] According to Antliff, Havel's contributions to theory emphasized creating and maintaining anarchist community. The contexualization of art in the radical political culture is extremely important because the cultural context of radicalism is central to understanding the relationship between art and politics.

Modernism encouraged a variety of styles and techniques and Antliff's study found that some anarchist artists experimented with non-traditional styles, which others continued in the realist tradition. Part of the modernist rebellion was against the requirement that art be representational – thus the insistence on stylistic freedom and tendency toward abstraction. This represented a challenge for artists seeking to communicate political messages to the general public or even within radical political communities. Artists rebelling against realism included cubists, futurists and Dada-influenced artist Man Ray (who occasionally produced realistic pieces). Antliff also examined artists who created realistic political aesthetic statements – George Bellows, Ludovico Caminita, Robert Minor, and Ben Benn.

Despite the modernist assault on realism, realistic images played a more important role in portraying and reflecting anarchist political action. Anarchist realism relied heavily on graphic art, cartoons, and drawings published in radical newspapers and political avant-garde magazines such as Emma Goldman's *Mother Earth* and *The Masses*. Curiously, given Goldman's own avant-garde proclivities and her avid embrace of Nietzschean individualism, her

---

83 Antliff, 95.

journal was relatively indifferent to the new modernist styles and the new trends in aesthetics, according to Peter Glassgold.[84] In most anarchist publications, the imagery was heavy with symbolic political content conveyed in a narrative message. Commonly portrayed images were of direct political actions, and included striking workers; the everyday lives of workers and their families; caricatures of greedy, wealthy capitalists as overweight or diabolical people; political demonstrations, and idealized artistic renderings of important political events such as the Haymarket massacre. Groups of protesters were often the focus of attention, emphasizing collective experiences and collective action. Some images overtly attacked religious beliefs and caricatured Puritan moralists like Anthony Comstock.[85] The image of the black cat (Sabot Cat) was common. It was a powerful IWW symbol borrowed from the French syndicalist movement and was widely recognized as a code for sabotage and "direct action" in the workplace. Sal Salerno noted that direct action for the IWW meant "actions that have real value for the worker."[86] The IWW also developed a particularly effective aesthetic tool – taking universally recognized popular tunes and creating political lyrics. The label "singing revolutionaries" attested to the popularity of their technique.[87]

Anarchist art also portrayed violent images. Artists

---

84 Peter Glassgold, ed., *Anarchy: An Anthology of Emma Goldman's Mother Earth* (Washington, DC: Counterpoint, 2001).

85 Comstock was the U.S. Postal Inspector. He initiated a robust attack on "lewd and lascivious" images and objectionable books, literature on birth control and contraceptives shipped through the U.S. mails. He often locked horns with Margaret Sanger and Emma Goldman.

86 Salvatore Salerno, *Red November Black November: Culture and Community in the Industrial Workers of the World* (Albany, NY: SUNY Press, 1989), 125.

87 The IWW *Little Red Songbook* is still in print today, and from time to time, the lyrics are adapted to contemporary topics.

Robert Minor and Ludovico Caminita, among others, vividly described the Haymarket bombing, violent encounters with the wealthy and powerful, street battles, and other images reflecting political confrontations. The mainstream press, on the other hand, portrayed only negative images. Stereotypical mainstream symbols such as the black flag; wild-eyed, crazed men wielding exploding bombs; and images of daggers and guns were common. Any collective action was portrayed as mob action. Affirmative anarchist ideals, on the other hand, never saw the light of day in the mainstream corporate media.

Modernism and individualism

How are we to explain the modernist withdrawal from the historical mission of art to reflect the culture and Modernism's subsequent retreat into individual and personal rebellion as the source of inspiration for art? The answer, in part, is the emergence of modern individualism. Modern individualism was born and matured over a long period of time, but came into its own at the turn of the twentieth century. Thomas Hobbes planted the seeds of contemporary individualism as early as the seventeenth century, and individualism was reinforced by John Locke, Jean Jacques Rousseau, and the early nineteenth century utilitarian philosophers. Individualism was, in part, a rejection of various external authorities, and consistent with challenges to authority in other settings as well. The Reformation challenged the control of the Catholic Church over the interpretation of religious teachings and replaced centralized authority with direct individual communication with spiritual powers. In art, too, named individual artists gradually replaced the anonymity of the medieval artists. Central to almost all post-Hegelian aesthetics was the primacy of the individual artist as the source for artistic inspiration and creativity. Modernism was the aesthetic "face" of individualism, mirroring the individualism in cultures generally.

But, there were many other cultural vectors at work in the early twentieth century that served to reinforce the idea of individualism and individual action and push the individual into the role of prime mover. The rapidity of the transition from rural to urban living, the rise of the individual as consumer, and the new field of psychology were all married to American "rugged" individualism and the Emersonian faith in individual self-reliance. The transition from the social context of the village to the anonymity of the urban industrial landscape left individuals alienated and adrift in a world of other autonomous individuals. The psychology of Sigmund Freud reinforced the power of individual insights and the inner world of imagination and dreams and freed the individual from societal control.

The centrality of the individual in the emerging consumer economy further exacerbated the tendency to preference individual autonomous action. The logic of the marketplace is based on the primacy of individual choice and the "freedom" to choose. The conflation of the idea of a "free" market and a "free" individual underlies contemporary individualism. The indifference to social responsibility or even social responsiveness was the price of individual freedom in a market society.

Cultural differences also manifested themselves within the anarchist community in the tension between individualist and social anarchism and between native and immigrant anarchists. Anarchists from both schools debated the relative merits of the two approaches, in part because of the interest in Max Stirner – Emma Goldman and Benjamin Tucker faced off, for example, while at the same time Goldman actively promoted Nietzsche's individualism.[88]

---

88 The debate was taken up in Europe as well. In 1909, in *La Sensibilité individualiste (The Anarchist Sensibility)*, French philosopher Georges Palante developed a defense of Nietzschean individualist anarchism, exploring the disjunction between individualism and what he referred to as an idealistic and optimistic—and ultimately unrealistic—anarchism. Classical anarchism attempted to heal this

But, privileging the insights of the individual can be problematic – especially for politics and for political action. Like individualist anarchism, Modernism celebrates the emotional and privileges the power of the individual; it places an emphasis on style (but no particular style) rather than meaning; it postulates that the role of art is to be provocative; it has no concern for addressing or reflecting a formal social agenda; it embraces the alienated rebel as the new model for heroism as a kind of elitism; and it equates art with the idea of freedom *as* expression. Unfortunately, just because individual anarchist artists were political did not necessarily make their art political; and political art can reflect either one individual's politics or social politics. If the assumption is that the sole source of inspiration for political art is the individual artist, anything other than personal choice or even whimsy may not guide the artist's intentions. There are also potentially serious implications for politics and political action in the conflicting agendas of individual artistic self-expression and collective direct action. Does political art move the culture to where the individual artist wants to go, or does it move the culture toward society's collective goals? The conflation of individual artistic self-expression and anarchist political theory served, in the end, only to exacerbate the artificial separation of art from politics and to divert art from a more comprehensive, social mission. While individualism is one way to experience one's

---

dichotomy by integrating individual freedom with social commitment but failed, according to Palante—individualism is "the sentiment of a profound antinomy between the individual and society." Individualism and anarchism are not compatible, he concluded: "Inner life and social action are two things that are mutually exclusive."Palante, Georges. *La Sensibilite individualiste (The Anarchist Sensibility)*, translated by Mitch Abidor (Paris: Folle Avoine, 1909). Also known as "Anarchism and Individualism." Available at www.marxists.org/archive/palante/1909/individualism.htm and www.theanarchistlibrary.org

freedom, individual freedom can also end up being solipsistic, narcissistic, and irrelevant.

Modernism as anarchism

In *Anarchy and Culture,* David Weir developed a different and very radical analysis of Modernism: re-interpreting Modernism as a radical political expression of individualist anarchist activism, a politics expressed as aesthetics. [89] He positioned the modernists as a third, anarchist alternative to the Marxists and prior avant-garde movements in the arts. Weir's argument merits some attention because it offers one interpretation of the modernist desire to integrate politics and aesthetics.

Weir built his argument on defining Modernism as the aesthetic expression of Stirner's brand of extreme individualism which is characterized by the following principles: it is a critique of all hierarchies and all forms of psychological or ideological control over the individual; it celebrates the social order as "endlessly and actively fragmenting;" it is a "politics of style;" it reflects the "constant interplay of both Enlightenment ideas and Romantic vision;" and it is internally contradictory. [90]

Weir defined culture as art, anarchism as individualist anarchism, Modernism as the idea of the avant-garde, and politics as individual attitudes, acts, and statements of aesthetic protest against the dominant hegemony. He contended that Modernism has eclipsed anarchism, it *is* anarchism and that "anarchism succeeded culturally where it failed politically." [91] Even though nineteenth century Marxist-inspired social anarchist political movements failed, Weir argued, the individualist anarchist impulse survived in the modernist (and even the postmodernist) tradition as an

---

89 David Weir, *Anarchy and Culture: the Aesthetic Politics of Modernism* (Amherst, MA: University of Massachusetts Press, 1997),.261.

90 Weir, 5, 12, 15 and 33.

91 Weir, 5.

"ahistorical, conceptual 'anarchism.'"[92] Modernism represented "the art of satisfaction, egoism, and fragmentation
… [and] the aesthetic realization of anarchist politics."[93]

Weir nevertheless recognized that Modernism did not
have a clear, radical political agenda. It had the potential to either mask genuine radical political agendas, or
worse, to embrace reactionary political agendas. Some of
the modernists, Weir observed, "were drawn to the authoritarian politics of the period, but their endorsement
of such politics is not necessarily reflected in their artistic
practice."[94] Despite the incongruities and political implications of lumping fascists and individualist anarchists together, Weir is determined to use his aesthetic brand of
anarchism as a unifying principle. His assumptions are
jaw-dropping. *"But regardless of the underlying ideology that
informs a particular Modernism,* many of these Modernisms
look the same because they are overlaid with anarchism –
not political anarchism, but anarchism in aesthetic form
[italics mine]."[95]

In his effort to merge art and politics, Weir also cited
Theodor Adorno to support his argument that "aesthetic
practice became a form of political action."[96] He based his
view of aesthetic politics on an interpretation of Adorno's
definition of an autonomous art. According to Weir,
Adorno proposed that art could be most effective if it remained autonomous and apolitical. This interpretation is
something of a misrepresentation of Adorno's more nuanced position on the relationship between autonomy and
engagement with the social reality. Adorno argued that art
is never totally autonomous in the sense of being entirely
separate and individual. Part of the reason for Adorno's
rigorous defense of autonomy was his concern about the

---

92 Weir, 262.
93 Weir, 169.
94 Weir, 262.
95 Weir, 201, my emphasis.
96 Weir, 162.

co-optation of art by the culture industry. At the same time, art had a responsibility to challenge the dominant culture – a decidedly political responsibility.[97] The only possible role for art was to remain always just out of reach of the tentacles of capitalist aesthetics but still engaged in political debate. To counter co-optation in his theory, Adorno went overboard to establish an independent and autonomous role for art. But, he never meant for art to be isolated from society. In fact, he argued in *Aesthetic Theory* that the social was embedded in art: "The double character of art – something that severs itself from empirical reality and thereby from society's functional context and yet is at the same time part of empirical reality and society's functional context – is directly apparent in the aesthetic phenomena, which are both aesthetic and *faits sociaux*."[98] Politics was never far from his thinking, and a social role for art was grounded in the dialectical relationship within the artwork. The relationship between the aesthetic and the political is expressed in Adorno's concept of the form which reflected this "double character" of artworks: "The liberation of form, which genuinely new art desires, holds enciphered within it above all the liberation of society, for form – the social nexus of everything particular – represents the social relation in the artwork; this is why liberated form is anathema to the status quo."[99]

Adorno did not merge art with politics but retained their independent qualities in a dialectical tension. Overall, Adorno was more interested in the universal message of art rather than the particular and subjective expressions of individual artists. The particular is always subsumed under the universal; the artist and the artwork are irrevocably linked to a larger sense of purpose and meaning.

Weir's analysis obviously presents problems for Modernism and anarchism both: either you claim all of

---

97 Adorno, *Aesthetic Theory*, 255.

98 Adorno, *Aesthetic Theory*, 252.

99 Adorno, *Aesthetic Theory*, 255.

modern art as anarchism, or you reduce anarchism to art. If Weir is correct, ultimately, the anarchist must ask, what are the implications for anarchism as a political theory if aesthetics is the only arena in which anarchism can operate effectively or can claim theoretical ground? His theory is open to criticism at several points. By removing the traditional concept of "politics" as a collective social activity and replacing it with individual acts of aesthetic rebellion and self-expression, the political dialogue is diverted from the broader critique of organized power structures such as the state, the organized tyranny of multinational corporations, racism, or religious fundamentalism, to focus entirely on cultural matters. Further, Weir does not discuss, and his approach would seem to be indifferent to the question of how Modernism was/was not a critique of capitalism. Indeed, many theorists argued that Modernism is just an aesthetic manifestation of capitalist consumerism and, as such, is not part of the solution but part of the problem. Weir's analysis forces the anarchist community to ask once again whether individualist anarchism is really a critique of capitalism or just its swan song, its eviscerated howl of frustration.

Weir also flirted with the destabilizing and relativistic notion that all art could (potentially) be "political." This belief paralleled American Pragmatist philosopher John Dewey's conclusion that "every experience is an aesthetic one" so that one is left with the question of whether any experience is really an aesthetic one or whether all experiences are aesthetic.[100] In emphasizing experience and the extension of the aesthetic across all human enterprise, both subjective and objective elements were sublimated to experience. Dewey, for example, even made a special effort to be non-judgmental: "The experience may be one that is harmful to the world and its consummation undesirable. But it has aesthetic quality."[101]

---

100   John Dewey, *Art as Experience*, (New York, NY: Minton, Balch, 1958).

101   Dewey, 39.

Weir's argument that Modernism *is* anarchist politics hinges on how politics is defined and whether politics is understood as collective or individual. The word "politics" comes from the Greek word for city – *polis*. While political theorists have debated for millennia the nature of the ideal political organization, the study of politics has continued to be shaped by the characteristics of a collective unit, not the individual. Traditionally politics has been understood as coordinated interaction among people to organize and to structure their personal and economic lives around mutually-agreed upon principles; individual politics, on the other hand, emphasizes individual actions – particularly acts of rebellion. This distinction is an important one, and a case will be made in the final chapter of this book that an anarchism that fails to recognize the mutuality of both social and individual contexts is inconsistent with the goal of creating political art.

Finally, there is no rationale for seeing Modernism as political action in and of itself. However much Weir would like to paint an entire aesthetic movement with the anarchist brush, he failed to make a case that Modernism is anarchism in political practice. His approach also served to trivialize more sophisticated political analyses of anarchism. While some modernist artists were political (and I will discuss many of them throughout this book), it will be clear that anarchism is much more than political art; and Modernism is much less political than anarchism. Indeed, Modernism often had other objectives that were hostile to radical and progressive politics.

THE LEGACY OF MODERNISM

MODERNISM AND ITS derivative impulse postmodernism are the aesthetic ocean in which we have been swimming since the late nineteenth century; and, as such, Modernism is too broad to pin down to a specific purpose, goal, or agenda. It has manifested itself in every area of the arts. In some ways it seems merely to be a term or convention to describe what took place in the arts since the Industrial Revolution. And, in that sense, it has no "legacy" since it is still a work unfolding.

Modernist art has no consistent style or content; it has no specific technique bearing its name. Sometimes it is described as a mood or an attitude; sometimes it seeks only to disrupt for the sake of disruption. At their best the early modernists made important stylistic statements as an aesthetic avant-garde: they broke with a previous aesthetic that was clearly defined and articulated in theme, technique, and style. But, they offered no equally compelling vision in its place. The classical role of art as representing collective meaning was abandoned to the whims and fantasies of the individual artist's vision.

Modernism celebrated the freedom of the individual artist, the freedom to experiment with content and style, and the freedom from the repression of all aesthetic standards and expectations. In turning art toward the subjective whims of individual artists, however, Modernism set the stage for the separation of art and the artist from any social context or cultural tradition. But, there may have been an ironic result of this conscious separation. In *Has Modernism Failed?* Suzi Gablik concluded that in abjuring traditional moral and aesthetic values, modernism ironically undermined the power of the individual artist to influence society:

> Individuality and freedom are undoubtedly the greatest achievements of modern culture. But insistence upon absolute freedom for each individual leads to a negative attitude toward society, and the sense of a culture deeply alienated from its surroundings. The desire for an unconditional world can only be realized, when all is said and done, at the cost of social alienation – in the absence of integration and union.

> The growing dependence on a market-intensive, professionally manipulated art world has resulted in artists losing their power to act autonomously and live creatively. This particular change happened without being instigated. It was non-deliberate. It happened because late capitalism, with its mass-consumption ethic, weakened the capacity of art for transmitting patterns of conscious ethical value. ... Whether or not this process can be reversed will depend on what we all now think of the hopes and ideals with which the modern era began – and whether we believe that art is related to a moral order, or that its function is purely an aesthetic one. [102]

While individual artists may or may not have been political actors, their art increasingly had no political role. In the process of freeing the artist from tradition and from any obligation to society, the meaning of art was also altered. Art for art's sake unwittingly became the slave to commodity capitalist aesthetics; the work of art was now just another object, another commodity, abandoned to the vagaries of the marketplace.

Left unresolved was the uneasy relationship between Modernism and capitalist aesthetics. As the twentieth century progressed, this issue became the focus of intellectual analysis and political and aesthetic debate. The early warnings of Walter Benjamin and Theodor Adorno blossomed into the cultural studies movement of the 1970s which focused its critique of Modernism almost entirely on capitalist aesthetics and the art of advertising as political power.

---

102   Gabrik, Suzi. *Has Modernism Failed?* NY and London: Thames & Hudson, 1984. Chapter 5, www.rowan.edu/open/philosop/ downey/Aesthetics/scans/Gablik/Baglikb.htm

CHAPTER 3

DADA, SURREALISM AND THE DREAM OF REVOLUTION

Sooner or later …the long smouldering fury of the dream of freedom is going to erupt. … [T]he whole ambition of the surrealists is to inspire it, to multiply it, to arm it, to free it, and to make it invincible.1

INTRODUCTION

ARTISTS AND PHILOSOPHERS MEASURE THE PULSE OF THEIR eras. They "read" and reflect on the messages conveyed, especially in times of uncertainty and change. They are central to distilling and interpreting the events swirling around them, to making manifest the meaning of culture shifts, and to bringing pattern and understanding to the many ways that people experience and express their realities. In many cultures artists are honored and respected as the bearers of new visions – an avant-garde channel through which cultural transformations are transmitted. At certain important cultural junctures, a major new

---

1 Anonymous, "1976: End of the 'American Way of Life,'" Arsenal/ Surrealist Subversion 3 (1976), in *Surrealist Subversions: Rants, Writings and Images by the Surrealist Movement in the United States*, ed. Ron Sakolsky (New York, NY: Autonomedia, 2002), 474.

aesthetic emerges to reflect a new awareness, a new focus, a new direction or vision. The early twentieth century was such a time of tremendous cultural upheaval, and Dada and Surrealism were at the cutting edge of the modernist avant-garde aesthetic response.

The idea of an avant-garde is in many ways the heart of the modernist impulse.[2] Change had always occurred historically in art, but the changes were subtle – changes in technique, changes in patronage and message, changes in scale and subject matter. But beginning in the mid-nineteenth century, the magnitude and speed of change accelerated with the monumental shifts in perspective and purpose that Modernism unleashed. Key to the modernist agenda was the idea of autonomy. Two senses of the term emerged. The first is the idea of the autonomous individual artist as the source of artistic inspiration who is free and independent from the constraints of bourgeois tradition and capitalist culture. The second, and more radical, sense of autonomy is the idea of the institution of art itself as autonomous and separate.

The latter was the inspiration for the radical extremes of the Dada movement. In order to free art from suffocation and repression by bourgeois society, the bourgeois meaning of art had to be rejected. The movement emerged after World War I in Western Europe as a nihilistic response to the profound despair over the rampant death and destruction resulting from the war, disenchantment with the political and economic realities of capitalism, and the dismemberment of traditional communal life by the introduction of the capitalist mode of production. Society was in upheaval; the old myths, the very foundations of society had failed. Everywhere writers and artists looked, the old world view had failed and Europe had been completely destroyed. The movement artists randomly selected the nonsense word *dada* to convey this nihilistic experience of nothingness.[3]

---

2   See Peter Burger, *Theory of the Avant-Garde* (Minneapolis: University of Minnesota Press, 1984.

3   Armand Lanoux, *Paris in the Twenties* (New York, NY: Golden

The Dada solution was to reconfigure art as performance and engagement with the world – to radically disrupt the dominant aesthetic meaning and integrate art and life in a new society. British writer Gavin Grindon argued that Dada artists adopted the public performance techniques of the activist protest movements of the era.

> Dada took a protest form. Their particular imagination of protest was indebted to the language of libertarian nineteenth-century working-class movements. These movements tended to account for protest and direct action in reactive terms of incitement, provocation, outrage, and offense. ... For the Dadaists, the artist-organizer was replaced by the artist-agitator.[4]

Historian Armand Lanoux concluded that "Dada was a kind of battering ram, capable of breaking down more than one kind of wall, of shattering more than one kind of privacy. [It] set out to destroy art."[5] Dada called for the ultimate destruction of art as a means of destroying the bourgeoisie. The Dadaists went one step further beyond a simple critique of bourgeois art – they rejected all meaning in art. In *Dada: Art and Anti-Art* Zurich painter and filmmaker Hans Richter (an active participant in the early days of the movement) recalled,

> Dada not only had no programme, it was against all programmes. ... [The] negative definitions of Dada arose from the rejection of what needed to be rejected. This rejection

Griffin Books/Essential Encyclopedia Arts, Inc., 1960), 44.

4 Gavin Grindon, "Surrealism, Dada, and the Refusal of Work: Autonomy, Activism, and Social Participation in the Radical Avant-Garde," *Oxford Art Journal* 34.1, 2011: 89.

5 Lanoux, 44.

arose from a desire for intellectual and spiritual freedom. ... It drove us to the fragmentation or destruction of all artistic forms, and to rebellion for rebellion's sake; to an anarchistic negation of all values, a self-exploding bubble, a raging *anti, anti, anti*, linked with an equally passionate *pro, pro, pro*![6]

Dada emerged at a point in European history when radical social movements were at their apex. They shared the call for revolutionary change with the various Marxist, socialist, and anarchist movements. The commitment to rebellion was central to the Dada aesthetic. Reflecting on the spirit of rebellion in *The Rebel*, Albert Camus wrote, "In every rebellion is to be found the metaphysical demand for unity, the impossibility of capturing it, and the construction of a substitute universe. Rebellion, from this point of view, is a fabricator of universes and a definition of art. The demands of rebellion are really, in art, aesthetic demands."[7] But, Dada had no plan, no ideology, no formal philosophical "solution" to the challenges of the era – only a message of refusal, destruction, and rebellion.

Although no particular identifiable style can be linked to Dada art, a variety of techniques such as collage, photomontage, nonsense words, and political pamphlets were employed (with ongoing bitter arguments over whom had first created the new techniques). Artist Marcel Duchamps' submission of a urinal as a work of sculpture to an art exhibition is often cited as the quintessential example of Dada outrageousness and the use of "ready-mades" in art. According to Dada poet, writer and drummer Carl

6   Hans Richter, *Dada: Art and Anti-Art* (London and New York, NY: Thames and Hudson, 1965 and 1997), 34-35. This is an excellent analysis of the world of Dada by a participant observer. His account also relies heavily on writings of other Dada artists.

7   Albert Camus, *The Rebel: An Essay on Man in Revolt* (New York, NY: Vintage, 1973), 221.

Wilhelm Richard Hüelsenbeck, who was active in Zurich and a founder of Berlin Dada, the manifesto was an especially important aesthetic tool: "The manifesto as a literary medium answered our need for directness. We had no time to lose; we wanted to incite our opponents to resistance, and, if necessary, to create new opponents for ourselves."[8]

There is general agreement that the Dada movement was born in Zurich, Switzerland in 1916 and spread quickly to other cities – Berlin, New York, and Paris. The central cast of characters was small, and the same people appeared in first one city, then the other. German émigré Hugo Ball was a prominent Zurich poet and founder of the Cabaret Voltaire – the site of many Dada events. Dada performances competed for outrageousness. One element central to all events was the practice of insulting their audiences to the point of instigating riots. Their goal was to wake the audience up; the audience, of course, delighted in the outrages and kept coming back for more. According to Richter, "the interplay of different arts was maintained in all our activities." Ball wrote, "I was convinced of this: a theatre which experiments beyond the realm of day-to-day preoccupations. ... A fusion, not merely of all art, but of all regenerative ideas. The background of colours, words and sounds must be brought out from the subconscious and given life, so that it engulfs everyday life and all its misery."[9] According to Ball, artists such as Wassily Kandinsky, Paul Klee, and Giorgio de Chirico also inspired style in Dada art.

Responding spontaneously to an element of chance and serendipity was another core objective in Dada:

> Even without going to extremes, the use of chance had opened up an important new dimension in art: the techniques of free association, fragmentary trains of thought, unexpected

---

8   Richard Hüelsenbeck, speech quoted in Richter, 103.
9   Richter, 35.

juxtapositions of words and sounds. In the field of visual art this new freedom had consequences that were possibly even more far-reaching.[10]

This idea of free play allowed Dada artists to explore endless creative variations in their art: using found objects, pasting random pieces of paper into new shapes and designs, or creating poems from words randomly strewn across a table.

Ball was influenced by some aspects of anarchism and was especially taken with Bakunin. In 1916 he created a Dada Manifesto which is characterized by the use of nonsense words and the rejection of everything (with a touch of absurdity for good measure) which can be seen in a representative phrase from the manifesto below:

> Dada psychology, dada German cum indigestion and fog paroxysm, dada literature, dada bourgeoisie, and yourselves, honoured poets, who are always writing with words but never writing the word itself, who are always writing around the actual point. Dada world war without end, dada revolution without beginning, dada, you friends and also-poets, esteemed sirs, manufacturers, and evangelists.[11]

Another key figure in Zurich was the Romanian poet Tristan Tzara, who also had connections with French writers André Breton and Louis Aragon. Tzara and Aragon especially played an important role in the transition from Dada to Surrealism – at least for a while before Tzara had a falling out with Breton.

Two other German artists, working in the realist tradition, also merit mentioning here: George Grosz and John

---

10 Richter, 55.

11 Hugo Ball, "Dada Manifesto," 1916. En.wikipedia.org/wiki/Hugo_Ball

Heartfield. While Dada was raging in Berlin, these two artists continued to develop popular art forms designed to reach the average person. Like the Dada artists, they were critical of bourgeois art. Grosz is noted for his satirical illustrations and acute political insights, Heartfield for his photomontages. They also collaborated on collages and other art projects. Their work appeared in the one and only volume of the satirical newspaper *Jedermann sein eigner Fussball* (every man his own football). The paper was subsequently banned, but their work continued to appear in other publications, and they subsequently created artwork for the German Communist Party. In 1933, Heartfield barely escaped the SS who came to arrest him. In an essay by the same name in *Grosz/Heartfield: The Artist as Social Critic*, Beth Irwin Lewis observed: "The strongest and most ironic tribute to the work of Heartfield came not in the Nazi attempts to destroy and discredit his work, but in their imitation of his techniques."[12]

Dada artists also shared their new vision in New York, according to Richter. Both American and European Dada artists gathered around photographer Alfred Stieglitz's 291 Gallery on Fifth Avenue. The American artist Man Ray was a central figure; the Europeans included visual artists Francis Picabia, Arthur Cravan, Marcel Duchamps, and Albert Gleizes. Marcel Duchamps painting, "Nude Descending a Staircase" was a big hit at the Armory Show in 1913, one of New York's first avant-garde exhibitions.

Writer and critic Roger Shattuck argued that the Berlin Dada movement was the most overtly political, responding in part to the terrible devastation of Germany after the war.[13] Berlin was embroiled in political rebellion, which was reflected in some Dada activities including left wing

---

12 See *Grosz/Heartfield: The Artist as Social Critic*. Minneapolis, MN: University Gallery University of Minnesota, 1980.

13 Roger Shattuck, "The D-S Expedition: Part I," *The New York Review of Books* 18, 9, May 18, 1972. http://www.nybooks.com/articles/archives/

publications and the disruptive performances that had been so successful in Zurich. However, Richter argued that Dada politics was as fragmented as the art: there was little understanding of political perspectives.[14]

> There was a revolution going on, and Dada was right in the thick of it. At one moment they were all for the Spartakus movement; then it was Communism, Bolshevism, Anarchism and whatever else was going on. But there was always a side door left open for a quick getaway, if this should be necessary to preserve what Dada valued most – personal freedom and independence.

Nevertheless, Richter concluded: "They may all have been 'anti' different things, and for different reasons – this certainly became the case later on – but every one of them was anti-authoritarian." At one point, their activities came to the attention of the police over an anti-militaristic song Richter had published in the periodical *Jedermann sein eigner Fussball.*[15] In another bold political statement, at the inauguration ceremony for the government of the new Weimar republic, Johannes Baader threw flyers from the gallery nominating himself first president. "On another occasion," Richter noted, "Baader interrupted former Court Chaplain Dryander, preaching in Berlin Cathedral."[16] Their most startling action took place at the First International Dada Fair in 1920. According to Richter, this was the climax of Berlin Dada.

> The tone was set by a number of provocative political pieces expressing hatred for the Authority that had "brought us to this." From

---

14 Richter, 109.
15 Richter, 111.
16 Richter, 126-127.

the ceiling hung the stuffed effigy of a German officer with a pig's head, bearing a placard saying "Hanged by the Revolution." The all-important prefix "anti-" seemed here to be directed against the ruling class rather than against art.[17]

The baton was passed to the French Dadaists who were then succeeded by the surrealists. Tristan Tzara and Hugo Ball were two important figures in the transition from Dada to Surrealism, along with French writer and poet Jacques Vaché. Poet Louis Aragon was involved in Dadaism between 1919 and 1924, when he collaborated with French poet André Breton and others to found Surrealism. As early as 1918-19, the work of Breton and Aragon and others appeared in Zurich Dada publications but their allegiances quickly shifted as they sought to assert a more intellectually disciplined aesthetic in Paris – Surrealism.

According to Richter's account there were constant power struggles in the Paris Dada community over leadership, aesthetic perspectives, and political positions. The acrimony was palpable, and at the center of the dis-ease was Breton. According to Richter, an uneasy peace lasted until 1921 when

a new dominant figure appeared, one who replaced the former caprice and confusion with strict authority and discipline: this was André Breton."[18] ... None of the anti-authoritarianism of Dada had rubbed off on him. None of the humour either. ... However much I might admire, indeed love, his *Nadja*, I could not bring myself to enter the magic circle in which contests between Surrealism

17 Richter, 133.
18 Richter, 187.

and Sub-realism, ex-and in-communication, adoration and damnation, never ceased.[19]

Over the next couple of years, Breton systematically broke with the artists. The internal conflicts continued, even between the early founders of the new surrealist movement. For example, both Tzara and Aragon were purged after their drift to the right and their embrace of Stalinism. The French surrealists formally rejected Dada (while at the same time adopting some of their techniques), arguing that Surrealism was its legitimate, and more political, successor. Breton went to some lengths to dissociate Surrealism from its aesthetic predecessor in what would become standard personal attacks on the Dada artists. Breton denounced Tzara, for example, over the merits of the Dada musical and theatrical performances, which Breton felt were passé and were no longer effective; and he downplayed the importance of Tzara's role in developing the 1918 *Dada Manifesto*. After their falling out, Breton even referred to Tzara as "a dangerous enough simpleton."[20] All of these personal conflicts were caught up in the larger political struggle between the dadaists, the surrealists, and the Communist Party, and it is interesting to speculate how much those internal battles affected the aesthetic battles. Tzara was subsequently critical of Surrealism's involvement with the Party (although he and Breton reconciled in 1929).

The attack on Tzara was also an attack on the essential practices of Dada because Breton was anxious to re-position Surrealism as the pre-eminent aesthetic movement. In "After Dada" Breton wrote:

---

19 Richter, 177-178.

20 André Breton, "Visit with Leon Trotsky," in André Breton, *What is Surrealism? Selected Writings*, Franklin Rosemount, Ed., translated by Samuel Beckett and others and introduced by Franklin Rosemount (New York, NY: Monad, Pathfinder Press, 1978), 230.

Dada, very fortunately, is no longer an issue; its funeral, about May of 1921, caused no rioting. ... Although Dada had, as they say, its hour of fame, it left few regrets. In the long run its omnipotence and its tyranny had made it intolerable. ... After all, there is more at stake than our carefree existence and our good humour of the moment. ... It seems to me that the sanction of a series of utterly futile "Dada" acts is in danger of gravely compromising an attempt at liberation to which I remain strongly attached. Ideas which may be counted among the best are at the mercy of their too-hasty vulgarization.[21]

In a more balanced assessment, surrealist historian Franklin Rosemount concluded that Dada had played an important role in the subsequent success of Surrealism:

Scandal for scandal's sake, rooted in a sort of maniacal skepticism, proved to be as redundant and as ineffective as the art for art's sake which it set out to undermine. Despite its ambitions, Dada destroyed very little. But this little was, in its way, of enormous significance. A whole network of cretinising illusions, pitiable self-deceptions, unforgivable pomposities; the "religion" of art, aesthetic complacency, the dreariness of a decayed classicism; the academies of impressionism, expressionism, fauvism, even cubism – all were overturned and swept aside by Dada. Only this Dadaist demolition, this clearing away of the debris, made possible a new departure. Dada was a remarkable ferment which, more or less, in spite of

---

21 André Breton, "After Dada," in Breton, *What is Surrealism?*, Part II, 18-19.

itself, enabled new and more powerful forces of subversion to gain time, to gather energy, to prepare themselves. ... Dada perished to make way for the infinitely more revolutionary intervention of surrealism.[22]

Breton is generally acknowledged to be the most important theorist of French Surrealism. The Dada movement's critique of Modernism and the new theories of the unconscious promulgated by Sigmund Freud were especially influential in the development of Breton's Surrealism. Breton was also an admirer of the works of Gustave Moreau, one of the best known French symbolist painters.[23] According to Marxist aesthetician Christopher Caudwell, surrealist artists were influenced by the symbolist content, incorporating their fantastical images and experimenting with alternatives to traditional form and structure.[24]

The surrealists tied the spirit of aesthetic rebellion to the political idea of revolution, embellishing and deepening the role of art in political change. Expanding on the outrage of the Dada art movement, Surrealism emphasized rebelliousness and negation as mechanisms to critique and challenge modernity and self-consciously shaped the art and politics debate in the twentieth century, a debate that continues today. The surrealists also employed new insights – in particular the science of psychology of Sigmund Freud. The Oxford English Dictionary (OED) defines Surrealism as a "movement in art and

---

22 Franklin Rosemount, "Introduction: André Breton and the First Principles of Surrealism," in André Breton, *What is Surrealism? Selected Writings*, Part I, 43.

23 David Walsh, "Gustave Moreau: An exhibit at the Metropolitan Museum of Art, New York City (June 1-August 22), *World Socialist Web Site*, July 14, 1999. http://www.wsws.org/articles/1999/jul1999/mor1-j14_prn.shtml

24 Christopher Caudwell, *Illusion and Reality* (New York, NY: International Publishers, 1937, 1977).

literature seeking to express the subconscious mind by any of a number of different techniques including the irrational juxtaposition of realistic images, the creation of mysterious symbols, and automatism." But, as we shall see, Surrealism aspired to be much more. Surrealism also aspired to play an active political role. The challenge for the radical community has always been how best to use radical art to impact radical politics: particularly, how to create art that does not exploit or manipulate, but rather illuminates a new world. The surrealists were the first artists to take up this political challenge as it an active element in their aesthetics.

The writers and poets were more prominent in French Surrealism that the visual artists although Breton also created collages and sculptures. In 1924, Breton published the first of several surrealist manifestos. He initially defined Surrealism as an artistic technique and a philosophical methodology that was grounded in the internal, psychological thought processes of the individual artist. The source of inspiration for surrealist art was the unconscious mind of the artist, from which the images emerged spontaneously and unedited. In an effort to break totally with traditional aesthetics, Breton called for the rejection of traditional styles and techniques for writing poetry and for poets to move beyond conscious thought processes to allow new images to emerge from the unconscious. The writing of poetry was to happen automatically, flowing out of the inner self.

> I resolved to obtain from myself what one seeks to obtain from [psychiatric] patients, namely a monologue poured out as rapidly as possible, over which the subject's critical faculty has no control – the subject himself throwing reticence to the winds – and which as much as possible represents *spoken thought*. ...
> I began to cover sheets of paper with writing,

feeling a praiseworthy contempt for whatever the literary result might be.[25]

Surrealism, Breton wrote, is "pure psychic automatism, by which it is intended to express, verbally, in writing, or by other means, the real process of thought."[26] But, Breton did not stop with simply jettisoning the traditional techniques and content of poetry or being open to new imagery. He expanded his 1924 definition of Surrealism over the next decade to encompass the political; and in the pamphlet, *What is Surrealism?* (1934), he "corrected" the apolitical implications of the earlier definition. This shift came, in part, as a response to the rise of fascism across Europe.

THE POLITICAL AESTHETIC OF SURREALISM

THE SURREALISTS WERE true modernists in that they were committed to rejecting the world around them and seeking alternatives: they embraced rebellion, they despaired over the political status quo, and they rejected the formalisms of traditional aesthetics. They wanted to make new, outrageous art; and they aspired to create the ideological and psychological climate for a new world through their art. As Walter Benjamin observed in *Surrealism: The Last Snapshot of the European Intelligentsia*, determining the relationship between art and politics is a big challenge: "Where are the conditions for revolution? In the changing of attitudes or of external circumstances? That is the cardinal question that determines the relation of politics to morality and cannot be glossed over."[27] While the surrealists were com-

---

25 André Breton, *What is Surrealism?* Lecture, Meeting of the Belgian Surrealists, Brussels, June 1, 1934. Pamphlet. www.surrealist. com. See also Breton, *What is Surrealism?* op.cit. and André Breton, *Manifestos of Surrealism*, trans. by Richard Seaver and Helen R. Lane (Ann Arbor: University of Michigan Press, 1972).

26 Breton, *What is Surrealism?*

27 Walter Benjamin, *Surrealism: The Last Snapshot of the European Intelligentsia*, 1929. http://www.generation-online.org/c/

mitted to bringing art and politics together, unfortunately, they were not always clear on how they would accomplish this objective. Nevertheless, this merger remained as a goal – even as their political thinking matured over time. Despite its self-conscious tone of political correctness and vangardism (as we have seen, Breton made a habit of "un-inviting" people to the surrealist table), Surrealism can be studied in the context of the dominant political and philosophical currents of the time. It paralleled in many ways the revolutionary energies of Marxism and Hegelian dialectical materialism, anarchism, and socialism. Surrealists were committed to creating art that distilled the energies and dreams of a revolution that was to be "truly extended into all domains," according to Breton. He saw Surrealism as the aesthetic manifestation of a Hegelian "*living*" movement, undergoing a constant process of becoming ... and a continuous sequence of acts." He advocated for a never-ending, dynamic, and activist Surrealism, always undermining the existent reality, perpetually subversive and iconoclastic, and committed to the expression of the "*necessity* of change."[28]

There were competing aesthetic and political agendas that attracted the attention of the Surrealists. On one hand, the potential for a creative process freed up to explore the unconscious human mind fascinated them. They believed that their receptiveness to the workings of the imagination and to the inner dream worlds opened up new pathways to aesthetic and political insights. On the other hand, they were deeply committed to political involvement. Early on they were attracted to Marxism and the libratory potential of the Russian Revolution of 1917 and they expressed deep concern and anxiety about the rise of fascist politics.

The politics of the mind

One of Surrealism's most significant aesthetic contributions was the transference of the desire for

---

fcsurrealism.htm

28 Breton, *What is Surrealism?*

freedom from the political world to the inner, psychological world of the individual. Surrealists believed that new symbols and new images would emerge from the unconscious to revitalize personal as well as political realities. They were especially fascinated with Sigmund Freud's interest in the power of the unconscious to shape the conscious through the mediating power of dreams. The surrealists adopted this insight as a political tool of analysis to provide a mechanism both to explain and to change the real world. According to Breton, poets could use the tool of automatic writing to free up creative and political energies buried in the subconscious mind and to activate them in the outer world. Surrealists believed that the way to revolution was to encourage dreaming and imagining a future that would constantly be recreated anew by celebrating the creative impulse and practicing artistic rebellion at the same time. As contemporary critic Roger Shattuck observed, "Surrealists turned to the unconscious not primarily for therapeutic purposes but for what they often called 'revelation.' ... Some of the early documents circulated within the group speak both of revolution and of 'Surrealist illumination.' The language is clear: The Surrealist revolution 'seeks above all to create a new kind of mysticism.'"[29]

Sensitive to the charge of escapism implicit in their psychologically-driven aesthetic, Breton drew a parallel between intuition and reason and between aesthetics and politics, focusing on their interactivity. Reflecting on the development of Surrealism, he described two epochs through which Surrealism passed as it clarified and defined its political position – an intuitive epoch and a reasoning epoch. "The first [1917-1924] can summarily be characterized by the belief expressed during this time in the all-powerfulness of thought, considered capable of freeing itself by means of its own resources." In the second epoch, Breton argued, surrealist politics was refined

---

29 Shattuck.

and strengthened. "No coherent political or social attitude, however, made its appearance until 1925. ... [when] surrealist activity entered into its *reasoning* phase. It suddenly experienced the necessity of crossing over the gap that separates absolute idealism from dialectical materialism."[30] In a rudimentary dialectical way, he proposed working interdependently in each reality to enlighten the other.

> Let it be clearly understood that for us surrealists, the interests of thought cannot cease to go hand in hand with the interests of the working class, and that all attacks on liberty, all fetters on the emancipation of the working class and all armed attacks on it cannot fail to be considered by us as attacks on thought likewise.[31]

The artist's thinking had to be aligned and interactive with the real world in order to make these connections between individual insights and collective political action.

Despite Breton's earnest desire to portray Surrealism as committed to political action, the surrealists were more interested in finding a way to inspire individuals to revolt from within than in mobilizing the masses. Their emphasis on the psychological (inner) world reinforced an individualistic rather than a social locus of political action. Surrealist aesthetics never clearly developed just how psychological and mystical insights would result in political action or inspiration for revolution. Instead, surrealists called for an art committed to changing the mind, believing that a "revolution" in thinking would open up new possibilities. This "revolution" would occur by freeing up the suppressed images and insights buried in the unconscious, the subversion of all thought.

Breton believed that it was the mission of surrealists to serve as a vanguard in creating new ways of freeing up

---

30 Breton, *What is Surrealism?*
31 Breton, *What is Surrealism?*

political thinking. While the surrealist techniques (especially automatic writing) were not clearly applicable to the political sphere, nevertheless, there was an effort to link the political to what Breton called the "poetic". Breton believed that Surrealism would liberate this lyrical element which could then be placed in the service of political revolution, noting that "we have accepted this legacy from the past, and Surrealism can well say that the use to which it has been put has been to turn it to the routing of capitalist society."[32]

Contemporary surrealists have attempted to expand on this poetic element. Surrealism went beyond the poetic impulse, Robin D. G. Kelley argued, to "restructuring the mind."[33] Further exploration in this tantalizing direction could shed light on exactly how minds are changed. In his introduction to *Surrealist Subversions*, Ron Sakolsky repeatedly affirmed the primacy of poetry and poetic action. The poetry in life is grounded in the desire of the heart for freedom; art is situated at the "crossroads of desire and action." The primary surrealist goal, according to Sakolsky, is "liberating imagination and desire."[34]

Surrealism and political activism

Historically, political movements have defined and used art in different ways; similarly, artists have turned their talents to creating and to supporting a variety of political agendas. Histories of the surrealist impulse have focused heavily on Surrealism as an aesthetic movement rather than a political movement. As we have seen, the political component of the surrealist vision was

32 Breton, *What is Surrealism?*
33 Robin D. G. Kelley, "Freedom Now Sweet: Surrealism and the Black World," in *Surrealist Subversions, Rants, Writings and Images by the Surrealist Movement in the United States*, ed. Ron Sakolsky (New York, NY: Autonomedia, 2002), 148.
34 Ron Sakolsky, "Introduction," *Surrealist Subversions*, 27-28.

not clearly articulated; and despite the surrealists' stated desire to align their art with the liberation of the working class, they never developed an activist politics of the street. Early on, Surrealism did make an effort to adopt a strong political position within the broader political context of turn-of-the-century Marxism by aligning itself ideologically with the working class and the politics of the Communist Party (CP). Almost immediately, however, the free spirited surrealist artists conflicted with the highly disciplined CP agenda.

The surrealists were soon swept up in the bitter struggles within the CP between Stalin and Trotsky. That epic power struggle spilled over into the surrealist camp when Aragon published a politically incendiary poem in 1932. He was arrested, and Breton defended him. But according to Franklin Rosemount, "The Stalinized CP used the 'Aragon affair' to accuse the surrealists of demanding special treatment for poets. Then, to the amazement of his surrealist comrades, Aragon himself sided with the party *against* them!"[35] Breton rejected the party's interference, and the growing resentment against party injunctions to get the surrealists in line with the Bolshevik imperatives. This led to personal antagonisms and a bitter falling out over Aragon's decision to align himself with the Stalinist wing of the CP.

Breton had joined the party in 1927; but as he explained in *The Second Manifesto*, the alliance was short-lived. In 1933, the party's Association of Revolutionary Writers and Artists expelled Breton; a year later the party officially adopted the Socialist Realism aesthetic mandated by Moscow. The shift from Surrealism to Socialist Realism was not something easily embraced by the surrealists, and efforts to align the two perspectives were doomed from the start. The two perspectives paralleled each other and danced together only briefly, having little in common beyond a vague commitment to "revolution." After

---

35 André Breton, *What is Surrealism?*, Part I, 118.

the break-up, Surrealism set its own independent path
and remained unconvinced that the party line of Socialist
Realism had anything to offer Surrealism. The feeling, of
course, was mutual.

Breton's uneasy six-year alliance with the Communist
Party quickly broke down over the issue of the political role of art. Socialist Realism as an aesthetic partner
to communism was still in the formative stages when the
debate began with the Surrealists, and aesthetic distinctions were soon drawn between the two approaches to
differentiate them. Historian and filmmaker Robert Short
observed that

> While the communists interpreted contem-
> porary events in the light of the inevitable eco-
> nomic collapse of capitalism, the Surrealists
> exposed the moral and cultural symptoms of
> the *débâcle.* [Surrealists] sought not so much
> to convince as to move – not so much to ar-
> gue the cause of a particular programme as to
> arouse the feeling of revolt and to prompt the
> demand that *something* must be done. While
> the communists instructed the proletariat in
> the strategy of revolution, the Surrealists were
> trying to bring about the emotional climate in
> which the revolution might break out.[36]

According to Short, Surrealists encountered ideological
difficulties reconciling their position with communism in
three particularly sensitive areas:

> the reconciliation of a generalized spirit of
> revolt with revolutionary action; the reconcili-
> ation of the idea of a "spiritual revolution" and
> its accompanying insistence on ethical "purity"

---

36 Robert S. Short, "The Politics of Surrealism, 1920-1936," *Journal of
   Contemporary History* 1, 2, 1966, mimeo, 6.

with the practical necessities of political effectiveness; [and] the reconciliation of an independent revolutionary art with the demands for propaganda and didacticism made by the communist party.[37]

The Surrealist idea of revolt for its own sake was not easily harnessed to the discipline required for ongoing revolutionary activity. The emphasis in Surrealism on the inner psychological life as a vehicle for understanding reality (sur-reality) directly challenged the materialist Marxist analysis of economic and class-based political forces as the drivers of social change. The personal explorations of the dreams of an inner world were likely to keep the individual dissociated from the real world politics. Finally, artists who demanded independent, personal freedom could not be counted on to convey a specific ideological perspective, no matter how revolutionary their intentions might be.

The basic difference between the surrealists and the communists had to do with their differing world views; Short concluded, "If both saw the revolution as the prelude to the founding of a world based on the desires of men, their ideas about the content of these desires were not the same. For the Marxists they were material while for the Surrealists they were primarily subjective and spiritual ... individual rather than social."[38] Short further concluded that Surrealism was not political at all and had had "no real affect on political theory; the Surrealists, observed André Masson, had to *dream* politically or cease to be. But they were unable at the same time to *act* politically."[39]

When Breton finally broke from the communists, he consciously opted to keep Surrealism independent of the political fray. "It is only too certain that an activity such as ours, owing to its particularization, cannot be pursued

37 Short, mimeo, 1.
38 Short, mimeo, 10.
39 Short, mimeo, 12.

within the limits of any one of the existing revolutionary organizations."[40] Remaining ideologically "pure," however, left the surrealists politically ineffective. Breton's shift to a more "political" tone in his rethinking of Surrealism may have heralded his own transition to a more activist role; but the movement, as a whole, remained, by choice, apolitical.

After rejecting the structured politics of communism, Breton recast Surrealism as a different kind of politics; and according to Shattuck, Breton was able to keep surrealist politics free of ideological positions and the Communist Party line. Shattuck concluded, "In the long run their political record is uncompromised. They did not allow themselves to be herded for long into the Communist Party corral. They defended Trotsky, refused to swallow communist fronts and the pap printed in *l'Humanité*, and they were among the first to circulate statements condemning the Moscow trials."[41]

Early twentieth century Surrealism did not long survive as a political movement, victim in part of its own in-fighting and lack of clarity. After being ousted from the Communist Party, Surrealists sought an ideological home in other Marxist ideological camps; but nothing ever came of those dalliances. Curiously, the surrealists did not align themselves with the social anarchist movements of that era. This may have been a result of their earlier squabbles with Dada anarchists.[42] Surrealism came under fire in later years from the Situationist International for flirting with the Communist Party and then abandoning politics entirely. According to situationist Raoul Vaneigem, "One of Surrealism's chief faults … is that it handed over all responsibility for the universal revolutionary project to Bolshevism."[43]

---

40 Breton, *What is Surrealism?*

41 Shattuck.

42 Raoul Vaneigem (Jules-François Dupuis), *A Cavalier History of Surrealism*, Translated by Donald Nicholson-Smith (Edinburgh and Others: AK Press, 1977, 1999), 14-16.

43 Vaneigem, *A Cavalier History*, 109.

Nevertheless, the surrealist idea and its stylistic innovations have persisted as a minor sub-text throughout the twentieth century. But, if we are seeking to develop a line of direct influence between surrealist art and politics – especially the *impact* of their political aesthetic on political reality – we will not find one. While it is true that they formulated political statements, they never developed a fully articulated political position and were generally not involved in the political activism of the day. Surrealism was, by and large, sidelined by its own posturing in the 1930s.

Surrealist art as a new politics

Surrealist artists believed at some level that they had an ethical responsibility beyond making art, and they were interested in exploring a new approach to politics in the context of envisioning a new world. In a recent essay "The Future of Surrealism," contemporary surrealists Philip Lamantia and Nancy Joyce Peters proposed that the Surrealist aesthetic was a new kind of politics: that what is enduring of Surrealism is its sense of freedom and love, its "subversion of positivist rituals," and its power to imagine "*another life* to oppose this life." Surrealism, they averred, "is the name of a new continent of the spirit" and will change how we think about both art and about politics.[44] Art must be not just at the service of politics but must shape politics. Surrealist artists believed that all elements of culture must be subject to the scrutiny and challenge of the aesthetic vision. They looked at every facet of the oppressive life of the modern era, and their goal was to teach people how to "see" in a new way. Under their incisive scrutiny, people were called to re-assess all prevailing cultural attitudes. Part of their success, they believed, lay in seeking to remain outside of all politics.

The key to unlocking the politics of Surrealism is to understand its vision of freedom. It manifested itself as the

---

44 Philip Lamantia and Nancy Joyce Peters, "The Future of Surrealism," in *Surrealist Subversions*, 230-234.

magic of rising expectations fueled by passion, always exploring and exploding the thin margins of repression and authoritarianism. In a short essay, "Dreaming, Playing, & Breaking Up the Existing Order," contemporary surrealist Gale Ahrens credited Surrealism with breaking "the power trap" in "ways that the authoritarian state cannot control," with rebellion its motivating action. [45] This subversive impulse is central to Surrealist art and action. Surrealism is at its best when the everyday is elevated to awareness and is transformed. However, Surrealism can be criticized on this point because in its desire to remain "free" and continuously creative and changing, it ended up being arbitrary and ephemeral, without a sustained agenda. By its own definition, it cannot be predictable but must remain ever alert to the need for new subversive thinking.

Surrealism and the aesthetics of consumer capitalism

Another worldview was emerging as a major competitor for the hearts and minds of people in the early twentieth century, one which offered a competing vision: the allure of consumerism and a world of infinite objects that the advertising dream factory fantasized. The surrealists never developed a meaningful response to this new world, a world in which the ideological battleground had shifted from the economic and political to the cultural. While they were openly critical of many facets of bourgeois culture, undermining at every turn the conventions of Christianity, the family, and nationalism, they failed to take up the challenge of the cultural manifestations of capitalism. According to Vaneigem, they "waged a war of mere harassment against bourgeois society" without addressing the emerging cultural hegemony. [46] They also failed to challenge seriously the emerging capitalist aesthetic (advertising) and the power of mass communication

---

45 Gale Ahrens, "Dreaming, Playing, & Breaking Up the Existing Order," in *Surrealist Subversions,* 251.

46 Vaneigem, *A Cavalier History,* 39.

media – although they certainly recognized its impact. Instead, they believed that life's value and fulfillment could be found through art and by imagining a better world – failing to see that capitalism had developed a sophisticated way to sell goods by imagining a false but appealing alternative world. Vaneigem concluded, "Little by little, as the dream of revolution broke up on the reefs of nascent Stalinism, but also as the society of the spectacle and of the commodity system inevitably co-opted anything that could be called artistic, Surrealism retreated to the heights of pure mind."[47]

Surrealism was also vulnerable from the beginning to co-optation by the competing consumer aesthetic. The emerging bourgeois culture of capitalist consumption and its powerful aesthetic of advertising images were already well-developed, although not to the level of today's sophistication and saturation. New and exciting visual ideas (like Art Nouveau) were quickly harnessed as a driving force for selling the message of capitalist abundance, economic growth, and production for personal pleasure. Instead of fulfilling political desires and dreams for a better future, desire was channeled into immediate gratification through consumption. According to Vaneigem, surrealist visual artists were especially vulnerable to co-optation: "Painting was a privileged sector of surrealist activity; it was also the sector most thoroughly co-opted by what the sociologists, in their eagerness to avoid any analysis of the spectacle and the commodity system, like to call 'the civilization of the image.'"[48]

American Surrealism

American artists never seriously engaged in the surrealist dialogue that was underway in Europe early in the twentieth century. By mid-century, the European movement was moribund. But in the 1960's a

47 Vaneigem, *A Cavalier History*, 105.
48 Vaneigem, *A Cavalier History*, 96.

revitalized contemporary surrealist movement came together around a group of artists and activists in Chicago.
Artists Franklin and Penelope Rosemont spent some time
in Paris early in the 1960's with the remnants of the surrealist movement, a visit that included several meetings with
Breton. The energies of the remaining French surrealists
inspired them even then. Returning to the United States,
they were firmly committed to spreading the artistic and
political message of Surrealism; and motivated by their inspiration, American Surrealism developed in Chicago and
expanded to radical, political, and artistic audiences across
the United States. Franklin Rosemont in particular was
determined to introduce the United States to the political
aspects of Surrealism:

> Although its poetry and painting alone are
> enough to situate surrealism among the most
> vital revolutionary currents of this century, it
> would be an error to presume that surrealism
> is concerned primarily with art or literature.
> … Art and antiart are imaginary solutions;
> surrealism lies elsewhere. … It cannot be em-
> phasized too strongly: Surrealism, a unitary
> project of total revolution, is above all a meth-
> od of knowledge and a way of life; it is *lived*
> far more than it is written, or written about,
> or drawn. Surrealism is the most exhilarating
> adventure of the mind, an unparalleled means
> of pursuing the fervent quest for freedom and
> true life beyond the veil of ideological appear-
> ances.[49]

American Surrealism was different from European
Surrealism. In many ways, it harkened back to the Berlin
Dadaists with their deep roots in political activism. By the

---

49 Rosemont, "Introduction," in Rosemont, *What is Surrealism?*, 24, 25,
   26.

1960's, anarchism was on the ascendancy on the left in the United States, the Situationist International dominated radical European aesthetics, and the influence of the old left had declined dramatically. Freed up from the rigidity of CP political ideology, the Chicago surrealists were free to experiment with alternative Marxist frameworks. Their ideas represented a rich and energetic fulfillment of the best in surrealist politics and aesthetics merged with an American anarchist political perspective. Further, their politics-as-art and their art-as-politics stances were firmly grounded in the particular American radical context. The Rosemonts went to Paris as young revolutionaries, steeped in the blossoming energies of the 1960's cultural revolution in the United States, the radical labor movement, the particular historical context of Chicago anarchism, and left politics generally. The energies of the 1960's were merged with the surrealist spirit of freedom and revolt in an effort to bring activism back into balance with theory. In many ways, American political activism revitalized a declining surrealist perspective.

Perhaps sensitive to criticisms of French Surrealism's disengagement from the elements of the political left, the Chicago surrealists established a solid foundation in the historical and contemporary social and political context of the city. The legacy of Chicago anarchism was apparent in their activities, especially their commitment to the vision of the Wobblies, the Industrial Workers of the World (IWW) – a powerful anarchist workers movement in the Midwest in the early part of the twentieth century. Often referred to as the "singing revolutionaries", the Wobblies consciously sought to bring the energies of art into everyday life and politics. They practiced what Gavin Grindon called the "art of social movements. … For a collective model of artistic production, we might look to the context of social movements, which have their own art taking the form of material culture and performance, which developed not from a tradition of aesthetic autonomy but of social conflict."[50]

---

50 Grindon, 86.

In "Surrealism: The Chicago Idea," Paul Garon, Franklin and Penelope Rosemont laid out the main principles of Chicago Surrealism: a commitment to revolt and revolution against capitalism; the practice of "poetry as praxis ...the process by which poetry is realized in everyday life;" the application of Freudian psychology "to break through the psychical and social obstacles separating desire from action;" an end to what they called "miserabilism" – the frame of thinking that keeps people under the control of the capitalist system; and a commitment to imagining a utopian future world.[51]

Like the early French surrealists, the American surrealists were fascinated with the manipulation of imagery (visual or print) to challenge and to distort common perception. This belief was most apparent in the visual arts. They believed that phantasmagorical and bizarre content could serve to undermine and break up commonly-held perceptions of reality. There was also a strong thread of utopian visioning in their art and politics as well as an abiding faith in the future.

Lamantia laid out the basic elements of the contemporary surrealist aesthetic in an essay critiquing contemporary American poetry. While he was speaking specifically of poetry, other contemporary Surrealist art forms reflect the same aesthetic elements:

> words [or images] set free from the prosaic prisons of social reality, images transformed by desire, poetry freed from the "laws" of nature, attentive to the becoming of unknown analogies, words purified by the rays of oneiric desire, language emancipated from the confines of speech, informed by the inner ear and disdainful of "music" other than the rhythms immanent in imaginary thinking, analogies whose *encounters* elicit every type of

51 Paul Garon, Franklin Rosemont, and Penelope Rosemont,

humor, and language becoming a means of infinite imaginary combinations. [52]

In 2002, Ron Sakolsky edited *Surrealist Subversions: Rants, Writings and Images by the Surrealist Movement in the United States*, the most complete collection of contemporary American surrealist work to date. Sakolsky concluded that the contemporary surrealist movement was an anarchist movement.

> Clearly, surrealism in the U.S. was steeped in anarchism, and anarchist theory and practice provided much of the revolutionary ardor that has characterized "Chicago Idea" surrealism from the very beginning. Several of the original band of Windy City surrealists were active as anarchists long before they encountered surrealism. ...Chicago surrealists and their transcontinental co-dreamers have always recognized themselves in anarchism's constant emphasis on freedom and direct action, its critique of the church, state and other authoritarian institutions, and its inherently countercultural dimension. At the same time, they remain critical of what they consider to be the rationalism and positivism that traditionally have dominated (and in their view disfigured) certain aspects of anarchist thought.[53]

CRITICISM OF DADA AND SURREALISM

SURREALISM – AND implicitly Modernism – was roundly criticized as it struggled to carve out a new aesthetic and respond to the political realities of a world teetering on

---

52 Philip Lamantia, "Poetic Matters: A Critique of the 'New American Poetics,'" in *Surrealist Subversions*, 287.

53 Ron Sakolsky, "Surrealist Subversion in Chicago: The Forecast is Hotter than Ever!" in *Surrealist Subversions*, 42 and 43.

the edge of total social and political breakdown. From the left came charges that it mirrored the values of bourgeois society. Surrealism's emphasis on art as a reflection and realization of individual's desires rather than as a challenge to the abuses of capitalism was perceived as succumbing to the seductions of the marketplace. Surrealism, the charges went on, relocated the locus of political action from the social and economic realms to the private actions of individuals transforming their own individual lives. Surrealism's fascination with the psychological roots of aesthetics and the phantasmagorical images dredged up from the unconscious of individual minds further removed it from effective political action by positing personal insights as the new ideological measure and the locus of revolutionary change. Finally, the surrealists were criticized for abandoning traditional aesthetic responsibilities. Art was freed up from any obligation to reflect social and cultural values and, instead, was to be appreciated for its own sake.

The most sustained criticism of Surrealism came from the Marxist left. Surrealism, the Marxists charged, had effectively severed art from any connection to or responsibility for the social and political reality. The surrealists had turned inward in a futile effort to rebel against the bourgeois status quo and the psychic destruction of the war, the argument went. They had sought to escape the status quo into a private aesthetic space. The crux of the problem with Surrealism for Christopher Caudwell lay in the fact that exploring the inner world of the individual detracted from the political and social imperative to take action.

> Finding himself ultimately enslaved by the social form and therefore still "bound to the market," the bourgeois rebel attempts to shake himself free even from the social ego and so to escape into the world of dream where both ego and external world are personal and unconscious. This is *surréalisme*, with the apparent

return of a realism which is however fictitious, because it is not the real, i.e., social external world which returns, but the unconscious personal world.[54]

Situationist Raoul Vaneigem was critical of Surrealism's focus on the individual as the locus of revolutionary energy, observing that Surrealism succeeded as an individual protest statement but not as a political force speaking for people collectively: "The Surrealist movement never did more than echo the kind of furious foot-stamping which, from Romanticism to Dada, had been the sole response of artists thwarted by the demobilizing combination (supplied courtesy of the commodity system) of a lifeless soul and a soulless life."[55]

So although Surrealism drew attention to each individual's potential for creativity in everyday life, it failed to spur the collective actualization of that creativity by means of a revolution made by all in the interest of all; instead, it invited the individual to lose his way twice over: to engage in a marginal activity which relied on Bolshevism to spark the revolutionary process, and to strive for a strictly cultural overthrow of culture.[56]

Walter Benjamin, too, was critical of the Surrealists. He praised the surrealists for attempting to revolt against the bourgeois world and its values in the name of complete freedom for the artist; but at the same time, he questioned whether they had successfully linked the idea of personal revolt with a disciplined revolutionary agenda:

---

54 Christopher Caudwell, *Illusion and Reality* (New York, NY: International Publishers, 1937, 1977), 270.

55 Vaneigem, *A Cavalier History*, 35.

56 Vaneigem, *A Cavalier History*, 52-53.

> Since [anarchist Michael] Bakunin, Europe
> has lacked a radical concept of freedom. The
> surrealists have one. They are the first to liq-
> uidate the sclerotic liberal-moral-humanistic
> ideal of freedom. … But are they successful
> in welding this experience of freedom to the
> other revolutionary experience that we have
> to acknowledge because it has been ours, the
> constructive, dictatorial side of revolution? In
> short, have they bound revolt to revolution?[57]

According to Rajeev Patke, the surrealists developed
only a partial critique of bourgeois art and were even less
successful on the political front. They failed to get at the
underlying mechanisms of bourgeois art – the political
and economic underpinnings of capitalism. Part of the
difficulty lay in their failure to take on a critique of advertising art. Another element was the lack of ideological
clarity.

> The attack on art launched by Surrealism
> lost its momentum in solipsistic esotericism.
> So did the political activism. Though Breton
> maintained a firm polemical grasp of the revo-
> lutionary intentions of the Surrealist move-
> ment, the political affiliations of the various
> Surrealists kept changing. … The free play
> of associations that was characteristic of
> Surrealism, and its Dada legacy, did not pre-
> pare its anarchist methods for a focused politi-
> cal *praxis*."[58]

The visual content of surrealist art is also problematic
from a political perspective. The surrealists were not interested in creating images with overt political content that

---

57 Benjamin, *Surrealism: The Last Snapshot.*
58 Patke.

one could read into the real world. Rather, they sought to distance their art from the more representational traditions of Impressionism, Naturalism, Symbolism, and other aesthetic schools working in a different way to heighten awareness of the real world. This, coupled with their lack of political focus weakened their commitment to revolutionary art.

The problem of surrealist aesthetic representation can be seen clearly in the art and politics of the Chicago surrealists. While a strong case can be made that they were activist revolutionaries I question whether surrealist art was the cause or effect of this particular aesthetic. It seems to me that the Rosemonts viewed Surrealism more as a broad political platform to actively challenge all aspects of contemporary life, and less as a specific style of art that would resonate visually with people desiring radical change. Both actions are necessary: art that inspires and motivates others to revolutionary change and artists who are inspired because they are actively engaged in revolutionary change. The weakness of either one of these elements potentially leaves the artist outside of the visionary energy driving change, or the revolutionary art is easily co-opted.

Ironically, Vaneigem argued, the effort to avoid co-optation may have directly contributed to Surrealism's turn away from the political.

> The [surrealist] painters lobby, never much interested in the political debate, was much relieved to see the movement taking a mystical tack. Already attached to the notion of the magic of the creative act, this tendency had everything to gain from a revitalization of myth centered on the idea of beauty and on art as a mirror of the marvelous. Such a perspective would allow the painters to devote themselves entirely to matters aesthetic

while loudly denying any concession to aestheticism.[59]

As a result, Vaneigem concluded, "the Surrealists took up the defense of myth, at a time when myth no longer existed, against the spectacle, which was everywhere."[60] A separate question – whether or not the aesthetic images appear as realistic or surrealistic – is whether the surrealist insights inspired people to take political action. Edgar Allen Poe was certainly a consummate artist of the surreal image, but his art did not inspire a social or a political revolution. Salvador Dali – one of the most financially successful surrealist painters, leaned far to the right politically. Surrealism's focus on the psychological, the bizarre, and extraordinary imagery of internal unconscious imagination had probably undermined its political impact. Surrealism may have opened up the possibility for new ways of seeing and may have led people to new personal insights or a more discerning and discriminating eye, but it did not necessarily get them to take political *action* on that new insight. The surrealist argument was that old imagery had to be destroyed. However, their alternative imagery did not result in a new, coherent vision. Surrealist imagery did little to make people aware of how they were oppressed, and it never rose to the level of inspiring them to change their world. It did not offer alternative visions for freedom from their social situation. The turn inward to escape a crumbling world had disastrous implications as art abandoned its traditional responsibilities to society. This question of the requisite interaction between active engaged by artists making revolutionary art will be taken up in subsequent chapters in greater detail.

Despite good intentions and a clear desire to be revolutionary, surrealists were not able to engage in and to sustain political action over time. If there is a weakness in

---

59 Vaneigem, *A Cavalier History*, 110-111.
60 Vaneigem, *A Cavalier History*, 113.

surrealist theory, it is that while it was good at identifying what to be against, where the flash points were, and the need to challenge everything, this openness to everything runs the risk of being far too diffuse and indiscriminate for sustaining political transformation. Surrealism, by definition, can have no plan, no conscious agenda; but the absence of a plan makes its political outcomes unpredictable. By the 1930's, Surrealism's role in the debate over the relationship between art and politics had waned in significance. Surrealism was a victim of its own internal inconsistencies and theoretical competition from Socialist Realism with its more overt revolutionary political message.

THE LEGACY OF DADA AND SURREALISM
MOST HISTORIANS MARK the period 1916-1930 as the high point of Dada. Hans Richter set the time span shorter – from 1915 to 1922. Roger Shattuck raised the question of whether Dada actually had a longer life: "Is it possible," he asked, "that the shape of time we should be contemplating begins somewhere back before the turn of the century with, say, *Ubu Roi* [the 1896 absurdist play], the shocking fusion of symbolism and anarchism, and ends soon after 1930 when modernism ran out of steam and capitulated to socialist realism?"[61] The 1924 publication of Breton's *Surrealist Manifesto* is another date marking the demise of the movement.

Dada faded almost as quickly as it had emerged. Gone were the rowdy performances and events. At a final *soirée* Breton climbed on stage, attacked the actors, and broke the arm of Pierre de Massot, after which the audience threw him and his colleagues out of the hall. The visual art, however, remained, and unlike the Surrealists who were

---

61 Roger Shattuck, "The D-S Expedition: Part I," *The New York Review of Books* 18, 9, May 18, 1972. http://www.nybooks.com/articles/archives/

primarily writers and poets, Dada art continues to impact the making of art and startle the viewer awake even to this day. Nevertheless, despite protestations, the great paradox of Dada remained: the demand to destroy art was intertwined with the desire to create a new kind of art. Richter described well the unresolved tension: "Proclaim as we might our liberation from causality and our dedication to anti-art, we could not help involving our *whole* selves, including our conscious sense of order, in the creative process, so that, in spite of all our anti-art polemics, we produced works of art."[62]

The essence of Dada was the provocative act; an action that sought to bring art and life together. Dada was characterized by rebellion for rebellion's sake, and Dada artists saw their rebellion as a political act. They even rebelled against art itself, advocating for the destruction of all art. While it was a posture that individual artists could adopt, it was, in retrospect, a bankrupt and empty political gesture because politics is about collective activity. According to Raoul Vaneigem, Dada's principle ideological tools of outrage included "deconsecrating culture, mocking its claims to be an independent sphere ... [and] playing games with its fragments," all in the name of destroying art and philosophy.[63] This separated it from reflective art, where the distance between artist and viewer is expected. But as contemporary art critic Peter Schjeldahl dryly concluded, Dada resembled a contemporary "publicity movement. ... Though hardly commercial, it anticipated a byword of modern advertising: forget the steak, sell the sizzle."[64]

In an interesting debate between Jess Cohn and Roger Farr over the merits of politics as performance or politics

---

62 Richter, 59.

63 Raoul Vaneigem (Jules-François Dupuis), *A Cavalier History of Surrealism*, trans. Donald Nicholson-Smith (Edinburgh and Others: AK Press, 1977, 1999), 8.

64 Peter Schjeldahl, "Young at Heart: Dada at MOMA," *The New Yorker*, June 26, 2006, 84-85.

as representation, the very core of Dada provocative actions came under scrutiny. Jesse Cohn rejected the argument that provocations are effective in communicating an anarchist agenda: "But resorting to pure dada can be a dead end as well. By presenting our politics as 'undecipherable,' we risk rendering them incommunicable; by making them 'unreadable,' we risk rendering them unintelligible. When we act crazy, we confirm the ideological assumption that *any* alternative to the status quo is crazy." Cohn concluded that Dada artists may have actually undermined their original political intent and should not be a model for contemporary political aesthetics.

Roger Farr disagreed, however, arguing that "The performative *affect* of punk [his example of contemporary dadists], for example ... *is* its political 'content.' ... '[U]nderstanding' the 'message' is not required during the performance because *the performance is the message.*"[65] Unfortunately provocative acts are limited to the immediate moment, and even the idiosyncrasy of the individual artist's expression. Although these acts may, in theory, awaken and inspire others to some future action, the ephemeral nature of the performance limits it range of effectiveness.

Kindred spirits of the Dada movement, surrealists kept the core ideas of Dada alive and transformed them in some ways. Hans Richter described the symbiotic relationship between Dada and Surrealism:

> They cannot be separated; they are necessary conditions of one another. ... They are basically a single coherent experience reaching like a great arch from 1916 until about the middle of the Second World War, a renaissance of meaning in art, a change in our field

---

65 Jesse Cohn, "The End of Communication? The End of Representation?" and Roger Farr, "The Intimacies of Noise," *Fifth Estate* 376 (2007), 40-45.

of vision that corresponds to a revolutionary change in the nature of our civilization.

All this grew naturally on the "crab-apple tree" of Dada that Breton proposed to cut down, but whose fruit was to nourish Surrealism, after the latter had grafted, pruned and tended the tree so that its fruit finally became a popular product in a way that Dada could never have attained. ... Surrealism gave Dada significance and sense, Dada gave Surrealism life.[66]

While Surrealism articulated a more or less coherent aesthetic philosophy, it did not make any significant impact on the world of politics. Surrealist's commitment to a personal and aesthetic rebellion isolated them from active engagement; and while André Breton flirted briefly with the Communist Party, the surrealist emphasis on the individual artist also precluded a coherent political perspective. Their reluctance to take up the narrow aesthetics of Socialist Realism is understandable and praiseworthy. In 1928, Breton revisited the question of the relationship between politics and art in a ringing attack on the Russian CP and a powerful defense of freedom of expression. In the "Manifesto for an Independent Revolutionary Art" (written in collaboration with Leon Trotsky and signed by Diego Rivera and others), Breton and Trotsky wrote:

True art, which is not content to play variations on ready-made models but rather insists on expressing the inner needs of man and of mankind in its time – true art is unable not to be revolutionary, not to aspire to a complete and radical reconstruction of society. ... We believe that the supreme task of art in our epoch is to take part actively and consciously

---

66 Richter, 195.

in the preparation of the revolution. But the artist cannot serve the struggle for freedom unless he subjectively assimilates its social content, unless he feels in his very nerves its meaning and drama and freely seeks to give his own inner world incarnation in his art.[67]

The Freudian psychological elements of surrealist aesthetics complicated achieving a clearly defined political philosophy. Surrealist inspiration is rooted primarily in the individual psyche, and the question that begs answering is whether an insight from an individual artist's subconscious can achieve political change. The imaginative force of surrealist art had its source in the dreams and subconscious of the individual. This individualistic perspective superseded any social role for art and any obligation on the part of the individual artist to address social issues. What the surrealists did accomplish was pushing the edges of creativity, opening up new visual directions, and advocating for art as a political act in and of itself.

The surrealist political agenda succumbed to two prevailing aesthetic forces: the rise of Socialist Realism and the overwhelming force of capitalist consumer aesthetics. The art world that they so strenuously resisted embraced the surrealists, and they became the newest darlings in that world that they so thoroughly despised. Today their paintings command astronomically high prices and are reverently hung in museums worldwide. Their political messages, however tepid, were neatly cauterized; and all that has remained in the cultural memory is a hint of their spirit of rebellion. Nevertheless, the movement is important to study because it was the first art movement to self-consciously address the central cultural, political, and aesthetic challenges that remain unresolved today.

---

67 André Breton and Leon Trotsky, "Manifesto for an Independent Revolutionary Art", in Rosemount, *What is Surrealism?*, 242-247, 243 and 245-246.

Like all artists, the surrealists were creatures of their contemporary intellectual environment. Rebellion was in the air, and social ferment swirled around them. Nineteenth century individualist anarchist ideas influenced surrealists; they were familiar with and accepting of Marxist analyses of the political situation; and they embraced the "new" psychological theories of Sigmund Freud. Their emphasis on psychology and the inner life of the individual's subconscious as the source of the artistic imagination was unique in the history of art.

In the introduction to *The Forecast is Hot*, contemporary surrealists Paul Garron, Franklin Rosemont, and Penelope Rosemont commented on the complex and contradictory surrealist commitment to challenging any and all fixed constructs:

> Too anarchist for most Marxists, too Marxist for most anarchists; too much in love with poetry and painting for most politicos; too involved in the revolutionary movement for most writers and artists; too immersed in theoretical inquiry for activists; too unruly for the professoriate; too rigorous in poetic matters for wheeler-dealers in the "Spirituality" racket; too devoted to the Marvelous for those afflicted with instrumentalist rationalism; too Freudian for the positivist/puritanical Left; too "wild" for conservative medical usurpers of psychoanalysis – surrealism continues to flourish in the only way it can: *outside* and *against* all the dominant paradigms.[68]

---

68 "Introduction," *The Forecast is Hot! Tracts and Other Collective Declarations of the Surrealist Movement in the United States 1966-1976*, eds. Franklin Rosemont, Penelope Rosemont and Paul Garon (Chicago: Black Swan Press, 1997), xxxiv.

Surrealists are still revered as symbolic of the rebellious artist. They set a standard against which all subsequent avant-garde artists seeking to make a political statement measure their own efforts. Their rebellion began with an effort to distance themselves from "academic" and traditional schools of art and find a way to respond to their alienation resulting from the horrors of The Great War. They gradually transitioned to a political perspective but never fully developed it. While they never satisfactorily resolved the relationship between art and politics, they were the first modern artists to attempt to bridge that gap.

The surrealists are also remembered for their efforts to devise new aesthetic techniques and new styles. Collectively, their work reflects a recognizable style and content: images of fantastic beings and worlds, signifying the strange, the humorous, the whimsical, and the weird; reflecting no reality except a sur-reality and the shadowy world of personal dreams. There is an absence of direction, of meaning; but there is a certain charm that haunts the viewer.

Surrealism was, if nothing else, a different reality, a suggestion of unfinished work to be completed, of dreams unrealized. In that way, Surrealism opened the door for potential aesthetic and political transformation. Rajeev Patke summed up the surrealist undertaking:

> Layers of convention and complacency had to be ripped away. The cleansing quality of violence had to be savored without distraction. Familiar modes had to be abandoned, their names erased, and new ones with no names discovered. ... Startling juxtapositions and wrenched transpositions had to convert surprise to shock. A state of perpetual shock had to be cultivated. Strangeness had to be returned to the familiar; the phantasmal had to

become as commonplace as the ordinary.[69]

Ultimately, however, after the dismantling of art, culture, and politics, what was left was the chaos of nothing, a fragmented world of disconnected pieces of the old world blown apart but never reassembled. When we look in the mirror of our culture, we can see the reflection that the surrealists held up for our eyes. If there is a message, the message is that the world will never be the same; and we have to create it anew. The surrealists took our world apart, but they gave us few tools to put it back together. After the dismantling, however, what still shines brightly is Surrealism's core impulse for rebellion and resistance and the insistence that art act for change.

---

69 Rajeev S. Patke, "Walter Benjamin, Surrealism, and Photography," paper presented at Workshop on 'Literature as Revolt in twentieth Century Europe', 17 August 1998, The University of Haifa, Israel (6the ISSEI Conference). www.sunwalked.wordpress. com/2009/12/17/interesting-paper-on-walter-benjamin-surrealism-and-photography-by-rajeev-s-patke

CHAPTER 4

SOCIALIST REALISM: **REAL LIVES, REAL PEOPLE, REAL POLITICS**

*The poem, the song, the picture, is only water drawn
from the well of the people, and it should be given
back to them in a cup of beauty so that they may
drink, and in drinking understand themselves.1*

INTRODUCTION

THE CREATION OF REALISTIC ART – THE REPRESENTATION OF
real and familiar images – can be traced back to the beginning of art itself. Realism in the service of politics also has
a long history. The rich and powerful have used realistic
representations to justify and to celebrate political leaders, spiritual beliefs, war heroes. Realism has also been
widely adopted to advance revolutionary political agendas. Realism was the most common style that nineteenth
century graphic artists used to highlight injustices and to
rally people to radical causes; and the style was especially
popular in Russia after the 1917 Revolution. Early examples of realist political messages include political cartoons,
socialist and communist iconography on posters and banners, World War I propaganda posters (developed by all

---

1   Attributed to Federico Garciá Lorca.

combatants), and literary works such as Upton Sinclair's graphic exposé of the meat-packing industry in *The Jungle*. Realism was the dominant political aesthetic style in the United States during the 1930's in depictions of the suffering of people during the Great Depression, in the exaggerated heroic images celebrating workers, in literary works, and in theater projects.

Socialist Realism was born in the political turmoil of Russia in the early decades of the twentieth century. Following the 1917 Russian Revolution Realism was the dominant political aesthetic. Most Russian artists quickly put their skills to work on behalf of the government. Some of the most talented visual artists in the Russian modernist-influenced World of Art Movement were soon engaged in creating attention-getting political graphic art. Despite their efforts to incorporate avant-garde modernist techniques – which can still be seen and appreciated in the political posters designed just after the revolution – Modernism was ultimately condemned by Josef Stalin as a manifestation of corrupt bourgeois culture.

In 1932, Stalin decreed in "On the Reconstruction of Literary and Art Organizations" that Socialist Realism was the only acceptable aesthetic in the USSR. Art was to serve as a propaganda weapon and while the parameters of the aesthetic would never be clearly defined, the understanding was that style and content would be dictated by the Central Committee of the Communist Party. Russian artists moved quickly to adopt the new party mandate and the strict stylistic limitations. Artists whose work was not deemed acceptable and artists who refused to follow the mandate either changed their styles, emigrated, committed suicide, or were even executed.

Socialist Realism quickly dominated the artistic landscape and was adopted by communist communities across the globe. Art was subordinated to politics, and artists used political and realistic imagery to sway public opinion and build solidarity. The proscribed and formulaic images were designed to illuminate the horrors of capitalism, to highlight and idealize the worker and cooperative economic activity, and to celebrate the successes of the Bolshevik revolution in particular and communism in general.

In the early 1930's, Socialist Realism had a significant impact on American art and aesthetic theory.[2] It became clear that capitalism had failed, and in response to the national despair generated by the Great Depression, the writers especially responded with calls for social change. They turned their talents and energies to developing a proletarian-inspired aesthetic theory grounded in a working class analysis. Hundreds of John Reed Clubs were organized by the Communist Party in 1929, bringing socially conscious artist together. The federal government's New Deal program, the Works Progress Administration (WPA), soon hired writers and artists all across the country and funded their work. All fields of art – photography, theater, film, art, and especially literature – turned to creating empowering images of people struggling and overcoming adversity. Most of these artists rejected the hard line that Stalin dictated. They developed an American

---

2 Even today, however, great effort is made to dissociate the socialist realist impact in the United States. Popular resources like Wikipedia, for instance, differentiate between Socialist Realism, Social Realism (apparently the acceptable American designation), and American Realism. Still another source coined the term "democratic Realism." The confusion is unfortunate, because the impact on the world of art by the Russian experience was, indeed, widespread, especially in Europe and the United States. Each country took the concept in its unique direction, but all worked with the same set of expectations: that art had an undeniable link with politics in the real world. In the United States, the political realism was shaped by a Russian-inspired Socialist ideology and political agenda. It did not emerge from isolation. I have chosen to apply the same term, Socialist Realism, in all geographic settings. The debates within specific settings clarify how each parsed the ideological positions.

version of Socialist Realism that reflected Marxist ideology. According to Donald Egbert, Marxism appealed to Americans because they shared some of the same values: "There are certain characteristics common to Marxism and the American democratic tradition, ... the virtues of a classless society, [and] ... an optimistic belief in progress and in the special importance of industrial and technological progress."[3] Egbert noted other influences on the emerging political aesthetic including individualism, some strains of anarchism, and William Morris's work in aesthetics.[4]

This new American radical aesthetic was formally adopted in 1935 at the First American Writers Congress. The Congress met for three days in New York City. Two-hundred-sixteen delegates from 26 states were present, and 150 writers attended as guests including representatives from Mexico, Cuba, Germany, and Japan. Over 4,000 spectators attended the sessions. The Congress was endorsed by many well-known and influential American writers: Erskine Caldwell, Jack Conroy, Theodore Dreiser, James Farrell, Michael Gold, Josephine Herbst, Meridel Le Sueur, Nathanael West, and Richard Wright among many others. Even writers such as Dos Passos, Ernest Hemingway, and John Steinbeck who did not attend subsequently adopted an aesthetic with strong political messages couched in realistic representation.

The debate among participants at the Writers Congress was often lively; and although the writers disagreed over specific ideological perspectives, they eventually reached general agreement on the basic principles of a new political aesthetic. The meeting also generated minor debates

---

3   Donald Egbert, *Socialism and American Art: In the Light of European Utopianism, Marxism, and Anarchism* (Princeton, NJ: Princeton University Press, 1967), 108.

4   For an extended discussion of non-Stalinist influences on American Socialist Realism, see Section V of Donald Egbert's "Introduction," in Egbert, *Socialism and American Art*, 85-128.

such as Kenneth Burke's proposal that American writers reject the terminology of "the masses" and "workers" and, instead, use the term "the people." Questions were also raised about the effectiveness of the Communist Party in the context of American politics. One of the official outcomes of the conference was the formation of the League of American Writers which the Communist Party sponsored. One year later the American Artists Congress was formed to develop a similar agenda for the visual arts. Other radical arts organizations soon followed – the Workers Dance League, the Workers Music League, and the Theater Collective.

In the new aesthetic, art was defined in social rather than personal or stylistic terms – not art for art's sake or to reflect the individual artist's vision but art necessitated by the economic and social reality. This radical aesthetic challenged the modernist ideas of the artist as alienated and isolated and the individual as the font of all creative energy. Instead, art would be motivated and inspired by a social, collectivist agenda that would produce not only different subject matter but also use different modes of expression. The insistence on a social dimension to art served, Joseph Freeman suggested, to ground the myths of the artist in reality.[5] Others, including editor of the *New Republic* Malcolm Cowley cautioned that the poet must not ignore politics but, at the same time, should be wary of limiting ideologies.

> All poets are automatically revolutionary:
> if they are genuine poets. They exhibit every
> idea they handle at the moment of its disin-
> tegration; they are the perpetual foes of ab-
> straction. What you demand is that they re-
> ject the Capitalist abstractions and accept the

---

5   Joseph Freeman, "Discussions and Proceedings," in *American Writers' Congress*, ed. Henry Hart (New York, NY: International Publishers, 1935), 170.

Communist. By assuming the world a poet
merely assumes that the present moment offers all the elements for a full statement of the
human situation.[6]

Despite disagreements over the finer points of ideology, most participants at the Congress were committed to
a "social" or "proletarian" art. In many ways, they echoed
the words of an earlier Industrial Workers of the World
(IWW) spokesman for social art, Bill Haywood.

Proletarian art would be very much kind-
lier than your art. There will be a social spirit
in it. Not so much boasting about personality.
Artists won't be so egotistical. The highest ideal of an artist will be to write a song which the
workers can sing, to compose a drama which
great throngs of workers can perform out of
doors. When we stop fighting each other – for
wages of existence on one side, and for unnecessary luxury on the other – then perhaps we
shall all become human beings and surprise
ourselves with the beautiful things we do and
make on the earth.[7]

Socialist Realism was not confined to the radical left;
its principles soon permeated official government policy
and practice although with a toned-down political message
and absent the label of Socialist Realism. Many of the left
and communist artists were involved from the start with
the Works Progress Administration/Federal Arts Project

6   Allan Tate to Malcolm Cowley, Correspondence December
1930-December 1934, quoted in Daniel Aaron, *Writers on the Left:
Episodes in American Literary Communism* (New York, NY: Octagon,
1974), 340.

7   Bill Haywood, attributed to Haywood and quoted in Max Eastman,
Venture (New York, NY: A.&C. Boni, 1927), 210.

(WPA/FAP), which was established in 1935 to provide financial support for unemployed artists by putting them to work on public art projects. By and large, policy was determined at the federal government level. Holger Cahill, the first national Director of the WPA/FAP (who credited John Dewey as his inspiration rather than the left), was committed to local control and, more importantly, local cultural expression. He attributed the success of the WPA/FAP to three basic policies:

> This creative drive has been stimulated and maintained because the Project has held to the idea of the unity of art with the common experience, the continuity between "the refined and intensified forms of experience that are works of art and everyday events, doings, sufferings, that are universally recognized to constitute experience"; because the Project has encouraged the closest possible collaboration between the artist and the public for which he works; and because it has held firmly to the idea of the greatest degree of freedom for the artist.[8]

REPRESSION OF SOCIALIST REALISM IN THE UNITED STATES

A BASIC PREMISE of cultural policy under the WPA/FAP was the government's assurance of artistic freedom and the clear separation of art and politics. Experience during the 1930's and in subsequent decades proved that this did not happen. The artists generally leaned leftward in their personal politics, and their art reflected the economic and political climate of the times. From its very inception the WPA projects were under attack from the right wing. We

---

8   Holger Cahill, "American Resources in the Arts," in *Art for the Millions: Essays from the 1930's by Artists and Administrators of the WPA Federal Art Project*, ed. Francis V. O'Connor (Boston: New York Graphic Society, 1975), 33-44, 40.

can trace the beginnings of the McCarthy Era (which we traditionally associate with the 1950's) to the closing down of the Federal Theater Project in 1939 on the recommendation of the House Un-American Activities Committee (HUAC). HUAC determined the Theater Project to be full of communists. Throughout its less-than-illustrious career, HUAC systematically attacked every facet of the arts and cultural work as being communist-inspired, from writers and theater workers to filmmakers and musicians.

The film industry received special scrutiny, in part, because film reached such a wide audience. Many artists working in the film industry had liberal and even further left political leanings, and their colleagues often subjected them to harassment and condemnation. Ronald Reagan got his start in politics by forming a right-wing artists' union in Hollywood – the Screen Actors Guild – which was instrumental in creating and maintaining mass hysteria during the witch hunt in the film industry. In 1947 at the openings of the HUAC hearings that year, Reagan and Walt Disney testified that there were many communists in the film industry. Subsequently, formal actions were taken against a high profile group that came to be known as the Hollywood Ten. They refused to testify when they were asked to disclose their relationship with the Communist Party (membership in which was not illegal). They were repeatedly asked, "Are you now or have you ever been a member of the Communist Party?" All ten were summarily fired, banned from work in the film industry, and blacklisted. Their names were even removed from previous film credits. The blacklist was expanded through the mid-1950's to include hundreds of actors, writers, dancers, illustrators in Disney's studio, screenwriters, singers, and musicians. Many famous artists made the "list"; many more careers were ruined by insinuation and gossip. Among the hundreds of blacklisted artists were such illustrious people as Lillian Hellman, Paul Robeson, Richard Wright, Leonard Bernstein, Will Geer, Lena Horne, Burl

Ives, Dalton Trumbo, Arthur Miller, Pete Seeger, Orson Welles, and Aaron Copland. In subsequent years some were able to continue their creative work – sometimes under false names or without attribution.

The right viewed Socialist Realism as a real threat to American culture, but criticism came from the liberal left as well. In 1950 in the midst of the McCarthy hysteria, a group of anti-Stalinist leftists and neo-conservatives formed the Congress for Cultural Freedom. Their stated goal was to oppose communism both at home and abroad. Many prominent intellectuals, such as John Dewey, Arthur Schlesinger, Jr., Bertrand Russell, Tennessee Williams, and Irving Kristol supported the organization. In 1967, the *Saturday Evening Post* and *Ramparts* magazines reported that the CIA had funded the organization for many years.

Despite the dark ages of the McCarthy Era and the subsequent suppression of politics in art, the core ideas of Socialist Realism were never seriously discredited. They were revived in the 1980's in the Cultural Democracy Movement in an effort to develop a more inclusive approach to political art. In "Reflections on Cultural Democracy," Don Adams and Arlene Goldbard developed the broad outlines of this new movement and contributed important theoretical work.[9] They positioned the Cultural Democracy Movement in opposition to both popular and high culture. Large media corporations controlled popular culture: "The consumer culture industries – movies, television, records, mass-market publishing, and so on – produce and disseminate the culture of technology ... [and] are concerned only with end products, with commodities." So-called high culture was also problematic: "The establishment arts institutions ... produce and disseminate

---

9   Don Adams and Arlene Goldbard, "Reflections on Cultural Democracy," mimeo, ca. 1980. See also Arlene Goldbard and Don Adams, *New Creative Communities: The Art of Cultural Development* (Oakland: New Village Press, 2006).

a parallel culture of status."[10] They also insisted that the Cultural Democracy Movement stay free of the rigid constraints that various leftist ideologies mandated and, instead, take on the larger challenge of critiquing culture production generally.

> While much oppositional artwork can be seen as part of the movement for cultural democracy, the movement's identity and historical significance ... do not lie in its alignment with particular political causes, but in the fact that it stands in opposition to the whole organization of culture in our society. ... culture itself is the arena in which social transformation can now begin. So our main work is to expose the false consciousness the dominant cultural systems promulgate, and to offer in its place the vision of a society founded on cultural democracy.[11]

Adams and Goldbard were also critical of the individual artist who stood outside of his/her community: "The artist ... is called on to play the part both of a person and of an artist. Of the two, that of person is more immediately important. ... He must enter the common arena and become a citizen."[12] They also refused to dictate a specific style or content of works of art: "Regardless of the medium or style or arena in which an artist works, the material of cultural work is consciousness."[13]

AESTHETICS OF SOCIALIST REALISM

SOCIALIST REALISM WAS well grounded in Marxist aesthetics. One of the central elements of Marxist aesthetics was

---

10 Adams and Goldbard, 1.
11 Adams and Goldbard, 3.
12 Adams and Goldbard, 6.
13 Adams and Goldbard, 17.

the commitment to the realistic portrayal of social reality in the context of human community. Marxist aesthetician Christopher Caudwell called for a lyrical, evocative style because it reflected collective inspiration. Writing about the tradition of harvest songs, he concluded that poetry played an active role reflecting not just the physical reality of the community but also the essence of it. "For poetry describes and expresses not so much the grain in its concreteness, the harvest in its factual essence ... but the emotional, social and collective complex which is that tribe's relation to the harvest. ... Not poetry's abstract statement – its content of facts – but its dynamic role in society – its content of collective emotion – is therefore poetry's *truth*."[14]

Socialist realist art portrayed people self-conscious of themselves as social, political beings, an art that evoked the idea of the social relationship itself. Caudwell believed that it was only through the full realization of the interaction and dialectical encounter between outer reality (including political reality) and inner sense that true art comes to be known. It requires engagement, interaction, and participation in the real world.

> All art is conditioned by the concept of freedom which rules in the society that produces it; art is a mode of freedom, and a class society conceives freedom to be absolutely whatever relative freedom that class has attained to. In bourgeois art man is conscious of the necessity of outer reality, but not of his own, because he is unconscious of the society that makes him what he is. He is only a half-man. Communist poetry would be complete, because it will be man conscious of his own necessity as well as that of outer reality.[15]

---

14 Christopher Caudwell, *Illusion and Reality* (New York, NY: International Publishers, 1937, 1977), 38.

15 Caudwell, 328-329.

Proletarian art also had a responsibility to contribute to the creation of a new world that realized the previously suppressed hopes and dreams of the community, according to Caudwell.[16]

Caudwell insisted on a concrete awareness and expression of reality. The artist had a duty to reflect the world as it really was: not abstractly but personally and intimately through emphasizing the collective nature of social existence and the deep need for relationship. The creation of art should reflect the social relationships that shape individuality. The artist is not alienated, but remains him/herself:

> This concrete world of life which gathers up within itself as a rounded, developing whole the divorced and simpler abstract worlds of man and Nature is the peculiar concern of the communist poet. He is interested in his own individuality, not in and for itself ... but in its developing relation with other individualities in a communicating world that is not just a fluid amorphous sea, but has its own rigidity and reality.[17]

Similarly, in *The Necessity of Art*, writer Ernst Fischer called for an art that had a moral component: the artist was, of necessity, called to reflect not only class awareness and the class struggle but also the moral goodness and rightness of that struggle. Art must be purposeful and meaningful.

> The artist's task [is] to expound the profound meaning of events to his fellow-men, to make plain to them the process, the necessity, and the rules of social and historical

16 Caudwell, 391.
17 Caudwell, 327-328.

development, to solve for them the riddle of
the essential relationships between man and
nature and man and society. His duty [is] to
enhance the self-awareness and life-awareness
of the people of his city, his class, and his nation. ... to guide individual life back into collective life, the personal into the universal, to
restore the lost unity of man.[18]

The artist had a responsibility to depict not only a representation of the objective reality but also the vitality of
the process itself. Ideally, through engagement with the
artist, the observer is drawn into art, participates in art
in an intimate way. Proletarian art celebrated the process
of becoming rather than leading the reader to a pre-or-
dained outcome. By engaging the reader in a process, a
new symbolic experience was created which drew people
together rather than isolating them – art as participation.
Grounding art in the historical and political realities of the
community resulted in a new aesthetic of relatedness, no
longer separated from the flux of experience.

Stylistic elements of Socialist Realism

Socialist Realism is easily identifiable by
its emphasis on the economic and political context in which
people live – in particular, its portrayal of the nature of
political and cultural oppression. Its specific content and
forms of expression address real and potential connections
with others as well as overt political analysis. Professor
Barbara Foley outlined three essential elements of proletarian literature: criticism of capitalism, realistic portrayal,
and an analysis of class relations:

The first of these is the critique of ideology. ... [P]roletarian literature lays out the

18 Ernst Fischer, *The Necessity of Art*, trans. Anna Bostock (London:
James Curry Ltd., 1990), 42.

imperative necessity for querying the forms of consciousness – notions of loyalty, of human potentiality, of common sense – that bind us, emotionally and conceptually, to the regime of capital. … [T]he second feature … is its aspiration to portray reality in its totality. … Finally, proletarian literature's focus on class as social relation of production, and hence on the unremittingly antagonistic relation between exploiters and exploited, does much to counter the mystifying proposition of common interest that underlies the rhetorics of nationalism and patriotism.[19]

Socialist realist imagery centered on the lives of working class people and their struggle against capitalism. There are many examples of American social realist art: in literature Jack Conroy's *The Disinherited*, John Steinbeck's *The Grapes of Wrath*, Meridel Le Sueur's moving short stories, novels, and novellas of workers and women; Dalton Trumbo's anti-war novel *Johnny Got His Gun* (which was made into a powerful film in 1971); in film *The Salt of the Earth* and *The Grapes of Wrath*; in music, the songs of Woody Guthrie; in photography the works of Dorothea Lange, Walker Evans, and Lewis Hine; in the graphic art of Ben Shahn and William Gropper; and the work of hundreds of literary, visual, and theatrical artists in the various Federal Arts Projects across the United States.

Common themes from everyday life were celebrated and honored in social realist art. Words and images were contextualized to a particular political community, to a particular struggle, to a vision, or often to the world of work. While there was a recognition that individuals were suffering economically, the art emphasized the social aspects

19 Barbara Foley, "The Continuing Relevance of Proletarian Literature in a Time of 'Endless War,'" *Fortune City*, March 2003. http://www.victorian.fortunecity.com

of suffering – the politics that affected people collectively. There was also a strong regional element to American Socialist Realism that was grounded in regional differences in culture and linguistic expression that spawned entire sub-genres in the various arts. This was a direct result of WPA policies encouraging local artistic expression.

There are special qualities which distinguish political art that are readily apparent in the choice of themes and content. "The People" are always present in political art. Political art speaks to people, about people, and for people. People are the subject and the object, the audience, the voice, the bearers of collective memory – the very reason for art. They are portrayed in their collective, heroic role as participants in the political struggle and the grand conversation about human freedom. Events portrayed in political art are often actual political events, or they are the politicization of everyday events. Historical events are recalled to awaken, to remind, to honor martyrs, to raise awareness of the shared experiences of oppression, to inspire people to resist and overcome.

The importance of representing people, especially working people, was a key element in Socialist Realism, coloring the way artists experienced and articulated the world around them. The worker was always central in the artist's consciousness. Years ago I had an exchange with author Meridel Le Sueur that highlighted how she saw reality through the eyes of working people. One afternoon, she and I decided to visit the James J. Hill (of railroad fame) mansion in Saint Paul, Minnesota. As we were admiring the incredible wood carving everywhere, I commented on the beautiful house Hill had built. She turned to me and in a rather stern voice admonished me, "Hill did not build this house, the workers did and don't forget it." Her message was about the importance of consciously choosing perspective and establishing a working class context.

Political art is not only passive portrayal; it also reaches out and draws in an audience. To be effective, political art must have a public vehicle for expression; and beginning in the 1930's, public political art adopted many popular forms designed to reach the intended working class audience. Federal Theater Project productions were well attended and enthusiastically praised, and the developing genre of film occasionally took on the challenge of realistic portrayal of the politics and economics of the Depression. Murals were an especially powerful medium for highlighting political issues because they were permanent and because they were in public places. In a world where visual arts had been limited to paintings hung in museums and the relative new medium of film which was already focusing on escapist entertainment, the mural brought both art and strong political messages to the street.

The government was an active patron of visual art in the United States. The support included commissioning many wall murals to grace the inside and outside of public buildings. Murals painted on walls in public places were designed around a strong narrative form, often with an overt political message. Professor of modern and contemporary art Sergio Cortesini noted, "The notion of mural art as a form of communication of a civil faith – as opposed to the solitude of easel work – was the key concept instilled by Section administrator Forbes Watson ... to document the first murals commissioned by the Treasury Department. 'Back of all great mural painting is a [social] belief. The painter shares this belief with the audience.'"[20] Style and content were suggested by the government, but were broad enough to allow for artistic freedom. Three subject areas were recommended – local history, local activities, and the postal system.[21]

20 Sergio Cortesini, "Depicting National Identities in New Deal America and Fascist Italy: Government Sponsored Murals," in *Kunst und Propaganda: Im Streit der Nationen 1930-1945*, edited by Hans Jörg und Nikola Doll (Berlin: Deutsches Historisches Museum, 2007), 38.

21 Cortesini, 38.

In contrast to American murals which contained images of common people, workers, women, and children, Cortesini observed that Italian murals commissioned by Mussolini's fascist government conveyed a different political message that "excluded the common man, and brought forth the hypothesized fascist superman. ... This resistance to celebrating everyday life ultimately resides in fascist diffidence for individuals as citizens and the private dimension of the family." Totalitarianism, according to Cortesini, can be "understood as the total absorption of the private into the public, or, in other words, the subordination of the values of private life (religion, culture, morality, affections) to the utmost political value – the state."[22] There were some content similarities designed to appeal to similar audiences. Both Italian and American murals praised "homespun rural communities as the repositories of authentic social virtues, and conversely, distrusting of bourgeois and capitalist individualism. ... [They] both eschewed images openly sympathetic to capitalism."[23]

American murals were unabashedly political. Donald Egbert observed that "the strongest Marxian influences in American painting have not come directly from Russia [but] ... from Mexico, mainly as result of the influence of the communist painter, Diego Rivera."[24] In his study of the murals that Rivera created in San Francisco in the 1930's, Anthony Lee explored how murals functioned as a medium communicating a political message and the impact that they had on the politics of the city.[25] From the beginning, Rivera's murals were controversial. Unlike public art prior to the 1920's which lionized individuals in power and depicted idealized metaphors of capitalist

---

22 Cortesini, 43.

23 Cortesini, 44.

24 Egbert, 103.

25 Anthony W. Lee, *Painting on the Left: Diego Rivera, Radical Politics, and San Francisco's Public Murals* (Berkeley and others: University of California Press, 1999).

success, Rivera's murals portrayed the common people in larger than life images. His work initiated a dialogue in San Francisco over the definition of "public" and highlighted the fundamental differences between the "competing ideological and political bases" of material progress represented by capitalism and the more overt politics of workers.[26] Instead of images depicting abstractions such as "Progress" or "Industry," Rivera's murals placed workers in prominent roles.

According to Lee, Rivera also deliberately introduced political symbols into the murals: "Rivera took pains to encode [the worker in his mural] ... He put a hammer and sickle (perhaps originally a red star) on his left breast pocket. He had him pull the crucial lever [of a machine] – deliberately Michael Goodman claimed – 'with his left hand (not right hand) ... because he is a radical.'"[27] The intent of the political artist was to engage a dialogue about political questions through the visual medium of the mural, according to Lee: "Those murals, I argue, represented the leftist artists' most startling moment of activism and cohesion – the moment when their work entered into meaningful dialogue with widespread working-class dissent."[28] Despite the power of Rivera's murals, however, Lee was skeptical that the murals had fostered much political activism: "Despite the symbolic emphasis on public culture in the city, 1930's murals could not be made to stand in for larger debates about political reform or revolution."[29] His conclusion seems to suggest that there are some limits to the effectiveness of political art to actually result in direct political action.

Nevertheless, Rivera's politically charged murals certainly got the attention of the power brokers in San Francisco and elsewhere. In San Francisco some of the

---

26 Lee, 49.

27 Lee, 109.

28 Lee, xix.

29 Lee, 160.

city fathers recognized themselves portrayed in the murals in less than flattering roles. In 1934, Nelson Rockefeller obliterated a mural he had commissioned by Rivera because it included an image of Lenin leading a May Day parade and because it was too critical of capitalism. Powerful images in public places of working people rising up against capitalism were perceived to be a threat. The power of politically-charged imagery in the public arena is still perceived (perhaps rightly) as a threat today. In 2011, the Governor of the state of Maine ordered the removal of a mural honoring the history of labor in the state that had been commissioned to decorate a wall in the Department of Labor. He said he had received complaints that the mural was unfriendly to business. Mike Alewitz, a contemporary political muralist who has been designing and painting murals since the early 1980's, has seen several of his murals erased for political reasons: one created in Austin, Minnesota, during the Hormel Strike of 1985-1986 that I will discuss below.

In *Insurgent Images: The Agitprop Murals of Mike Alewitz*, Paul Buehl and Mike Alewitz outlined some of the key characteristics of contemporary political murals. Generally, murals address specific local issues in addition to incorporating transcendent themes. Exploitation is a recurring theme with the people often portrayed as challenging or defeating the power structure. Most murals include images of people in action, their faces reflecting emotion about the topic of the mural. Historically, murals addressed class issues; but by the 1970's, mural art incorporated new subject matter including race, gender, gender preference, or anti-war messages.[30] Murals continued to focus on local communities. The Chicago Public Art Group, spearheaded by artist William Walker, created an estimated 250 community murals in the city of Chicago during the 1970's. The murals were situated in neighborhoods, were created

---

30 Paul Buhle and Mike Alewitz, *Insurgent Images: The Agitprop Murals of Mike Alewitz* (New York, NY: Monthly Review Press, 2002).

with neighborhood involvement, and often addressed local community concerns.[31]

In 1986 in the midst of a bitter strike between the local meatpackers union P-9 and the Hormel Company in Austin, Minnesota, the men and women of the striking community worked with Alewitz to create a 16 x 80 foot mural on the wall of the P-9 Austin Labor Center. Alewitz explained his reasons for coming to Austin to work on the mural:

> One of the reporters asked me why I was willing to come here, since I was from out of town. I told her … in my opinion, this wall on this building is the most important wall in the United States today. Because the P-9 strike is the most important labor struggle that has taken place in this country in decades. And if I had a choice of any wall to paint on, it would have been this one.[32]

The P-9 mural is a classic example of Alewitz's content and style: colors are bright, and the mural is filled with powerful images of people. His murals usually contain a large, central human figure that dominates the action portrayed. In the P-9 mural, the central figure is a woman with long, flowing, black hair, swinging a huge meat cleaver. She is in the act of hacking off the head of a huge serpent representing the all-consuming Hormel Company. The bloody cleaver had "P-9" printed on it. A second large figure is holding a torch aloft. Across the length of the mural is a banner bearing the words of an old Wobbly quote: "If blood be the price of your cursed wealth, good God we have paid in full." The serpent is also an important figure in the mural. It is shown squeezing the buildings of the

---

31 Community Media Workshop Newstip, "Chicago Muralists Heralded," October 20, 2005. http://www.newstips.org
32 Buehl and Alewitz, 36-37.

Hormel plant where there are lines of workers marching into the plant in an eerie scene reminiscent of the classic German film *Metropolis*. A second banner on the mural bears the words, "One for All and All for One." The mural was dedicated to Nelson Mandela, who was imprisoned at the time, with the message, "International Labor Solidarity, Abolish Apartheid."

The mural had to be protected day and night from vandalism by people who were not supportive of the strike. The community was bitterly divided. Austin was a classic example of a company town, and people who opposed the strike felt that Hormel had given a lot to the town. The thought that workers would challenge their benefactor was unacceptable. Unfortunately, in 1987 the United Food and Commercial Workers (UFCW) forcibly took over the P-9 center, replaced P-9 as Hormel's union, and destroyed the mural. According to Buehl and Alewitz, "When the Washington-based UFCW trustees snatched control of the local, their stooges shut off the security light so as to encourage vandalism and sought to contract for a Twin Cities crew to sandblast the mural off the wall. No union sandblasters would accept the work; and despite a local judge's restraining order, the bureaucrats' flunkies proceeded with the sandblasting themselves."[33]

The role of the artist

Proletarian writers and artists were, more than anything else, dedicated to a narrative of commitment and passionate involvement. The artist was not simply an observer and a recorder but also an active participant engaged in the political struggle. "Indeed, it is largely this intimate relationship between reader and writer that gives revolutionary literature an activism and purposefulness long since unattainable by the writers of other classes," editors of the *Partisan Review* William Phillips and Philip

---

33 Buehl and Alewitz, 47.

Rahv observed.[34] Midwestern writer Meridel Le Sueur
made a similar case that art was social, and the writer
should be passionately committed to transmitting a message of political struggle and empowerment, inspiring the
people to hope and to action.

In Martin Espada's study of political poetry, *Poetry Like
Bread: Poets of the Political Imagination*, he explored the nature of political art, its content, and the role of the political
artist. The task of the political poet (and the political artist
generally) is to awaken the people, to rouse them to take
collective action. The voice is an active voice, and most
often the political poet speaks with a collective voice: his
country, her tribe, their race, class, gender, sexual orienta-
tion. Where the self is expressed, it is a self always set in
the context of a specific community.

There are four powerful "voices" or narratives that the
political poet uses – the voices of the prophet, the mourner,
the rebel, and the muse of change.

Political poet as prophet. Like the Old Testament prophets
of the Bible, the political poet acts to warn, to awaken, to
arouse, to inspire. As poet and writer, Le Sueur eloquently
described the inspiration for her art:

> You wrote in the Socialist world more like
> a prophet, a conduit for the suffering of your
> people. A cry out … a whoop or a holler – more
> like the ballads of the people come to sing sor-
> row – a common sorrow. I also took this from
> the Hebraic prophets who were educators,
> singers, warners [sic]. … I look upon writing
> as revealment, underground, subversive expo-
> sition. I mean exposing the enemy. Remarks
> on Kansas caves, underground journals,
> newspapers, leaflets, posters, mass chants. To

34 William Phillips and Philip Rahv, "Recent Problems in Revolutionary
Literature," in *The Anxious Years*, ed. Louis Filler (New York, NY:
G.P. Putnam's Sons, 1963), 339.

write to expose and to rouse, awaken, wake
up. Watch out. Art as action, as deep image of
struggle and not bourgeois reflection.[35]

The role of prophet calls for a deeply committed self-consciousness on the part of the political artist and a sense
of responsibility for effecting social change.

Political poet as mourner. The poet also has an obligation
to articulate and to share the emotional context caused
by oppression or political violence. The awareness of anguish, death, and suffering is a staple theme in political
poetry, precisely because it recognizes and honors the
personal nature of political awareness as well as identi-
fies the source of suffering. Others also shared the suffering; it is not just a private experience; it is a shared
event, a public event. Reading the literature of the Great
Depression, It is impossible not to understand that an important part of survival and resistance was that the suffering was so apparent, so public, so shared. As a result,
people took comfort in knowing that they were not the
cause of it.

In our contemporary, desensitized world, we don't like
to recognize, let alone honor, suffering. It is fashionable
in the United States today to criticize those who focus on
any kind of victimization as being "too negative." Those
actions are part of a concerted effort at massive cultural
denial about the level of violence and suffering in our
culture. Recognizing the violence that is so endemic in
our culture – whether individual or collective – lifts the
cloud of uncertainty over political stories of pain and sorrow. But, the voice of suffering in political poetry is never
self-defeating or pitying but rather is joined with a righ-
teous anger that moves the reader to action against the
cause of that suffering. This awareness and recognition

35 Meridel Le Sueur, *Journals*, n.d. A complete collection of Le Sueur's
   writing journals are archived at the Minnesota History Center,
   Saint Paul, Minnesota.

can be instrumental in motivating political resistance and change.

Political poet as rebel. Finally, the voice of rebellion and resistance is loud and clear in political poetry. Strengthened by the knowledge of shared grief, the political poet tells us that we can also find the courage to rebel. In the poem "The Common Grief," Honduran poet Roberto Sosa memorialized the Disappeared – bringing together in the poem both the victims of political violence and the women who grieved for them.[36] Jack Hirschman (United States) reminded us in the poem "Haiti" that no matter how oppressed people are, they will eventually rebel and rise up against their oppressors. [37] In Martín Espada's (United States) poignant and powerful poem "Federico's Ghost," an airplane pilot spraying the fields with insecticide poisons a young migrant boy picking tomatoes. He becomes a martyr for the other workers who begin a silent campaign of sabotage to honor his spirit: "Still tomatoes were picked and squashed/ in the dark, /and the old women in camp/ said it was Federico."[38] Ernesto Cardenal (Nicaragua) puts it even more simply in his poem "The Peasant Women from Cuá": "Their dreams are subversive."[39] Claribel Alegría's (Nicaragua) poem "From the Bridge" is a powerful metaphor about one person's transition from victim of oppression to revolutionary resistance. She challenges the reader to understand and to respond to the suffering and death of oppressed people by contrasting those who would continue to bind up the wounds of the oppressed and those who would change the situation that creates the pain in the first place. In the poem she moves herself and the reader from victim and passive observer to the fierce

---

36 Martin Espada, ed., *Poetry Like Bread: Poets of the Political Imagination* (Willimantic, CT: Curbstone Press, 1994), 219.

37 Espada, 149.

38 Martin Espada, "Federico's Ghost," in Espada, 130.

39 Ernesto Cardenal, "The Peasant Women from Cuá," in Espada, 86.

revolutionary poet who is able "to peer out/through these pitiless/scrutinizing eyes/to have my claws and this sharp beak."[40]

Muse of change. The political poet can also serve as a muse of change – to keep the people's vision and hope bright. The poet as prophet must be filled with hope for the future, writes guerrilla fighter/poet Otto René Castillo (Guatemala) in an untitled poem: "For a thousand years I carry our name/like a tiny future heart,/ whose wings begin to open tomorrow."[41] In the poem "Immigration Law," Margaret Randall writes, "Give me a handful of future/to rub against my lips."[42]

Political art resonates with a purity of passion and an aesthetic of empowerment – the power of the idea, the power of lived experience, the power of passionate resistance, of change, and of transformation.

CRITICISM OF SOCIALIST REALISM

MORE THAN ANY of the movements to be explored in this book, Socialist Realism came under the most sustained and virulent attack because it was extremely effective and threatening to other forms of representation. Despite its obvious popular appeal in the thirties, the political potential of this aesthetic perspective was soon buried under the weight of criticisms from across the political spectrum. In the United States, from the left, the center, and the right, Socialist Realism was entangled in competing political theaters: debates about Stalin's efforts to mandate a circumscribed Socialist Realism, repression by the federal government, criticisms from both the liberal and radical left, and the rabid anti-communism of the McCarthy Era from the right. Some criticisms were valid; others, however, were misguided or even purposely manipulated to discredit an aesthetic that in many ways continues to be effective today.

---

40 Claribel Alegría, "From the Bridge," in Espada, 33.

41 Otto René Castillo, "Let's Go Country," in Espada, 105.

42 Margaret Randall, "Immigration Law," in Espada, 182.

The mutual exclusivity of politics and art

Criticism was aimed at two levels: at the actual content and context of the realist portrayals and at the political messages embedded in the artwork. Critics of proletarian literature rejected the inclusion of political subject matter such as working class issues. Socialist Realism was also faulted for a lack of symbols – it was too didactic. Because some communistic art celebrated work and the worker, any art depicting workers was, therefore, suspect because it might be "political" art. Other critics rejected the inclusion of any references to political ideology in works of art, particularly Communist ideology. "Real" art succeeded, the circular argument went, precisely because it was not political. Political art, some critics argued, is an oxymoron. Political art cannot be art precisely *because* it is political. The inclusion of politics as subject matter spoils the purity of the art; the aesthetics of the practical and the everyday squelches the Muse. Politics is realism; art lies in the realm of the ideal. Literary critic Irving Howe argued that art and politics should be separate, that politics was a 'violent intrusion" into the literary imagination, that there was an irreconcilable conflict between rational ideology and fictional art: "The novel tries to confront experience in its immediacy and closeness, while ideology is by its nature general and inclusive."[43]

Driven at times by an almost hysterical need to denounce this new aesthetic even as it succeeded, the critics further argued that true art was "reflection," not "action"; and it was an experience of the senses, not of the cognitive processes. Phillips and Rahv concluded that excluding politics in toto from the art form was necessary; proletarian writers were not "great" writers because they allowed the intrusion of politics into their art. What made art great was that it remained aloof, rising above the political landscape. Introducing politics into art was not only heresy, it

---

43 Irving Howe, *Politics and the Novel* (New York, NY: Avon, 1957, 1967), 22.

wasn't even "art"; it was propaganda. Literature that dealt with political questions was incapable of truly reflecting the complexities of the human spirit.

Theodore Adorno developed a more nuanced but equally penetrating critique of Socialist Realism. His personal political affinities were Marxist, but his criticism spared no one. His intent in *Aesthetic Theory* was to develop an aesthetic that remained aloof of narrow ideological claims to art – capitalist aesthetics, the fascist appropriation of Futurism, the retreat of Surrealism into bourgeois individualism and what he saw as the "authoritarian" nature of Socialist Realism. At the same time, he demanded that art must have a social function. While his theory in general is very complex, his critique of Socialist Realism is concise and focused. In a passage criticizing Bertolt Brecht's work, for example, he noted that while Brecht "wanted to provoke social change," his art was probably "socially powerless." Furthermore, "Brecht by no means deceived himself on this score. Its effect is captured by the English expression of *preaching to the saved*. ... His didactic style, however, is intolerant of the ambiguity in which thought originates: It is authoritarian."[44] Adorno insisted that true art remain autonomous yet, at the same time, embedded in social realities. His critique of Socialist Realism included the role of the Communist Party in Russia.

> During World War I and prior to Stalin, artistic and politically advanced thought went in tandem; whoever came of age in those years took art to be what it in no way historically had been: a priori politically on the left. Since then the Zhdanovs and Ulbrichts have not only enchained the forces of artistic production with

---

44 Theodor W. Adorno, *Aesthetic Theory*, Edited by Gretel Adorno and Rolf Tiedemann, Translated with a translator's introduction by Robert Hullot-Kentor (Minneapolis: University of Minnesota Press) 1997.

the dictate of socialist realism but actually broken it; socially the aesthetic regression for which they are responsible is transparent as a petty bourgeois fixation.[45]

Adorno's definition of an effective political art can be seen in his critical comments about the didactic nature of Socialist Realism: "Among the mediations of art and society the thematic, the open or covert treatment of social matters, is the most superficial and deceptive. The claim that a sculpture of a coal miner a priori says more, socially, than a sculpture without proletarian hero, is by now echoed only where art is used for the purpose of 'forming opinion.'"[46] He dismissed Emile Zola's naturalism, for example, with the observation that "it was always uncertain if the artistic stance of growling and raw technique really denounced such things or identified with them. Real denunciation is probably only a capacity of form which is overlooked by a social aesthetic that believes in themes."[47] He observed at one point that Socialist Realism was "simply childish."[48]

Adorno's critics have accused him of being an elitist who sought only to return to the classical traditions of nineteenth century art. But, his position on "fine" art, vis a vis popular art, was more nuanced. He was critical of capitalist aesthetics which he dismissed as "kitsch" and "ready-made clichés," but he did not rule out a role for art with broad appeal to the masses that had been created independently from the culture industry: "When art has allowed itself, without condescension, to be inspired by a plebian element, art has gained in an authentic weightiness that is the opposite of the vulgar."[49]

45   Adorno, *Aesthetic Theory*, 254.
46   Adorno, *Aesthetic Theory*, 229-230.
47   Adorno, *Aesthetic Theory*, 230.
48   Adorno, *Aesthetic Theory*, 250.
49   Adorno, *Aesthetic Theory*, 239.

Echoing the criticism of mass culture by Max Horkheimer and Theodor Adorno in *The Dialectic of Enlightenment* and Clement Greenberg's scathing criticism of "kitsch" popular art, Louis Menand argued that Socialist Realism functioned in the cultural arena similar to advertising and to other popular media. Any aesthetic dictated from "above – whether it was initiated by the left or the dominant culture – was a form of tyranny. … Mass culture … was strictly a top-down affair. It was imposed on the masses by businessmen … and its function was to convince people that life under capitalism is natural and good. … There was thus no difference between Hollywood movies and the Socialist Realism of Stalin's Soviet Union. Realism had become a method of domination."[50]

The debate over the separation of art and politics has been an ongoing one. Critics have long been uneasy, for example, about how to evaluate the work of Leni Riefenstahl, the filmmaker who created some of Hitler's most compelling Nazi and anti-Semitic propaganda. The Nazi's were masters at bringing art and politics together in powerful visual messages. Critic Charles Taylor explored the complex interrelationship in a recent review of books written about Riefenstahl. His review began with the assertion that "Riefenstahl has been central to the arguments about whether politics can be separated from art, whether form can be separated from content."[51] The dilemma was clear: could Nazi propaganda be appreciated as "art" because of the skill and artistry it embodied, or are we obligated to reject it outright because of its volatile political content? Taylor agreed with Susan Sontag's reflections on Riefenstahl's artistic merits. In a 1975 essay for *The New York Review of Books*, "Fascinating Fascism," Sontag wrote:

---

50 Louis Menand, "Unpopular Front: American art and the Cold War," *The New Yorker*, October 17, 2005, 206.

51 Charles Taylor, "Ill Will," rev. *Leni Riefenstahl: A Life*, by Jurgen Trimborn and *Leni: The Life and Work of Leni Riefenstahl*, by Steven Bach, *The Nation*, May 7, 2007, 44.

"Anyone who defends Riefenstahl's films as documentaries, if documentary is to be distinguished from propaganda, is being ingenuous. In [her film] *Triumph of the Will,* the document (the image) is no longer simply the record of reality: 'Reality' has been constructed to serve the image."[52]

Allan Antliff examined the relationship between art and the personal politics of the artist in the problematic behavior of the anarchist graphic artist Robert Minor. Immensely talented, Minor walked away from the practice of his art; and according to Antliff, "He would dismiss the revolutionary relevance of art, announcing that henceforth he would dedicate himself to political work."[53] His actions were widely analyzed and criticized at the time, including by the communists who resented his attacks on Lenin's anti-union position and the Bolsheviks. Writer and critic Max Eastman framed the communist argument against Minor as a critique of anarchism. As part of a broader effort to undermine anarchism as a political theory, his critique hinged on portraying the anarchist artist as outside of the revolutionary milieu. Eastman took his analysis to its logical conclusion: not only was the anarchist artist isolated from the politics of class-based revolution, but he/she was actually an apologist for the liberal bourgeoisie.[54]

Emma Goldman quickly challenged Eastman's harsh denunciation of the artist's role in revolutionary change. The artist was not outside the working class, she argued; the revolutionary aesthetic impulse was available to everyone. "Anarchism is a natural philosophy of artists," she wrote; "Why so exclusive, dear Max? ... Surely you want

---

52 Susan Sontag, "Fascinating Fascism," rev. of *The Last of the Nuba* by Leni Reifenthal and *SS Regalia* by Jack Pia, *The New York Review of Books,* February 6, 1975. www.nybooks.com/articles/archives/1975/feb/06/fascinating-fascism/

53 Allan Antliff, *Anarchist Modernism: Art, Politics, and the First American Avant-Garde* (Chicago and London: The University of Chicago Press, 2001), 183.

54 Antliff, 207.

the worker to become the creator rather than the creature of his conditions. Unless the worker grasps that society must be organized on the basis of the freest possible scope for expression, the future holds very little chance for either the artist or the worker."[55]

Socialist Realism as a threat to artistic freedom

According to several critics, the rigidity of Marxist determinism excluded proletarian art from ever being "true" art. The more deterministic the substance of art, the more it undermined individual artistic freedom, Phillips and Rahv argued.

> Its literary "line" stems from the under-standing of Marxism as mechanical material-ism. In philosophy, mechanical materialism assumes a direct determinism of the whole superstructure by the economic foundation. … The literary counterpart of mechanical ma-terialism faithfully reflected this vulgarization of Marxism. But its effects strike even deeper: It paralyzes the writer's capacities by creating a dualism between his artistic consciousness and his beliefs, thus making it impossible for him to achieve anything beyond fragmentary, marginal expression.[56]

Daniel Aaron argued in *Writers on the Left* that political content in art restricted artistic creativity and freedom of expression and that the conversion to Marxism by many artists was a "defective romanticism." Aaron argued that art could be only an individual expression; communism is antithetical to the creative artist because it demands

---

55 Emma Goldman, "An Unpublished Letter," *Freedom*, (October-November, 1919): 5, 6, 7; quoted in Antliff, *Anarchist Modernism*, 208.

56 Phillips and Rahv, 341.

submission to the "group mind." Aaron saw communism as a monolithic concept into which all writers of political realism could be placed. Writers closer to the monolith were rejected as "proletarian" writers. The writers who "escaped the deadly influences of communism" are the "better" writers he argued – those American literary figures who while initially fascinated with the idea of revolution, ultimately came to see the error of their ways. Writers like John Steinbeck, John Dos Passos, and Hamlin Garland, for example, had moved from the left to the extreme right of the political spectrum. Aaron's final criticism of proletarian writers was that they were out of touch with American realities; revolution was not about to occur; and those who believe that it would were bankrupt in both their thinking and their art.[57]

Others shared similar concerns about the dangers of a political party line dictating art. In their 1938 *Manifesto: Towards a Free Revolutionary Art*, surrealist Andre Breton and communist Leon Trotsky criticized the rigidity of the Communist Party's version of Socialist Realism on several grounds.

> No authority, no dictation, not the least trace of orders from above! Only on a base of friendly cooperation, without the constraint from the outside, will it be possible for scholars and artists to carry out their tasks, which will be more far-reaching than ever before in history. ... Every progressive tendency in art is destroyed by fascism as "degenerate." Every free creation is called "fascist" by the Stalinists.[58]

---

57 Daniel Aaron, *Writers on the Left* (New York, NY: Octagon, 1974).

58 Andre Breton and Leon Trotsky, *Manifesto: Towards a Free Revolutionary Art*, 1938. http://www.generation-online.org/fcsurrealism1.htm

Breton and Trotsky concluded that true revolutionary art had to be independent. To counter the socialist realist decree from the Russian Communist Party, they called for communist artists to form the International Federation of Independent Art. "The communist revolution is not afraid of art. It realizes that the role of the artist in a decadent capitalist society is determined by the conflict between the individual and various social forms which are hostile to him. This fact alone, insofar as he is conscious of it, makes the artist the natural ally of revolution."[59] Art must come from within the individual artist, they argued, not be dictated by a central committee: "The artist cannot serve the struggle for freedom unless he subjectively assimilates its social content, unless he feels in his very nerves its meaning and drama and freely seeks to give his own inner world incarnation in his art."[60] In *Anarchist Modernism* Allan Antliff raised a similar criticism. He defended the subjectivity of the individual artist as the source of art and took special exception to Socialist Realism's conscious suppression of individual expression. Antliff concluded that "the artist became an accessory to politics."[61]

Socialist Realism and capitalist advertising aesthetics
Curiously, Socialist Realism never incorporated a sustained critique of capitalist aesthetics. While socialist realists made the criticism of capitalism as an abstract ideology a centerpiece of aesthetics, they did not critique capitalist aesthetics as such. Artists and writers did find popular culture distasteful, according to Aaron. During the 1920's, for example, the banalities of American popular culture so appalled many American writers and intellectuals that they withdrew into bohemian ghettos such as Greenwich Village or into their own inner worlds. Some even fled to Europe. By and large, they were more

---

59 Breton and Trotsky, *Manifesto*.
60 Breton and Trotsky, *Manifesto*.
61 Antliff, 209.

interested in escaping the emerging middle class mass media than confronting it. Instead, by the 1930's they focused their energies on developing an alternative aesthetic without directly confronting advertising art. The shift to greater engagement with the real world around them may have been a result of the obvious collapse of the capitalist consumer economy.

THE LEGACY OF SOCIALIST REALISM

THE PORTRAYAL OF real people, real environments, and real life events always resonates with people, but not necessarily with art critics. The current popularity of reality television programs makes this statement more than obvious. We like to look at the lives of others and ourselves and imagine ourselves in other situations. The portrayal of realistic contexts in programming as well as advertising almost always guarantees an attentive audience. We are comfortable with realities that we recognize; we like to see things that we know; yet we are still open to exploring the known in different settings, with different resolutions. Realism is visually compelling; a significant portion of the message is transparent to us. Socialist Realism worked because realism works. The failure of the capitalist economy in the 1930's opened up an opportunity for an alternative discourse, and art played a central role in making sense of the cultural impact of the Great Depression. The realistic images and the embedded narrative reflected real time personal, social, and political events as people grappled with the effects of widespread suffering.

Socialist Realism also took up again the classical challenge of creating meaning in art. Although the idea of purposeful art and universal meaning had languished under early modernist aesthetics, social realist artists felt compelled to speak about ethics and values and to make judgmental statements about the world. The power of shared symbolism was again honored, and strong narrative messages were conveyed in all art forms. Growing as it did out of hope inspired by a real revolution in Russia and ripening in the efforts of people to overcome the pain and anguish of the Great Depression and create a more just world, Socialist Realism sought to breathe the rarified air of great art. The artificial realism of the culture industry was, for a time, superseded by powerful real images and real people seeking to build a better world. Socialist Realism connected people with the politics of their time, illuminated their exploitation, raised the question of alternative political realities, and pointed the way to a better future.

There is, however, room for serious criticism of the rigidity that the Russian Communist Party imposed on art. The debate over ideology distracted artists from fully exploiting the dialectic interaction between the real and the potential in service of a new world. A more creative and open realism was already clearly working for capitalist aesthetics, but it was stifled on the left. Only one realistic narrative could be tolerated – the worldview created by capital. Further, some of the socialist realist terminology was alien to the American scene – recall the debate about the use of the word "worker" versus "the people". America had never accepted that there are sharp class distinctions in the country and they continue to hold to the ardent belief that anyone can "make it."

Nevertheless, as Professor Richard Pellis and others have pointed out, these critics were shouting into a vacuum. Socialist Realism became the dominant aesthetic in Western Europe, Russia, and the United States in large part because realism, or a realistic portrayal of life, is highly effective.

In the early 1930's however, those who rejected proletarian literature were usually on the defensive. No matter how eloquently they celebrated the universality of art or the writer's dedication to this craft, they seemed unable to

grasp that these ideals were simply less appealing to intellectuals at present than the desire to play a more direct role in American life.
For most writers during the depression, the
problem was not how to remain free but how
to become more committed.[62]

The advertising industry knew that realism worked;
governments knew that it worked, and the radicals did as
well.

62 Richard H. Pellis, *Radical Visions and American Dreams: Culture and
    Social Thought in the Depression Years* (New York: Harper & Row,
    1973), 186.

CHAPTER 5

THE SITUATIONIST INTERNATIONAL: **ART AS DIRECT ACTION**

The Society whose modernization has reached the state of the integrated spectacle is characterized by the combined effect of five principal features: incessant technological renewal; integration of state and economy; generalized secrecy; unanswerable lies; and eternal present.[1]

INTRODUCTION

FOLLOWING ON THE HEELS OF SURREALISM AND THE DADA-influenced Lettristé movement, a new radical aesthetic emerged in France in 1957 to challenge both Socialist Realism and Surrealism – the Situationist International (SI). The SI took great pains to reject any references to "isms" – including their own – in part because they felt that their approach to art was spontaneous and could not be formally systematized. It was also a rebuke of Socialist Realism. In *The Revolution of Everyday Life*, situationist Raoul Vaneigem observed, "The world of -isms ... is never anything but a world drained of reality, a terribly real seduction by falsehood."[2] This view is consistent, of course, with

---

1   Guy Debord, *Comments on the Society of the Spectacle*, Trans. Malcolm Imrie (Sheffield: Pirate Press Publications, 1991).

2   Raoul Vaneigem, *The Revolution of Everyday Life*, Trans. by Donald

the modernist wariness of prescriptive aesthetic agendas. In deference to their sensitivity, I will not refer to them as situationists or their theories as situationism.

While the members of the SI saw themselves as the successors to Surrealism, they argued that they had expanded the vision of the Surrealists to reflect a more intentional political agenda coupled with a sophisticated critique of all aspects of consumer society. Art, they believed, should not be a retreat into the self-reflective world of the individual unconscious but should play an active role in political action in the here and now – Art *as* protest/action; protest/action *as* art. According to Guy Debord, one of the principle theorists of the SI, they "took up the dropped threads of Surrealism but with an eye to sharpening the politics of artistic expression and expanding and extending the very idea of art itself. Like the Dadaists and surrealists, they saw themselves as rebels and critics of the dominant society including its art."[3] Their approach merged art and politics into art as empowerment and action grounded in everyday life. "Revolution is not 'showing' life to people," Debord observed, "but making them live. ... Getting them to speak for themselves in order to achieve or at least strive toward an equal degree of participation."[4] This was a philosophy of action, of lived aesthetics; there was no waiting for a revolution; it could be actualized now by living everyday life as art. As political theorist Gilles Dauvé explained,

---

Nicholson-Smith (London: Left Bank Books and Rebel Press, 1994), 24.

3   Guy Debord, "Report on the Construction of Situations and on the International Situationist Tendency's Conditions of Organisation and Action," (1957), in *Situationist International Anthology*, ed. and trans. Ken Knabb (Berkeley, CA: Bureau of Public Secrets, 1981), 18.

4   Guy Debord, "For a Revolutionary Judgment of Art," (February 1961), in *Situationist International Anthology*, 6.

> Previously the most lucid artists had wanted to break the separation between *art* and *life*: The S.I. raised this demand to a higher level in their desire to abolish the distance between *life* and *revolution*. "Experimentation" had been for Surrealism an illusory means of wrenching art out of its isolation from reality: the S.I. applied it in order to found a positive utopia. The ambiguity comes from the fact that the S.I. did not know exactly whether it was a matter of living differently *from now on* or only of *heading that way*.[5]

While there are strong parallels between Surrealism and the SI, their differences illustrate the uneasy tension inherent in the relationship between art and politics: does political action change the art, or does art change politics? The SI believed that Dada and Surrealism failed in their efforts to bring art and politics to bear on changing the culture. According to Debord, they were both ineffective because "Dadaism wanted to *suppress art without realizing it*; Surrealism wanted to *realize art without suppressing it*. The critical position later elaborated by the Situationists, has shown that the suppression and the realization of art are inseparable aspects of a single *supersession of art*."[6]

The SI was especially critical of Surrealism's embrace of the unconscious as the fountain of revolutionary change and transformational energy calling it occultism and spiritualism. "The error that is at the root of Surrealism is the

---

5 Gilles Dauvé (Jean Barrot), *Critique of the Situationist International*, trans. Louis Michaelson (Berkeley: Red-eye 1, 1979). This essay has been reprinted twice, first as a pamphlet re-titled "What is Situationism ?" (Unpopular Books, London, 1987) and second in the anthology *What is Situationism ? A Reader*, ed. Stewart Home (AK Press, London, 1996). http://www.libcom.org

6 Guy Debord, *The Society of the Spectacle* (Detroit: Black and Red, 1983), 191.

idea of the infinite richness of the unconscious imagination. … We now know that the unconscious imagination is poor, that automatic writing is monotonous, and that the whole genre of ostentatious surrealist 'weirdness' has ceased to be very surprising," Debord concluded.[7]

Raoul Vaneigem was also critical of Surrealism's overemphasis on subjectivity because individual insights did not necessarily lead to collective political outcomes. Vaneigem concluded that Surrealism "failed to spur the collective actualization of that creativity by means of a revolution made by all in the interests of all." The separation of intention from political action was a fatal flaw in the surrealist aesthetic. The surrealists "ought by rights to have turned themselves into theorists and practitioners of the revolution of everyday life, [but] were content to be mere artists thereof."[8]

The SI, however, may have gone to the other extreme. In rejecting art as personal and subjective, they resurrected and revitalized the outrage of the dadaists against art itself; and like the dadaists, they sought to distance themselves from the traditional role of the artist. They called for the destruction of art as objectification. In its place they demanded that life become an artistic act – art as activism and lived experience. In the process, however, art itself may have been a victim. In a recent assessment of the SI, John Moore argued, for example, that the SI threatened the freedom of the individual artist and creativity itself.[9] Despite Moore's concerns, however, the SI did not suppress individual expression, but it did expect responsiveness to a real political context.

---

7   Debord. "Report on the Construction of Situations," in *Situationist International Anthology*, 19.

8   Raoul Vaneigem (Jules-François Dupuis), *A Cavalier History of Surrealism*, Translated by Donald Nicholson-Smith (Edinburgh and Others: AK Press, 1977, 1999), 52-53.

9   John Moore, "The Insubordination of Words: Poetry, Insurgency and the Situationists," *Anarchist Studies* 10, 2 (November 2002), 151.

AESTHETIC ELEMENTS OF THE SITUATIONIST INTERNATIONAL PERSPECTIVE

THE SI MADE several important conceptual contributions to the aesthetics of politics. They built upon, but moved beyond, Dada and Surrealism to develop a sophisticated critique of capital's oppressive cultural hegemony in the postmodern world – what they termed the *spectacle*. Instead of advocating that art remain aloof and alienated, they challenged capitalist aesthetics head on. By focusing on this critique, they echoed Horkheimer and Adorno's criticism of the cultural industry and Walter Benjamin's warnings about the power of mass communication techniques.

The SI formalized four principles to guide their aesthetic. They coined the term *spectacle* to describe the capitalistic cultural hegemony, the new hegemony of capitalist production; they developed the aesthetic technique/action of *detournement* (a direct action tool aimed at undermining the spectacle by using its own symbols against it); they explored the concept of the *dérive* (practical techniques for changing behavior and attitudes to move from passivity to action); and they promoted the conscious creation of political/aesthetic *situations* as contexts for collective revolutionary action.

The spectacle

Early Marxist critiques of capitalism focused on control of the means of production but largely overlooked the cultural implication of the limitless production of goods for consumption. Not until mid-twentieth century was a sophisticated analysis of the driving force behind capitalist aesthetics developed by the SI. Their critique exposed the political and aesthetic tools used by capitalists to fuel constant consumption through control of advertising images. They called it the spectacle – a term that the SI coined to describe the totality of the economic/social/cultural relationship that capitalism created to perpetuate imbalances of economic and political power. The spectacle was the constructed capitalist vision in which we now live, the bubble of friendly, entertaining oppression in which we move.

The spectacle is the symbolic objectification of the capitalist system in its cultural phase, and represents a more contemporary analysis of Marxist aesthetic principles. Various theorists refer to this process as the "fetishization of commodities," the "reification of desires," "displaced meaning," or "commodity meaning." The spectacle is an artificial culture stands outside of and is antithetical to individual human intervention and control. Many contemporary theorists have built on the work of the SI arguing that through the mechanism of an every-changing world of commodities meaning continually reconstructs itself; and this reconstructed meaning-in-process, in turn, shapes human character and human society to its own end. There is general agreement that commodity consumption and the spectacle created to perpetuate it continually reshape social values.

The objects present in our environment exert their control over us by shaping our collective behavior. Karl Marx identified this alienated, independent power of consumer goods as the "fetishization of commodities." According to Marx, mass-produced objects are alienated from the worker and are no longer invested with the personal power of their makers. Instead, objects take on a life of their own as they enter an impersonal marketplace. As abstract objects disconnected from any social reality, they are then fetishized and serve as pacifiers to divert our attention from the loss of control over our economic lives. They are empty of personal meaning, of social meaning, of collective human meaning. Things in a consumer society say *me* rather than *we*. Their purpose is to please the individual owner rather than to cement a social relationship with the creator of the object or to invite the consumer to participate in any collective interaction or communication. Thus, the meaning of the consumer product is individually, not collectively, determined. The individual is given only very limited choices shaped by the cultural industry.

According to Guy Debord, "The spectacle is not a collection of images, but a social relation among people mediated by images."[10] Echoing in some respects the early insights of Adorno and Benjamin, Debord developed a sophisticated Marxist analysis of the construction of images in a technological society and their insidious control over contemporary culture:

> At the technological level, when images chosen and constructed by someone else have everywhere become the individual's principal connection to the world he formerly observed for himself, it has certainly not been forgotten that these images can tolerate anything and everything; because within the same image all things can be juxtaposed without contradiction. The flow of images carries everything before it, and it is similarly someone else who controls at will this simplified summary of the sensible world; who decides where the flow will lead as well as the rhythm of what should be shown, like some perpetual, arbitrary surprise, leaving no time for reflection, and entirely independent of what the spectator might understand or think of it.[11]

Debord concluded, however, that the spectacle is not just a matter of imagery, but a holistic political mechanism for shaping and controlling reality: "The spectacle cannot be understood as an abuse of the world of vision, as a product of the technology of the mass dissemination of images. It is, rather, a *Weltanschauung* which has become

---

10 Debord, *Society of the Spectacle*, 4.

11 Guy Debord, *Comments on the Society of the Spectacle*, (Verso, 1998), pp. 27-28.

actual, materially translated. It is a world vision which has
become objectified."[12]

In a consumer society spectators remain passive, ea-
gerly anticipating a continually re-created spectacle that
reinforces that passivity. The SI argued that the spectacle
is all pervasive and, thus, complicates the possibility for a
clear and independent political response: "People are to a
great extent accomplices of propaganda, of the reigning
spectacle, because they cannot reject it without contesting
the society as a whole."[13]

Debord's theories are also consistent with semiotic cultural theorists like Sut Jhally. According to Jhally, the
abstract sign represents a whole package of condensed
meaning: "traditional Marxist concepts such as reification
are not sufficient analytical tools, because we have moved
from a phase where the commodity-form was dominant
to one where the *sign-form* prevails. ... Objects lose any
real connection with the basis of their practical utility and
instead come to be the material correlate (the signifier)
of an increasing number of constantly changing abstract
qualities."[14] According to Jhally, this shared symbolic
meaning creates a kind of ersatz community. The process of creating true, shared meaning – meaning created
by people themselves – is ruptured in a consumer society.
Instead of objects being collectively agreed-upon representations of the collective social reality, individual consumers mediate objects. This constructed collective meaning that emerges from the many isolated individual acts of
consuming does not happen accidentally or mysteriously.
The advertising industry manipulated consumer reality

---

12 Debord, *The Society of the Spectacle*, Paragraph 5.

13 Internationale Situationniste #8 (January 1963), "Ideologies,
    Classes and the Domination of Nature," in *Situationist International
    Anthology*, 105.

14 Sut Jhally, *The Codes of Advertising: Fetishism and the Political Economy
    of Meaning in the Consumer Society* (New York, NY: St. Martin's
    Press, 1987), 11.

through the conscious construction of symbols designed to perpetuate the idea of consumption for itself rather than to reflect real relationships between people. According to Jhally,

> Only once the real meaning has been systematically *emptied* out of commodities does advertising then *refill* this void with its own symbols. ... *The fetishism of commodities consists in the first place of emptying them of meaning, of hiding the real social relations objectified in them through human labour, to make it possible for the imaginary/symbolic social relations to be injected into the construction of meaning at a secondary level. Production empties. Advertising fills. The real is hidden by the imaginary.*[15]

The signs and symbols that the advertising industry creates touch all aspects of our lives – psychologically, sociologically, spiritually, economically, and, of course, politically. They effectively shape and control us at all levels because they are designed to satisfy basic human needs such as the need for closure to experience, the need for social relationships and their representation of collective meaning, and the individual fascination with novelty. They also come to represent our culture as a whole giving us a sense of continuity across time with other people, a kind of false collective meaning. Consumer products are consciously encoded with meaning, according to Jhally: "A code is the store of experience upon which both the advertiser and the audience draw in their participation in the construction of 'commodity meaning.'"[16] Meaning is communicated through these signs or codes which function in the culture as myths function in culture generally. This need for shared meaning is just as important as the more

---

15 Jhally, 51.
16 Jhally, 140.

immediate needs of material comfort and personal gratification. As Jhally observed, "Meaning is not secondary. It is constitutive of human experience."[17]

According to Jhally, capitalism has a monopoly on the distribution of these signs and codes and through advertising consciously creates complex new meanings that include the products that they are promoting. These signs and codes are part of our empirical reality – they are not alien to us which is why they work – but they are rearranged and reprioritized to meet the needs of capital:

> Advertising borrows its ideas, its language, and its visual representations from literature and design, from other media content and forms, from history and the future, from its own experience, and also from the specific experiences and discourses of its particular targeted market; then it artfully recombines them around the theme of consumption. Through advertising, goods are knitted into the fabric of social life and cultural significance.[18]

Both cultural meaning and personal meaning, then, come to be identified with the process of consuming until, according to Jhally, "Consumption replaced community, class and religion as the defining feature of social life."[19] In the spectacle all art is subject to capitalist manipulation. The process of commodification of everything – even art and imagery – keeps the spectacle alive and self-perpetuating, and the media that capital controls serve to sustain and to perpetuate the spectacle through manipulation of messages and images.

---

17 Jhally, 189.
18 Jhally, 142.
19 Jhally, 192.

Détournement

The SI consciously developed political actions and aesthetic tools to challenge and to subvert the
hegemony of the capitalist spectacle. Breaking the hold of
the spectacle on art, culture, and meaning required attack-
ing the spectacle from all sides. One of their solutions was
to appropriate and undermine the symbols of the spectacle, to turn them against the spectacle, and to adapt them
to serve a new revolutionary agenda. To accomplish subversion, the Situationists developed the political-aesthetic
technique of detournement. Analysis and critique of the
spectacle was not sufficient: the situationist artist must act.
These overt political-aesthetic actions illuminated a way
to simultaneously subvert and transform the spectacle and
create new meaning. The SI called for activists to devise
mechanisms and events to expose the inherent contradictions, breaks, and dissonances in the spectacle – actions
that were intended to make the power of the spectacle visible and transparent.

Detournement actions are not abstract or surreal; they
are grounded in a specific context that is familiar to the
observer. The SI sought to create a break from the artificial consumer world of here and now and to open up the
possibility for a new and better world here and now. Art
becomes political action based on a kind of appropriation
and transformation of the artificially constructed world,
making it real by exposing the capitalist version of the wiz-
ard behind the curtain pulling the strings. The technique
of detournement is essentially an aesthetic technique of
realism; and because it is grounded in the real world, the
meaning of the detourned symbol are readily apparent to
the average person: *"The distortions introduced in the detourned
elements must be as simplified as possible, since the main force of
a* detournement *is directly related to the conscious or vague recollection of the original contexts of the elements.* Detournement *is
less effective the more it approaches a rational reply,"* according

to Debord and Gil Wolman.[20] The visual symbolic materials for creating detournement are lying all around us, and the activist need only change them enough to introduce the possibility of change.

Another way to think about detournement is as a living collage in which the observer plays an active role deconstructing a broken world and constructing a new one with the pieces. Detournement is a political application of the early Dada technique of *montage*, which was widely applied in film in particular. Russian filmmaker Sergei Eisenstein raised the idea of montage to a new level of sophistication, where the viewer/audience participates with the artist in constructing a new reality out of the pieces of the old. According to Eisenstein,

> The strength of *montage* resides in this, that it includes in the creative process the emotions and mind of the spectator. The spectator is compelled to proceed along that selfsame creative road that the author traveled in creating the image. The spectator not only sees the represented elements of the finished work, but also experiences the dynamic process of the emergence and assembly of the image just as it was experienced by the author.[21]

According to the SI, "The two fundamental laws of detournement are the loss of importance of each detourned autonomous element – which may go so far as to lose its original sense completely – and, at the same time, the organization of another meaningful ensemble that confers on each element its new scope and effect."[22] Detournement is

20 Guy Debord and Gil J. Wolman, "Methods of *Detournement*," in *Situationist International Anthology*, 10-11.

21 Sergei Eisenstein, *The Film Sense*, trans. and ed. Jay Leyda (New York, NY: Harcourt, Brace and World, 1975), 32.

22 Internationale Situationniste #3 (December 1959), "*Detournement* as

successful because people recognize the new political message which previously had been latent or obscured.

Debord and artist Gil Wolman described the dialectical nature of detournement as a conscious process of taking disparate bits of images filled with old meaning and joining them in such a way as to create a synthesis to make a new aesthetic statement: "The mutual interference of two worlds of feeling or the bringing together of two independent expressions supersedes the original elements and produces a synthetic organization of greater efficacy."[23] Because this method is grounded in reality and everyone can know it, it avoids any tendency toward utopian idealization. We can participate in creating the new world and see it emerging from the old. Debord was not apologetic about "borrowing" the images and the meanings that advertising created: "Plagiarism is necessary. Progress implies it. It embraces an author's phrase, makes use of his expressions, erases a false idea, and replaces it with the right idea."[24]

In recent years the international graphics art collective Adbusters has revived and revitalized the SI agenda. They describe themselves this way:

> We are a global network of artists, writers, environmentalists, teachers, downshifters, fair-traders, rabble-rousers, shit-disturbers, incorrigibles and malcontents. We are anarchists, guerilla tacticians, meme warriors, new-Luddites, pranksters, poets, philosophers, and punks. Our aim is to topple existing power structures and change the way we live. ... We will change the way information flows, the way institutions wield power, the way the food, fashion, car, and culture industries set their agendas. Above all,

---

Negation and Prelude," in *Situationist International Anthology*, 55.

23 Debord and Wolman. "Methods of *Detournement*," 9.

24 Debord *Society of the Spectacle*, 207.

we will change the way we interact with the
mass media and the way in which meaning is
produced in our society.[25]

In *Design Anarchy*, Adbusters describes the concept of
detournement with phrases like "a sudden unexpected moment of truth," "a rupture in the normal practices of politics and society which destroys the regime's monologue,"
and "we smash the hall of mirrors."[26] They summed up
the SI technique of detournement as follows: "Debord
proposed detournement as a way for people to take back
the spectacle ... Literally a 'turning around,' involved re-
routing spectacular images, environments, ambiences and
events to reverse or subvert their meaning, thus reclaim-
ing them."[27] Over the years Adbusters has developed and
marketed many successfully detourned anti-advertising
campaigns: the Shell Oil symbol floating above dead fish
washed up on a shore; two Marlboro cowboys on horse-
back with the sun setting behind them, one looking at the
other saying, "I miss my lung, Bob"; a detourned Absolut
Vodka ad with the title "Absolut impotence"; and a poster
designed for PETA with a bloody cow's head on it, with
the title, "Do you want fries with that? McCruelty to go."
They are also the creators of Buy Nothing Day which
challenges the whole idea of the consumer society.

As they look to the future and the development of a
revolutionary alternative reality, Adbusters outlined the
central aesthetic principles and objectives that they believe
will guide the transition to a sustainable society. In their
1964 *First Things First Manifesto*, they concluded as follows:

The perspective – the aesthetic – of our sustainable future has yet to take hold. But we can

25 Kalle Lasn, *Design Anarchy* (Vancouver, BC: Adbusters Media
    Foundation, 2006), n.p.

26 Lasn, n.p.

27 Lasn, n.p.

speculate: It's an honest, simple way of being. It follows organic cycles and mimics nature's ways. It is not so much about being moral or good as being a little bit wild and fiercely determined, like crabgrass growing through cracks in the concrete. It's about "being" rather than "having" and "process" rather than "form."[28]

Detourned images of the capitalist spectacle were not the only source of ideas for SI art. According to John Moore, first and foremost the SI were creators, poets, imaginers, and insurgents themselves. They especially emphasized the importance of creating new imagery for a future world.

The "new creators" – as Vaneigem calls the practitioners of poetry in the situationist sense – are precisely that: creators, but also creators of the new. They are not restricted to shifting through the detritus of existing culture in order to plagiarize and detourne those materials – although such procedures might play a limited, secondary role in their practice.[29]

The biggest challenge for political artist/activists in the future, according to Adbusters, is a struggle for the imagination of the world. They developed a "to do" list for achieving the goals first set forth by the SI: creating a democratic means of communicating through such tools as the control of memes, practicing detournement, creating cognitive dissonance, and demarketing through such techniques as Buy Nothing Day, paradigm shifting, and educating people about true cost economics.

A question remains, however. Does detournement really work to change perceptions and to destroy the power

28 Lasn, n.p.
29 John Moore, "Insubordination," 158.

of capitalist aesthetics? The SI was very sensitive about this question of effectiveness. They were wary of the inherent potential danger of merely perpetuating the iconography of the spectacle, because while the detourned image is changed, the original intent of the ad remains latent in the image. How powerful that image remains or whether the detournement backfires and the power of the capitalist image might even be amplified is unknown.

Derivé

The concept of derive or "drifting" was an important tool for opening up the possibility for change. Derive may have been an attempt to replace the Dada idea of random chance and the surrealist mystical imagination with a more concrete means of imagining, defining, and experiencing a new world. In some ways, derive is a sophisticated critique of contemporary urbanism, which Debord abhorred. As an architect, Debord was interested in the relationships of physical space to social relations but in his writings the concept of derive is obscured in vague, allusional language, in part because the concept is not limited to the built world. As a technique, derive has the potential of changing both geographical and internal psychic spatial relationships. Debord describes it as a practical technique to teach individuals how to break with the status quo, change overt behavior, and open up physical and psychic space and develop new patterns of thought. Its intention is to destabilize "what is" in order to entertain the possibility of "what if." A "will to playful creation" drives derive, according to Debord, by undertaking "a passional journey out of the ordinary through rapid changing of ambiances" into a "new mode of behavior."[30] It is a conscious randomization, the outcome of which is to create "behavioral disorientation."[31] At other times derive is referred to

---

30 Debord, "Report on the Construction of Situations," 24.
31 Guy Debord, "Theory of the *derive*," in *Situationist International Anthology*, 53.

as an experience, one in which "chance plays an important role."[32] The SI practiced derive as a free-floating process for rethinking the real world – not just by imagining it but by studying the real world and by creating alternative frameworks or "situations" to address complex problems. Debord asserted that the SI had developed practical applications for urban design.[33] According to an anonymous article on the Angelfire website, "Situationists used psychogeography to criticize the machine-like rationalized environment of Modernist urban space arguing instead for a more organic approach to urban design." The SI called this new approach unitary urbanism, "the opposite of a specialized activity." It thrived on establishing independent autonomous physical environments:

> Unitary urbanism consisted of making different parts of the city communicate with one another. To them this new urbanism could only flourish in the lands that were out of the spectacle system. These lands were the places that made up "constructed situations." … Their message is so clear that unitary urbanism is related to construction of situations. By constructing situations people actually would create the temporary zones isolated from existing conditioning of everyday life.[34]

Derive urban environment experiments were designed as "wanderings" through the city landscape to explore how

32 Debord, "Theory of the *derive*," 51.
33 Debord, "Theory of the *derive*," 53.
34 Anonymous. "Section C. Situationists' Notion of Urban Space." http://www.angelfire.com/ar/corei/SI/SIsecc.htm See also "Section A. The Last *Avant-gardes*: Situationists." http://www.angelfire.com/art/corei/SI/SIseca.htm and "Section B. "Methods of Situationists." http://www.angelfire.com/art/corei/SI/SIsecb.htm

people lived in a city and how they used cities. The goal was to understand how neighborhoods worked (or didn't) to create a cohesive environment. The theoretical and political objective was to challenge how borders of all sorts – including arbitrary geographical borders – operated in people's lives, according to Debord: "The most general change that the derive leads to proposing is the constant diminution of these border regions, up to the point of their suppression."[35]

The situation

The concept of the situation which lies at the heart of the SI aesthetic is linked to the idea of derive in an important way. The situation is an active intervention designed to create a rupture with the culture of the spectacle. Once the reality had been shaken up and new ways of seeing the world emerge, the next step is expanding and creating autonomous spaces (both physically and psychically) for the new world to come into being. A situationist, then, by definition is one who lives in these new constructions. According to Debord, a primary principle of the spectacle is passivity and "non-intervention," while the principle of the situation is active engagement. The situation is a political and social space, active and lived, not passive.

Newly-established situations also require moving acts of detournement from the level of just another new (more radical) advertising campaign to putting into action the new symbols in the new situations. These political acts are not just random or disembodied. Situations are at once activist and creative – they present an opportunity to clear a space for undertaking alternative actions. The goal is to occupy these new situations, create new meaning within them, and to empower individuals to act together. It is not sufficient to just break with the status quo; something new has to take its place. Debord describes situations as "collective ambiances" consciously constructed:

---

35 Debord, "Theory of the *derive*," 53.

> The construction of situations begins on the ruins of the modern spectacle. … [T]he most pertinent revolutionary experiments in culture have sought to break the spectator's psychological identification with the hero so as to draw him into activity by provoking his capacities to revolutionize his own life. The situation is thus made to be lived by its constructors. The role played by a passive or merely bit-part playing "public" must constantly diminish, while that played by those who cannot be called actors but rather, in a new sense of the term, "livers" must steadily increase.[36]

Situations were designed to bring people together in active political environments: "People's creativity and participation can only be awakened by a collective project explicitly concerned with all aspects of lived experience. The only way to 'arouse the masses' is to expose the appalling contrast between the possible constructions of life and its present poverty."[37] The social context of political action is central to SI theory. Establishing a social context gives the situationist action a quality of immediacy and grounding in reality. In this sense, the SI is consistent with traditional social anarchist theory with its emphasis on decentralization and local autonomy.

The organizational sites for situationist politics were the worker's councils – small, engaged groups exercising self-management through democratic engagement, which were networked with other councils in similar democratic processes.[38] Explicit in the idea of worker's councils was

---

36 Debord, "Report on the Construction of Situations," 24-25.

37 Internationale Situationniste #6 (August 1961), "Instructions for Taking Up Arms," in *Situationist International Anthology*, 64.

38 See especially Rene Riesel, "Preliminaries on the Councils and Councilist Organization,"270-282 282 and Raoul Vaneigem, "Notice to the Civilized Concerning Generalized Self-Management,"283-289

a ringing denunciation of Communist Party structure. Several elements were key to creating effective councils. In many cases, the SI talked about occupation of physical and political space as mutually required, even referring consistently to occupational movements. Workers councils could be established in a variety of settings such as neighborhoods, factories, and schools. Because the passivity engendered by the spectacle had to be overcome, people had to be engaged for true change to take place. The SI rejected the historical models of unions and party membership (which encouraged "leadership" and passive membership) in favor of situationally established government. In July 1966, the 17th Conference of the SI adopted the "Minimum Definition of Revolutionary Organizations," that stated in part: "Such an organization refuses to reproduce within itself any of the hierarchical conditions of the dominant world. The only limit to participating in its total democracy is that each member must have recognized and appropriated the *coherence of its critique.*"[39] In an effort to avoid dictating how the councils would operate in detail, the SI position on formal political organization structure was deliberately left undeveloped, with the assumption that each council would shape its politics to its specific situation.

There is also an element of celebration inherent in the situation. Since it is designed as an alternative to the poverty of the current reality, hope and joy represent a more positive experience. Gavin Grindon observed as follows:

> Between the works of Bakhtin, the Situationist International and modern anarchist theory, particularly the writing of Hakim Bey, there is a continual return to a shared

in *Situationist International Anthology*, ed. and trans. Ken Knabb (Berkeley, CA: Bureau of Public Secrets, 1981).

39 In *Situationist International Anthology*, ed. and trans. Ken Knabb (Berkeley, CA: Bureau of Public Secrets, 1981), 223.

constellation of ideas. ... Each theorises joy and desire as the basis of a culturally and politically radical event which they variously term as a "carnival," "festival," "situation," or a "temporary autonomous zone." In each case this event embodies a number of related qualities. It is seen as a politically radical fusion of life and art, a realization of joy and desire in the form of a broadly anarchistic micro-society.[40]

CRITICISM OF THE SITUATIONIST INTERNATIONAL

THE IMPORTANCE OF the SI to radical aesthetics has led to a serious analysis of their ideas, in part because their theories continue to provide a very trenchant analysis of capitalist aesthetics. Criticism, however, has come from several quarters, and the views of these critics warrant some attention here.

A collective or individual analysis?

Several Marxist critics charged that the SI had fallen into the same trap as the surrealists – relying too heavily on individual subjectivity and abandoning the concept of class in favor of an individualistic analysis. In *Critique of the Situationist International*, Gilles Dauvé noted that the Castoriadis rejected traditional Marxist theories of class and "re-found the revolutionary project entirely on the subjective discontent of workers, women, homosexuals, racial minorities, etc., who no longer form a class (the proletariat) opposed to the 'order-givers' (capitalists and bureaucrats) but merely a mass of oppressed individuals."[41] He charged that Castoriadis accepted as a given the spectacle's appeal to the isolated individuals and their particular wants and desires to find fulfillment,

40 Gavin Grindon, "Carnival against capital: a comparison of Bakhtin, Vaneigem and Bey," *Anarchist Studies* 12, 2 (2004), 148.
41 Dauvé, 2.

over and against the collective social relations of a group of people with similar political objectives. Dauvé concluded that the "SI was an affirmation of individuals to the point of elitism."[42]

However, the SI had already anticipated some of these charges of elitism and individualism by developing their own analysis of individualism – the individual acting within the context of the collective. They believed that under the spectacle, individual self-expression was already compromised, necessitating radical engagement with others to undermine the hegemony of the spectacle and to overcome the poverty of bourgeois individualism: "Real individual fulfillment, which is also involved in the artistic experience that the situationists are discovering, entails the collective takeover of the world. Until this happens, there will be no real individuals – only specters haunting the things anarchically presented to them by others."[43] The SI analysis of the spectacle concluded that people were manipulated individually (through their own complicity) as consumers. The radical challenge was how to move them from being individual consumers within the spectacle who thought that they were happy, to encourage them to adopt a new, more comprehensive vision where they could fulfill a "true" individual reality, in the context of a more fulfilling collective reality.

Recuperation by capitalism

One of the most serious charges leveled at the SI was that they were too close to the spectacle and were, thus, subject to co-optation or *recuperation*. There were important theoretical challenges that the SI faced in positioning themselves vis a vis the capitalist spectacle and, at the same time, using the products and tools of the

42 Dauvé, 11.

43 Internationale Situationniste #1 (June 1958). "Preliminary Problems in Constructing a Situation," in *Situationist International Anthology*, 44.

spectacle against itself. American anarchist Bob Black denounced the SI as just another avant-garde manifestation of consumer culture:

> The Situationists had to find a way to take from the system (what else is there to take from?) without being taken in by it. They characterized these possibilities as polarities: detournment (roughly: "diversion") and recuperation (roughly: "recovery"). To turn the system's images against it was to detourn, to divert them. But to be "turned" in turn – in the argot of the intelligence community – was to be recuperated, recovered by the system as art, as ideology, as any of many fragmentary forms of specialisation or partial opposition.[44]

Adbusters was also wary of recuperation, noting that "corporations appropriate criticisms, use them to improve their PR techniques." This idea posed an interesting challenge for future radical aesthetics: "Is it still possible to do anything outside of the capitalist model. Outside of 'the marketing aesthetic'?"[45] Anne Moore agreed: "Perhaps ... activists should start thinking about whether or not we want to participate in representation at all. ... In the worst-case scenario, culture jamming dismantles the master's house with the master's tools, and then provides the master with blueprints for a better house and better tools."[46] Moore was skeptical about the effectiveness of SI techniques: "a meaningful change to a system will not

44 Bob Black, "The Realization and Supression of Situationism." www.library.nothingness.org

45 Lasn, n.p.

46 Anne Elizabeth Moore, "Branding Anti-Consumerism: The Capitalistic Nature of Anti-Corporate Activism," in *Realizing The Impossible: Art Against Authority,* eds. Josh MacPhee and Erik Reuland (Oakland: AK Press, 2007), 293-294.

come about if it recreates the current system (even, if once recreated, it is more amusing)."[47] Finally, John Moore observed, "Like the deconstructionists, the situationists, far from escaping from the trap of postmodernity, in many ways become definitive and characteristic of it."[48]

Relying on cleverly manipulating the images of capitalist aesthetics by detourning them has another downside. The extensive use of mass media to shape and to control the cultural agenda (what Benjamin would call "mechanical art") breeds passivity resulting in a docile viewer who is unlikely to be open to change or to take political action. To play around with the visual objects that the advertising industry created may provide only a more entertaining experience but still result in a passive response.

Bob Black, too, was not optimistic about the future of the SI's ideas and tactics. In a biting critique he argued that the ideas of the SI have been thoroughly recuperated – in part, because of a failure of sustainability.

> Since 1972 unchaperoned by any organization, situationism has been available for various uses, some dubious. Punks pilfered it for subliminals. Museologists curated it. Marxist academics at Telos explained it away as Frankfurt School philosophy as harmless as they are. Pro-situ hustlers like Tom Ward traded on their expertise in it. SI veterans reminisced about it, but only the ones who'd been excluded. Anarchists either maligned it or miscegenated with it. Poseurs congratulated each other for having heard of it. Somewhere, workers might have appropriated it, although this is sheer speculation.[49]

---

47 Anne Moore, "Branding Anti-Consumerism," 292, 294.

48 John Moore, "Insubordination," 146.

49 Black, "The Realization and Supression of Situationism."

Nevertheless, despite these concerns adbusting tactics provided an opportunity for continued education and provocation.

Lack of commitment to a revolutionary agenda

Despite the SI's radical rhetoric, Dauvé argued that the SI was not very revolutionary and dismissed their efforts across the board. He charged that the SI was engaged in frivolous activities that embraced protest for its own sake and that they had no clear political vision, no collective agenda, no well-defined set of tactics except to disrupt the spectacle. Dauvé's criticism of the SI is perhaps the most damning because he placed their work in the broad context of a critique of modernist and postmodernist politics.

> The common trait of all modernism is the taking up of revolutionary theory by halves. … Its axiom is to call, not for revolution, but for liberation from a certain number of constraints. It wants the maximum of freedom within the existing society. Its critique will always be that of the commodity and not of capital, of politics and not of the state. Of totalitarianism and not of democracy.[50]

Detournement, in particular, was open to criticism as a revolutionary tactic. Critics charged that it was merely a safety valve to relieve the frustrations of people who felt powerless to confront the spectacle. Detournement shifted the focus from a revolutionary agenda to tinkering with the status quo. In critiquing the contemporary detournement work of Adbusters, for example, Rob Levy concluded, "Their spoofs of commercials and mock advertisements tend to create self-fulfilling narratives that reinforce the dominance of the economic genre and the power of

---

50 Dauvé,15.

media."[51] In "Branding Anti-Consumerism," Anne Moore argued, "At the heart of the failure to recognize the inability of culture jamming to institute social change seems to be a confusion on the part of activists over the differences between parody and politics. ... Humor is not action."[52]

Levy does not dismiss the Adbuster situationist tactics out of hand, noting that "Potential seems to lie in subverting the system through *decentered*, localized actions such as their legislative initiatives (though potentially reformist) and direct actions against consumer culture." He goes on, however, to observe that without a clear revolutionary vision, these tactics will likely remain useless: "Yet, these cannot and will not succeed until they are accompanied, time and time again, by a precisely outlined set of values, meanings, and alternative ways of seeing and talking about the world. Whether such a language can be articulated is the essential question of modern oppositional politics."[53]

Marxists, in particular, were critical of the SI for its lack of rigor in analyzing the capitalist economic foundations of the spectacle. According to Dauvé,

> The S.I. had no analysis of capital: It understood it, but through its effects. It criticized the commodity, not capital – or rather, it criticized capital as commodity, and not as a system of valuation which includes production as well as exchange. ... Debord makes the spectacle into the subject of capitalism, instead of showing how it is produced by capitalism. He reduces capitalism to its spectacular dimension alone.[54]

---

51 Rob Levy, "The Politics of Language in Social Movements of the Information Age," in *Design Anarchy* (Vancouver, BC: Adbusters Media Foundation, 2006), n.p.

52 Anne Moore, "Branding Anti-consumerism," 291

53 Levy," n.p.

54 Dauvé, 6.

The anonymous reviewer of two books about the SI by Ken Knabb and Stewart Home agreed: "As Barrot (Dauvé) suggests, the works of the SI leave the impression that a further analysis of production is unnecessary."[55] In addition, the SI never undertook a serious analysis of the mass media corporate power structures behind the spectacle and the advertising industry that undergirds capitalist aesthetics. They had only a weak critique of centralized authority, of the state, or of power relations in any guise. The SI addressed only the symbols of the spectacle, working within the context of its visual products. Other relevant political questions they did not address adequately include how did the spectacle get to be so all-embracing? Why did the SI not see any potential for revolutionary external forces, instead, seeking to challenge the system of oppression only from within? How does using the tools and tactics of the enemy produce difference, or is it just a reshuffling of mutually agreed-upon fragments of reality?

The SI: art and the artist

At the theoretical level, the SI seemed to argue for not only maintaining a distance from "art" and the art community but also for rejecting all art as objectification and representation. The SI described their approach to art as follows: "Is the SI an artistic movement? We are artists only insofar as we are no longer artists: we come to realize art."[56] According to John Moore, the SI was never really interested in making art; Debord "fetishizes action at the expense of art, as if the two were *necessarily* incompatible and not complementary – or integral – modes of

---

55 Anonymous, "Whatever happened to the Situationists?" Rev. Ken Knabb, Ken. *Public Secrets* and Stewart Home, ed., *What is Situationism? A Reader,* Aufheben, 7, Autumn 1998. http://www.libcom.org

56 Internationale Situationniste #9 (August 1964), "Questionnaire," in *Situationist International Anthology,* 139.

practice."[57]They took this position, in part, to avoid the trap of recuperation by the art community although they were less successful avoiding recuperation by the advertising industry. They were well aware – from their own criticisms of Dada and Surrealism – that art could easily be appropriated for non-revolutionary ends; and working with the tools of the spectacle made them especially vulnerable to co-optation. Bob Black observed as follows:

> No avant-garde tendency ever tried harder, fully aware of what was at stake, to escape the curator's clutches than did the Situationists, even in their initial phase of intervention in the art scene. They knew that their Futurist, Dadaist, Surrealist and Lettrist fore bearers had been, in their word, recuperated, that is, recovered by and for the existing order. An order which showed itself as the spectacle, the "organization of appearances." Art – already image – is the easiest of all specialties to recuperate. All you have to do is ignore it or, if that doesn't work, buy it.[58]

Further, the SI essentially perpetuated the image of the artist as individual rebel. There is a certain romantic caché about the artists on the cutting edge who make a political statement. In its artistic, creative mode, individual action provides an example of how we might all break out of existing modes of thought, of image, of action. By standing out, being outrageous, the individual sharpens the distinction between human action and the deadening standardization of the status quo. But, in the end it does not create political change.

The problem of individualism

The SI did not adequately address the problematic role of the individual in a mass consumer

---

57 John Moore, "Insubordination," 152.
58 Black, "The Realization and Supression of Situationism."

culture that treated the individual as an isolated and independent unit. The SI did recognize that the spectacle was a world built on individualism and was aimed at controlling people as individuals – especially as individual consumers: "This society tends to atomize people into isolated consumers, to prohibit communication. Everyday life is thus private life, the realm of separation and spectacle."[59] Nevertheless, they did not make a strong case that their approach could be any different. Gavin Grindon saw an uncomfortable affinity between the SI's interest in the individual's self-fulfillment and the capitalist message that consumption equaled self-gratification: "Radical subjectivity, as a theory of social organization born of individualist self-interest, here appears to bear a disturbing resemblance to neoliberal laissez-faire theories, the very ideological foundation of the world [Raoul] Vaneigem is attempting to oppose."[60] Because consumer culture appropriates and distorts the idea of "freedom" by masking it as individual power, true individuality is compromised. Capitalism can never respectfully self-actualize individuals.

The SI also did not challenge the rationale behind the underlying individualist ethic of consumer society. At the core of our society is the sacred icon of individualism. It is hostile to community which is seen as a threat to self-fulfillment and unrestrained personal action. The central ethic in a consumer society is the unquestioned belief in the power and importance of the individual consumer. Consumers think of their own desires first. Detournement, for example, was aimed at inspiring the individual consumer to become enlightened and perhaps rebel against the spectacle. But, when the satisfaction of individual desires becomes the primary motivating force in the life of a community – as it has in consumer society – the only

---

59 International Situationniste #6 (August 1961), "Elementary Program of the Bureau of Unitary Urbanism," in *Situationist International Anthology*, 71.

60 Grindon, 158.

mechanism left to inspire change is an individual action. There is no effective mechanism to inspire collective acts of rebellion. Appeals to collectivity are only made at the point of building a new reality in new situations.

Consumerism and unbridled consumption

Despite a weak analysis of individualism, the SI was an early critic of the unrestrained growth of the capitalist system and its logical outcomes – overproduction and unbridled consumption. While they raised concerns about consumerism, their analysis described it in a limited way, as a phenomenon that rationalized the spectacle and inhibited true self-fulfillment, rather than in the context of the overall demands that capital placed on workers and the environment.

The SI's critique of consumption narrowly focused on concerns that consuming created false desires that masked real desires:

> But for the most part these goods have no use except to satisfy a few private needs that have been hypertrophied to meet the requirements of the market. Capitalist consumption imposes a general reduction of desire by its regular satisfaction of artificial needs, which remain needs without ever having been desires – authentic desires being constrained to remain unfulfilled (or compensated in the form of spectacles). The consumer is in reality morally and psychologically consumed by the market.[61]

Because nothing stands between the consumer's wants and the object to be consumed, desire becomes reality. Consumer desire undermines politics because it

61 Pierre Canjuers and Guy Debord, "Preliminaries toward Defining a Unitary Revolutionary Program," in *Situationist International Anthology*, 307.

reduces the interpretation of freedom to individual consumer choice. Consumer freedom is a false freedom; individual "desire" is enclosed desire channeled into choosing only *what* to consume, not *whether* to consume. As Vaneigem noted, "Whatever you possess possesses you in return. Everything that makes you into an owner adapts you to the order of things."[62] Further, consumer desire disempowers. It is not active. It is passive. To consume is to be manipulated – to follow another's direction, another's siren call, another's choice. It wants to be fed; it does not feed. It does not create, it does not give. A post-SI theory must take up this important critique of unbridled consumption particularly in light of the global environmental crisis.

More recently the Adbusters artists have focused their criticism on the problem of excessive consumption and the broader implications of unrestrained economic growth on environmental sustainability. One of their most important legacies that will surely influence political aesthetics in the future is their warning about the dangers of consumerism and its potential for destroying the self and destroying the planet. As they believe, the whole process of capitalist consumption must be reversed, and a new kind of meaning must be created by radical artists empowering themselves and adopting a revolutionary agenda: "I am not a decorator, a packager – I am the author, the storyteller, the creator of meaning." A radical aesthetics would have different goals such as "instead of increasing desire, try reducing it"; and to save the planet, "make waste visible" and teach the world to share.[63]

Sustainability of action
Perhaps the most troubling aspect of the SI approach is the failure to theorize a mechanism for sustained political activity. Like the marketplace,

---

62 Vaneigem, *The Revolution of Everyday Life*, 154.

63 Lasn, n.p.

detournement is, by definition, ever changeable, ever attentive to the "new," to changing consumer iconography.
This changeability serves to continually destabilize it.
Temporary autonomous situations are just that – temporary. In the spectacle, there can be no closure – only an
endless cycle of new replacing old, hope replacing disillu-
sionment through a new purchase. As Lewis Hyde noted,
"The consumer of commodities is invited to a meal without
passion, a consumption that leads to neither satiation nor
fire."[64] The consumer reality is everywhere characterized
by the fragmentation of experience which belies any continuity, so it is all the more imperative that a radical aesthetic address continuity and sustainability of action. The
human need for coherence, order, and balance is disrupted
in a consumer society. While there is some suggestion in
the SI literature that situations are created to develop and
to nourish a stable, predictable new world, the actual practices of detournement and derive seem to be haphazard,
disconnected, limited in time and space.

THE LEGACY OF THE SITUATIONIST INTERNATIONAL
ONE OF THE most important contributions of the SI was
the shift to a new concept of cultural politics. For the first
time, the spotlight was turned to the now ubiquitous mass
media, the capitalist aesthetic of advertising, and the consumer culture. The SI understood that an important political battleground had manifested itself in the cultural arena, and they aimed their tactics at the heart of the makers
of capitalist meaning.

The SI developed a very tightly-focused criticism of
capitalist aesthetics and targeted the real world manifestations of capitalism – advertising imagery. They also provided conceptual tools for undermining the effectiveness
of capitalist art. Situationist art itself was the method used
to attack capitalist art; it was visual; it was political; and the

---

64 Lewis Hyde, *The Gift: Imagination and the Erotic Life of Property* (New
York, NY: Vintage, 1983), 10.

content exposed the capitalist vision and made it transparent, undermining its political power. The detourned image was, effective or not, a political statement. It was also a frontal attack. The SI went right to the heart of the capitalist message and was able to intervene and destabilize its impact. While both Surrealism and Lettrism attempted to avoid a direct visual confrontation with capitalist aesthetics by deconstructing or by making traditional imagery surreal, the SI did not back away. In a culture increasingly stimulated by visual messages, the SI was especially effective in outlining what was at stake – the freedom that came from understanding the tools of manipulation and how to disarm them.

While their work was visually compelling as critique, it was not as effective envisioning an alternative future. Although their work directly addressed the power of capitalist aesthetics, they did not have an effective method for collectively empowering people. They could point out the enemy and the enemy's tactics; but once people were enlightened, they did not have a political mechanism to inspire them to change the reality of which they were newly aware. Nevertheless the situationist versions of the councils were briefly effective, especially in the 1968 uprisings in France. Despite the fact that they were temporary, they nevertheless provided a working model for future versions of the core idea: the creation of situations as part of a broader occupation movement outside of the spectacle.

Several critics were not optimistic about the potential for success of the SI agenda. Echoing earlier criticism of Surrealism, an anonymous reviewer observed, "Of course, these second wave situationists thought that their focus on character etc. was indeed carrying theory and the revolution forward. This was part of their tendency to reduce revolution to essentially a problem of consciousness: their own consciousness."[65] However, another anonymous defender of the SI took issue with these critics (many of

---

65 Anonymous, "Whatever happened to the Situationists?"

whom were in the academy) and vigorously defended both the SI's continuing importance and staying power:

> Despite the attention the SI receives, and the attempts over the years by various toss-pots to claim them for modern art or cultural studies, the SI remains in some sense irrecu-perable. The continued attempts by organized knowledge either to dismiss or co-opt the SI itself provides evidence of the enduring an-tagonism of their ideas, as does the conscious echo of their approach in a number of contem-porary struggles.[66]

---

66 Anonymous, "Whatever Happened to the Situationists?" Academic criticisms and attempts at co-option following the death of Debord in 1994 are detailed by T.J. Clark & Donald Nicholson-Smith in their article "Why Art Can't Kill the Situationist International," *art journal(!)* (October, 1997).

CHAPTER 6

THE POSTMODERN DIGRESSION: **WARMED OVER MODERNIST AESTHETICS**

The postmodern era ... is basically a tired, spirit-less recycling of used-up fragments, announcing that the development of art is at an end.1

INTRODUCTION: THE NATURE OF POSTMODERNISM

WE CANNOT REALLY SPEAK OF POSTMODERNISM AS A SPECIFic, well-defined philosophy. In many ways, it is merely a continuation of the modernist impulse taken to its extremes or perhaps its logical conclusion. Grounded in early twentieth century philosophies of Modernism and nihilism, postmodernism is broadly expressed as the rejection of any fixed theory and the fragmentation of knowledge into multiple relativistic discourses. Postmodernism has no standards, no objective set of beliefs or ideas against which actions can be measured, no ideal upon which to reflect. It has no vision of the future, no coherent dream. It seeks only to rearrange the cultural constructs and memes of the past. As a result, there is only subjective knowledge

---

1 John Zerzan, "The Case against Art," In *Elements of Refusal*, by John Zerzan, 54-62 (Seattle: Left Bank Books, 1988), 61. http://www.primitivism.com/case-art.htm

that is always conditional. In *The Twilight of American Culture*, Morris Berman called postmodernism a "philosophy of despair masquerading as radical intellectual chic … the counterpoint to the civilizational collapse going on around us."[2] Nevertheless, postmodernism does concede the centrality of something called "experience" – and especially individual experience. However, in rejecting any standard by which an experience can be evaluated, every experience had relative merit. By repudiating everything, postmodernism was left to sift through the broken pieces of intellectual structures. According to Brian Morris, "The so-called postmodern condition – with its alienation, cultural pastiche, fragmentation, decentred subjectivity, nihilism – describes, however, not so much a new paradigm or epoch but, rather, the cultural effectives of global capitalism."[3]

Despite the fragmentation that characterizes postmodernism, we can begin to describe the continually shifting detritus of the postmodern phenomenon as much by what it says it is not as by what it appears to be. In *Hiding in the Light,* media theorist Dick Hebdige provided a tongue-in-cheek, but accurate, description of how the randomness of the "postmodern" has influenced every aspect of contemporary culture:

> When it becomes possible for a people to describe as "postmodern" the décor of a room, the design of a building, the diegesis of a film, the construction of a record or a "scratch" video, a television commercial, or an arts documentary, or the "intertextual" relations between them, the layout of a page in a fashion magazine or critical journal, an

---

2   Morris Berman, *The Twilight of American Culture: Ideas of Creativity in Western Culture* (New York, NY: W.W. Norton, 2000), 63.

3   Brian Morris, "Reflections on the 'New Anarchism,'" *Social Anarchism* 42 (2008-2009): 47.

anti-teleological tendency within epistemol-
ogy, the attack on the "metaphysics of presence," a general attenuation of feeling, the collective chagrin and morbid projects of a post-
War generation of baby boomers confronting
disillusioned middle-age, the "predicament"
of reflexivity, a group of rhetorical tropes, a
proliferation of surfaces, a new phase in commodity fetishism, a fascination for images,
codes and styles, a process of cultural, political or existential fragmentation and/or crisis,
the "de-centering" of the subject, an "incredu-
lity towards metanarratives," the replacement
of unitary power axes by a plurality of power/
discourse formations, the "implosion of meaning," the collapse of cultural hierarchies, the
dread engendered by the threat of nuclear
self-destruction, the decline of the university,
the functioning and effects of the new minia-
turized technologies, broad societal and economic shifts into a "media," "consumer," or
"multinational" phase, a sense (depending on
who you read) of "placelessness" or the aban-
donment of placelessness ("critical regional-
ism") or (even) a generalized substitution of
spatial for temporal coordinates – when it becomes possible to describe all these things as
"Postmodern" (or more simply using a current
abbreviation as "post" or "very post") then it's
clear we are in the presence of a buzzword.[4]

While this passage is a humorous digression from a
more serious exploration of the postmodern phenomenon,
it certainly highlights the lack of a cohesive and coherent definition and the fragmentation and relativism that

---

4 Dick Hebdige, *Hiding in the Light: On Images and Things* (New York,
NY: Routledge, 1988), 181-182.

characterizes the era. Postmodernism is everything; and, thus, it is nothing.

AESTHETICS IN THE POSTMODERN ERA

POSTMODERN AESTHETICS, SUCH as it is, is one expression of the broader postmodern perspective. In the absence of a coherent conceptual framework, the fragmentation and diversity of perspectives continues, and there is no formal postmodern aesthetic theory that one can describe with any consistency. Paraphrasing the encounter between Humpty Dumpty and Alice in Louis Carroll's *Through the Looking Glass*, postmodern aesthetics means, Humpty Dumpty might have observed, "just what the artist chooses it to mean – neither more nor less." Art critic Harold Rosenberg noted that "There does not exist between artist and public a common outlook as to what is appropriate and important. … Each art has its own public, and within each art here are additional publics."[5]

What has come to be called postmodernism in the arts took shape in the middle of the twentieth century. Some hints of postmodernism had already emerged early in the twentieth century as criticisms of Modernism. Predecessors included some aspects of both the dada and surrealist movements. The dadaists took the more radical position arguing that all art ought to be destroyed, all symbols challenged and deconstructed. Surrealists, as we have seen, opted for the random eruptions of visions from the individual sub-conscious; Lettrists deconstructed and simplified images in an effort to destroy representation. Change followed change: neo-Dada was a retroactive revival of Dada; Abstract Expressionism was promoted as a unique American aesthetic. Action Painting (a term coined by Harold Rosenberg) emphasized art as performance, as action, and the artist engaged. By the late 1950's,

---

5   Harold Rosenberg, "Spectators and Recruiters," in *Discovering the Present: Three Decades in Art, Culture and Politics* (Chicago: University of Chicago Press, 1973), 127.

Minimalism had raised the deconstructivist impulse to a fine art. Everything was taken out of the picture. "Less" was all the rage; the result was what painter Dushko Petrovich called "the avant-garde of the rectangle."[6] In rapid succession, post-minimalism succeeded and rivaled Minimalism encompassing everything Minimalism left out: body art, performance art, conceptual art, land art, protest art, process art, anti-art art, and so on.[7] One theory followed swiftly on the heels of the previous theory, but none defining the *oeuvre* of the postmodern phenomenon as a whole. In a recent review in *The New Yorker,* art critic Peter Schjeldahl, expressing frustration with the fragmented nature of postmodernist aesthetics, concluded that since the abstract expressionists, aesthetics has moved from one narrative to another without any particular theory taking hold and dominating the art scene: "Then those movements [the New York School and Minimalism], too, disintegrated, and it's been pretty much one damn thing after another ever since."[8]

In the absence of aesthetic coherence, we are left with only a dizzying array of changing styles that are difficult to categorize; and all styles have equal merit. In general, however, all of these styles have a common characteristic: the recycling of previous cultural symbols. This relativism resulted in a retrograde quality to the art that Fredric Jameson described as depthless and superficial.[9] Art in the postmodern world becomes just another commodity according to Petrovich: "Almost everyone would agree that the art world has become a kind of spectacle. Much of the work is repetitive and derivative in a way that starts

---

6 Dushko Petrovich, "A painter's call for 'a practical avant-garde,'" *The Boston Globe,* March 4, 2007. http://www.bostonglobe.com

7 Petrovich.

8 Peter Schjeldahl, "Big Bang: Abstract Expressionism on full show at MOMA," *The New Yorker,* October 18, 2010, 95.

9 Frederic Jameson, "Postmodernism, or the Cultural Logic of Late Capitalism" *New Left Review* 146, 4 (July-August, 1984): 53–93, 60.

to resemble planned cultural obsolescence."[10] Rosenberg agreed: "In the art world today all past modes of painting and sculpture are converted into the contemporary. … The mind oriented to the past is thus disposed to reject 'modernism' in its entirety as a manifestation of cultural disintegration."[11]

POSTMODERN CRITICISM OF CAPITALIST AESTHETICS

MANY CRITICS OF postmodernism agreed that the primary challenge facing aesthetic theory in the postmodern era is how to interpret the preeminent role of capitalist aesthetics in shaping the culture. Modernism defined itself as a critical alternative to formal academic art schools and traditional aesthetics; postmodernism attempted to position itself in opposition to the aesthetic of capitalism, lending the criticism a decidedly political tone. Early on, Walter Benjamin, Max Horkheimer, and Theodor Adorno developed formal critiques of the cultural industry; and their work has had a strong influence on the postmodern cultural studies movement. Other critical voices include the ongoing influence of the Situationist International (SI), art critic John Roberts, Frederic Jameson, and Daniel Bell.

Criticism of capitalist aesthetics matured as a conscious body of critical theory with the rise of the academic cultural studies movement in the 1960's. Their research produced a body of literature dedicated to a critique of consumer society, the burgeoning phenomena of mass culture, and the power of mass communication media and its impact on art. These critics raised anew the concerns about the dangers of recuperation by capitalism, the absence of revolutionary potential, the fragmentation of meaning, and the limitations of and uncertainty about the effectiveness of the individual artist. The one element in postmodern aesthetic theory upon which all critics agreed and that became a truism was that the ideological battleground had

10 Petrovich.

11 Rosenberg, "Spectators and Recruiters," 130.

shifted from the political to the cultural arena. There was also consensus that the mass media was the omnipresent purveyor of aesthetic messages, overpowering all other aesthetic expression in the culture.

The loss of meaning and purpose

The absence of any agreed-upon collective meaning in postmodern aesthetics had a cascading effect on cultural communication and its representation. Relativism and fragmentation coupled with the celebration of individualism reduced meaning to subjective expression, denied any social role for aesthetics, and effectively destroyed any alternative narratives and explanatory frameworks. In the absence of any shared meaning, the traditional aesthetic questions of truth, beauty, meaning, and purpose were reduced to one simple formula: everything is meaningful, and knowledge is fragmented. In postmodernism, human agency is reduced to a tentative experiential reaction to a constantly changing reality. We can know only the small, the local, the limited experience of the individual; and what we know is always temporary. The bankruptcy of postmodern theory resulted in art without intrinsic meaning. According to Daniel Bell, postmodern art has failed us: "A culture of recycled images and twice-told tales is a culture that has lost its bearings. ...The practitioners of 'postmodernism,' by and large, have substituted pastiche for form and cleverness for creativity. ... Much of this was foreshadowed by Pop Art, an art which largely recycles images through collages or juxtaposition."[12] The absence of meaning is the result, in part, of the absence of a coherent alternative narrative that could provide an explanatory model for grounding us in a shared cultural reality. According to Sven Birkerts,

> The explosion of data – along with general societal secularization and the collapse of

---

12 Daniel Bell, "Modernism Mummified" *American Quarterly* 39, 1 (1987): 122-132, 130.

what the theorists call the "master narratives" (Christian, Marxist, Freudian, humanist ...) – has all but destroyed the premise of understandability. ... To see through data, one must have something to see through *to*. One must believe in the possibility of a comprehensible whole. In philosophy this is called the "hermeneutic circle" – one needs the ends to know which means to use, and the means to know which ends are possible. And this assumption of ends is what we have lost.[13]

Contemporary art critic Jed Perl is equally critical of postmodern art. In a recent review he wrote: "I keep looking for a key, a theme, a pattern," hoping to find meaning in postmodern art. ... "What I eventually realized was that I was looking for emotional or intellectual coherence when in fact those were values that the artists and their supporters had either rejected or perhaps simply lost track of; it is difficult to say which." Perl coined the term "laissez-faire aesthetics" to describe the current art climate that is, he believes, merely another face of consumerism – "just right for a new breed of high-end shopaholics. ...This is not easy to explain," he continued, "although it surely has something to do with the rapacity of our new Gilded Age, and with the nihilism of an art market eager to dress each and every new trend in a few moth-eaten costumes from the trunk labeled Dadaism." He concluded, "What laissez-faire aesthetics has left us with – in the museums, the galleries, the art schools, and the art magazines – is a weakening of conviction, an unwillingness to ever take a stand, a refusal to champion, or even surrender to, any first principle."[14]

Like many strains of modern art, postmodern art is apolitical for the most part. According to Munira Mirza,

---

13 Sven Birkerts, *The Gutenberg Elegies: The Fate of Reading in an Electronic Age* (New York, NY: Fawcett Columbine, 1994),75.

14 Jed Perl, "Cash and Carry Aesthetics" *The Baffler* 20 (2012), 18-27.

postmodern aesthetics "sneers at the idea of meaning, truth, beauty and all that. In that sense, modern art is neither left-wing nor right-wing, because so much of it rejects the notion of truth and meaning, which must inevitably characterize any politics."[15] Postmodern art's indifference to politics is a function of several factors: the preoccupation with individual expression; a tendency to avoid representation and to embrace abstraction, and, of course, the conscious rejection of coherence and meaning. John Roberts also criticized the lack of meaning in postmodern art, arguing that its impact on politics is negligible and that it lacks revolutionary potential: "Despite postmodernism's purported attack on elitism, its critique of autonomy is judged as having produced little in the way of actual transformative social institutions and collective cultural practice."[16]

The individual artist and artistic freedom

In many ways, postmodernism is Dada resurrected but without the passion and confrontation. Like Dada, postmodernism celebrates the assault on traditional art, opting instead for individual expression, meaninglessness, and relativism. Freedom of expression for the individual artist continued to play a central role in the postmodern cultural experience. Standardization was debilitating, and art must relentlessly escape standardized style. The result, of course, was that categorizing or even interpreting art was impossible. In the absence of any agreed-upon aesthetic principles, the individual artist was left to his or her own devices. "What is postmodern art?" we ask the postmodern artist. "Whatever interests me," is the response. "What is your art trying to say?" we ask

---

15 Munira Mirza, "Is modern art a left-wing conspiracy?" *Spiked*, November 22, 2007. http://www.spiked-online.com

16 John Roberts, "After Adorno: Art, Autonomy, and Critique." Paper delivered at apexart, London. March 8, 2000. http://www.apexart. org/residency/roberts.htm

the postmodern artist. "Whatever I want it to say," is the response. Richard Kearney observed that in this environment of uncertainty and relativity, "the postmodern artist does not claim to express anything because he does not claim to have anything to express."[17] The result was art that was freely expressed but absent intrinsic meaning.

The postmodernist movement has had a disproportionate influence but an inconsequential impact on aesthetics – despite its pretentions to being on the cutting edge. Paradoxically, if there is no shared context of cultural meaning against which the individual artist can position his/her art, both the individual art and the artist become less relevant. Jameson calls this phenomenon "the waning of affect." Historically, the artist held a privileged position in Western cultures, honored as a visionary and a weathervane of cultural progress. The postmodern artist is no longer special, unique, and original. There is only the craft, the art itself, the assemblages of making. The absence of any shared meaning affects artistic styles as well, as Jameson noted; it means "the end for example of style, in the sense of the unique and the personal, the end of the distinctive individual brushstroke (as symbolized by the emergent primary of mechanical reproduction). … Feelings are now free-floating and impersonal."[18] The postmodern artist becomes merely a *"bricoleur* … someone who plays around with fragments of meaning which he himself has not created," philosopher Richard Kearney concluded.[19] In the absence of an organizing principle, art becomes only data, information.

Harold Rosenberg was an early advocate of postmodern art. In 1952, in "The American Action Painters," he

17 Richard Kearney, *The Wake of Imagination: Ideas of Creativity in Western Culture* (Hutchinson, London/University of Minnesota Press, Minneapolis, 1988, London and New York, NY: Routledge, 2004), 5.

18 Jameson, 64.

19 Kearney, 13.

invited American audiences to learn about and appreciate the new trends in American art. Painting became a performance, an act, and the artist rather than the object created defined the art: "The act-painting is of the same metaphysical substance as the artist's existence. The new painting has broken down every distinction between art and life."[20] These action paintings were, however, private acts by individual artists: "Only the individual can communicate experience, and only another individual can receive such a communication."[21]

Rosenberg also saw the dark side of postmodern art: its isolation and the absence of any sense of valuation. In 1971, in the "De-definition of Art" he observed: The post-art artist carries the de-definition of art to the point where nothing is left of the art but the fiction of the artist. ... In the end everyone becomes an artist," and we might conclude, every work of art, every action, is of equal value. On a critical note, he concluded that "who regards anything he makes or does as art, is an expression of the profound crisis that has overtaken the arts in our epoch."[22] He also concluded that the postmodern artist lives in his own world, is disconnected from culture as a whole, and is essentially irrelevant.

> Unlike the art of nineteenth-century America, advanced paintings today are not bought by the middle class. Nor are they by the populace. Considering the degree to which it is publicized and feted, vanguard painting is hardly bought at all. ... Despite the fact that more people see and hear about works of art

20 Harold Rosenberg, "The American Action Painters," Art News 1/8, Dec. 1952. http://www.pooter.net/intermedia/readings/06.html

21 Rosenberg, "The Herd of Independent Minds," in *Discovering the Present*, 27.

22 Harold Rosenberg, *De-definition of Art* (Chicago: University of Chicago Press, 1983, 12-13).

than ever before, the vanguard artist has an audience of nobody. An interested individual here and there, but no audience.[23]

Aside from his admiration for action painting and Abstract Expressionism, Rosenberg was generally wary of postmodern art. In a 1966 essay entitled "Virtuosos of Boredom," he described the aesthetics of boredom:

> What is distinctive about today's art is that boredom is no longer left to chance. The new works insist on their utter greyness. ... In accompanying movements the spectator has passed from the imaginative tension of Action Painting, through the amused relaxation of Pop clichés, to the dazzle of Op, to, finally, the bafflement and boredom of paintings and sculptures deliberately denuded of sensibility.[24]

Rosenberg went on, however, to argue that this was a conscious tactic on the part of the artist, in actions reminiscent, perhaps, of the excesses of Dada: "the tiresome art work evokes the heroic days of modernism when art was created without thought of the spectator's response, and the artist was solitary and free."[25] In this vein, the American art scene subsequent to Abstract Expressionism is often referred to as Neo-Dada.

The consumer culture: the postmodern dilemma

The postmodern era can best be characterized as the final victory of capitalist aesthetics. The advertising industry and mass media have overwhelmed

---

23 Rosenberg, "The American Action Painters."

24 Harold Rosenberg, "Virtuosos of Boredom," in *Discovering the Present*, 120-121.

25 Rosenberg, "Virtuosos of Boredom," 122.

alternative aesthetic visions. In the consumer culture, all aspects of art – iconography, style, design, and purpose – were eventually appropriated and subordinated to the whims of the capitalist market. Without an intentional message, all new art was soon co-opted into the consumer aesthetic; and postmodernism became merely a new, improved capitalist aesthetic lacking any revolutionary potential. Fredric Jameson summed up the problem: "What has happened is that aesthetic production today has become integrated into commodity production generally."[26]

Max Horkheimer and Theodor Adorno (along with Walter Benjamin) were early critics of capitalist aesthetics – in particular, the power of the mass media and technology to shape consciousness and to control culture. Through their criticism, the groundwork was also laid to frame future discussions about the relationship between politics and art. Adorno concluded that capitalist aesthetics was destructive to true art; and, therefore, true art had to remain autonomous. Capitalist art was specifically designed to control message and perception according to Horkheimer and Adorno: "The withering of imagination and spontaneity in the consumer of culture today need not be traced back to psychological mechanisms. The products themselves ... are so constructed that their adequate comprehension requires a quick, observant, knowledgeable cast of mind but positively debars the spectator from thinking."[27] Although Adorno focused on the modern era, his critique is even more relevant in the postmodern era, in part, because of his insights into the power of mass media and the control of the advertising industry in shaping aesthetics. His analysis underlies most postmodern criticism of contemporary art and culture.

---

26 Jameson, 56.

27 Max Horkheimer and Theodor Adorno, "The Culture Industry: Enlightenment as Mass Deception," in *Dialectic of Enlightenment*, Mieke Bal and Hent deVries, eds., trans. Edmund Jephcott (Stanford: Stanford University Press, 2002), 100.

According to Adorno, the mass media served to maintain social control through several aesthetic conventions: standardization, playing on emotions, amusing the masses, and co-opting new art. Standardization guaranteed a level of comfort with the status quo resulting in a population resistant to change generally. Consumers are trained to welcome the endless re-runs of popular television series; to recognize the McDonald's golden arches icon, and are comforted and reassured by the fact that the hamburgers will taste the same worldwide; to await with great anticipation the formulaic movie genres that produce sequels and prequels; and to sleep comfortably every night in the knowledge that a brand name is a guarantee of product uniformity and a level of known quality.

Mass media productions are also carefully designed to appeal to raw emotional expression, inducing catharsis and releasing social pressures. Adorno rejected Aristotle's notion of catharsis as an aesthetic principle because it was "a purging action directed against the affects and an ally of oppression."[28] Most television and film programming is designed for entertainment, not enlightenment. According to Horkheimer and Adorno, this programming is consciously designed to distract people from the realities around them: "Amusement itself becomes an ideal, taking the place of the higher values it eradicates. … Amusement always means putting things out of mind, forgetting suffering, even when it is on display. At its root it is powerlessness."[29] John Roberts concurred with Adorno's position: "Mass culture offers compensatory forms of libidinal gratification, and as such, functions overall as a form of social repression. The pleasures of mass culture negate the promise of happiness of autonomous art."[30]

---

28 Theodor W. Adorno, *Aesthetic Theory,* Edited by Gretel Adorno and Rolf Tiedemann, Translated with a translator's introduction by Robert Hullot-Kentor (Minneapolis: University of Minnesota Press) 1997, 238.

29 Horkheimer and Adorno, 115 and 116.

30 Roberts, "After Adorno."

And finally, co-optation was one of the primary ways that capitalist aesthetics disarmed political challenges to its messages. Like those early critics who argued that capital eventually recuperated the avant-garde, Terry Eagleton found postmodern art had fallen prey to the same tendencies: "Postmodern culture is, among other things, a sick joke. ... Art has indeed been integrated with everyday life; but this has happened in the form of advertising, public relations, the media, political spectaculars, the catwalk and commodity, which is not quite what the Futurists and Surrealists had in mind."[31]

Adorno warned that the consumer culture was designed to continually expand its feverish search for the new, the exciting, the provocative by seducing and co-opting all art and turning it into just another commodity. He argued that ultimately all avant-garde art is eventually superseded in the same way that the consumer aesthetic embraced and exploited Surrealism.[32] To be free of the commodity culture, he concluded, art needed to maintain its autonomy. To remain true to a mission of meaning and purpose, it had to remain aloof from the corrupting culture around it.

Rosenberg was also critical of mass culture, pointing out how mass culture is inauthentic:

> The significant distinction is between the formulated *common experiences* which are the substance of mass culture and the *common situations* in which human beings find themselves. The common situation is precisely what the

---

31 Terry Eagleton, "Future Fetishists and Artists Who Don't Paint: How the Revolutionary Aims of the Avant-garde Led to the 'Sick Joke' of Postmodernism." Rev. Alex Danchev, ed. 100 Artists' Manifestos: From the Futurists to the Stuckists. The Times Literary Supplement. March 23, 2011. http://entertainment.timesonline. co.uk/tol/arts_and_entertainment/the_tls/article7173276.ece

32 Adorno, *Aesthetic Theory*, 229.

common experience with its mass-culture texture conceals, *and is often intended to conceal.* ...
To penetrate through the common experience
to the actual situation from which all suffer requires a creative act – that is the say, an act
that directly grasps the life of people during,
say, a war, that grasps the war from the inside,
so to speak, as a situation with a human being
in it.[33]

Echoing Jameson's concerns, Kearney was critical of
the tendency for capitalist aesthetics to consume all imagery and to subvert critical voices.

In many postmodern works the very distinction between artistic-image and commod-
ity-image has virtually faded. The practice
of parody and pastiche, while it frequently
intends to subvert the *imaginaire* of contemporary "late capitalist" society, often ends of
being co-opted or assimilated. Even the dissi-
dent images appear to be swallowed into the
"ideology of simulacrum" which prevails in
our consumer age. Indeed the suspension of
subjective inwardness, referential depth, historical time and coherent human expression
– four losses listed by Frederick Jameson as
symptomatic of postmodernism – is now becoming *de rigueur* in certain circles.[34]

Further, there is no real autonomy for the artist in the
consumer aesthetic, in the same way there is no real choice
for the consumer. Every element, according to John Berger,
is carefully managed. "Capitalism survives by forcing the
majority, whom it exploits, to define their own interests as

---

33 Rosenberg, "The Herd of Independent Minds," 18-19.
34 Kearney, 4-5.

narrowly as possible. This was once achieved by extensive deprivation. Today in the developed countries it is being achieved by imposing a false standard of what is and what is not desirable."[35] Clement Greenberg pointed out that in general, capitalist consumer aesthetics is the art of mass culture: "The notion of the postmodern has sprouted and spread in that same relaxing climate of taste and opinion in which pop art and its successors thrive [middlebrow art]. It represents wishful thinking for the most part; those who talk about the postmodern are too ready to greet it." For Greenberg, postmodern art was "easy" art; real art was "difficult."[36] Rosenberg was concerned, too, arguing that avant-garde art had succumbed to "fashion." The irony, of course, is that "In the fashion world, freshness and shock do not represent the emergence of the new but are mere artifices for refurbishing the familiar."[37]

The cultural industry and capitalist aesthetics: What is to be done?

Frederic Jameson was extremely skeptical about the potential for an effective revolutionary postmodern aesthetic response to the hegemony of capitalist commodification.

> For political groups which seek actively to intervene in history and to modify its otherwise passive momentum ... there cannot but be much that is deplorable and reprehensible in a cultural form of image addiction, which, by transforming the past visual mirages, stereotypes or texts, effectively abolishes any practical sense of the future and of the

---

35 John Berger, *Ways of Seeing* (London: British Broadcasting System and Penguin Books, 1972), 152.

36 Clement Greenberg, "Modern and Postmodern," William Dobell Memorial Lecture, Sydney, Australia, October 31, 1979, *Arts* 54, 6 (February 1980). http://www.sharecom.ca/greenberg/

37 Rosenberg, "The Avant-Garde," in *Discovering the Present*, 86.

collective project. ... Yet if postmodernism is a historical phenomenon, then the attempt to conceptualize it in terms of moral or moralizing judgments must finally be identified as a category-mistake.[38]

He went on, however, to argue "that we make at least some effort to think the cultural evolution of late capitalism dialectically, as catastrophe and progress all together."[39] Producing real political change will require not only challenging the existing cultural and political forces of power and control in the mass media but also creating real and realizable alternative political, economic, and organizational expectations.

The need for a critical stance. The adoption of a reflective, critical stance has important implications for political aesthetics according to Jameson: "No theory of cultural politics current on the Left today has been able to do without one notion or another of a certain minimal aesthetic distance, of the possibility of the position of the cultural act outside the massive Being of capital ... [However], distance in general (including 'critical distance' in particular) has very precisely been abolished in the new space of postmodernism."[40]

Adorno, too, argued that to resist the allures of the marketplace, true art must be reflective. Mass media art makes us comfortable in the here and now, in the immediate experience, and consciously shields us from reflecting on our world because reflection might result in a change of perspective. If art is to offer an alternative vision, the current illusions must be swept aside. Transformation requires that a dialectic be engaged: the thesis of capitalist aesthetics must be critiqued and challenged for a new synthesis to emerge. This requires that the artist position him/

---

38 Jameson, 85.
39 Jameson, 86.
40 Jameson, 87.

herself as critical observer, seeking new ways of seeing. Adorno concluded that art must always assume a critical role in opposition to the culture industry: "Whether art in turn becomes socially irrelevant – empty play and decoration of social bustle – depends on the extent to which its constructions and montages are simultaneously de-montages, destroying while receiving the elements of reality and shaping them freely as something other."[41]

Aesthetics and politics. Adorno was deeply skeptical about the potential for art to free itself from the domination of the capitalist aesthetic and from the power of the mass media to shape and to control political expression. He had seen the results of mass media in the service of fascism in Germany and how the United States government used similar techniques to communicate the political propaganda of the New Deal and the Second World War. According to Adorno, art played an important role in shaping a political agenda. The culture industry used a variety of tools to maintain control of the political message, but politically-aware artists also had a parallel role to play in undermining capitalism. Adorno argued that if art were to have any effect on politics, it had to be autonomous; but at the same time, the link between the art and the social context had to be maintained.

Realizing that his argument for an autonomous art raised serious questions concerning the political effectiveness of art, Adorno attempted to clarify and to strengthen the dialectical relationship between the individual artist and society. He argued that political issues would be expressed in the artwork through the artist's knowledge of society. According to Adorno, political messages were embedded within the form of the artwork itself and not conveyed through any overtly political imagery: "The liberation of form, which genuinely new art desires, holds enciphered within above all the liberation of society, for form – the social nexus of everything particular – represents the

---

41 Adorno, *Aesthetic Theory*, 255-256.

social relation in the artwork; this is why liberated form is anathema to the status quo."[42]

At several points in *Dialectic of Enlightenment* Horkheimer and Adorno noted the absence of political tension in the art created by the culture industry: "Technology reduced the tension between the culture product and everyday existence" blending the culture industry with empirical reality to create a zone of comfort that continually reinforces and reassures the public.[43] The content of television sit-coms and dramas, for example, is designed to undermine class consciousness by presenting a classless society without class tensions, wrapping in an idealized, happily consuming middle class. Real class-based economic and social tensions are addressed only sporadically in documentary programming such as historical reflections on the Great Depression. But, real economic issues are seldom directly confronted in the context of contemporary settings. Instead, political and economic realities are only a minor footnote to the steady diet of smiling, happy faces of people who drive nice cars, who shop with a certain abandon, and who never seem to go to work.

True art would not appease the public but jar it into a state of shock – what Adorno called a "shudder" – a sudden awareness of the false reality presented by the culture industry: "This experience is contrary to the weakening of the I that the culture industry manipulates."[44] A redemptive political art, according to Adorno, internalizes and articulates the political tensions in society: "What crackles in artworks is the sound of the friction of the antagonistic elements that the artwork seeks to unify."[45] By incorporating contradictions into the artwork, the social is always embedded within the art, rendering what Adorno called socially critical zones that illuminated the political flash

---

42 Adorno, *Aesthetic Theory*, 255.

43 Horkheimer and Adorno, 101.

44 Adorno, *Aesthetic Theory*, 245.

45 Adorno, *Aesthetic Theory*, 177.

points: "where it hurts; where ... the untruth of the social situation comes to light. It is actually this against which the rage at art reacts."

There are, nevertheless, problems with Adorno's political position. Despite his contention that the social/political agenda is embedded within the dialectic of autonomous art, his proposals for translating that insight into direct action are unclear. By emphasizing that redemption will be achieved through his idea of autonomous art rather than through collective action that the art inspired, he continues to privilege the insights of the individual artist and trusts that he or she has a true grasp of the political environment. Art by itself, however enlightened the artist might be, will not result in collective action.

Adorno's concept of autonomy could easily be misinterpreted because it de facto assumes that what is not autonomous must be in collusion with capitalism. If all non-autonomous art is likely to succumb to being seduced by the consumer culture and easily co-opted, how then does autonomous art become something other than ephemera? The price of autonomy could also be the loss of a meaningful link between art and the day-to-day politics of social change.

His discussions of the form and content of autonomous art are also vague and generally unhelpful in a political context. What does it mean to include "tensions" in the artwork? Contradictions? Suffering? It is one thing to argue that a work of autonomous art includes a dialectical interaction between the empirical reality and a potential alternative reality and another to understand how the artist is to render these tensions. He also appears to be skeptical of realism – primarily because of its prominence in capitalist aesthetics: "Through its unavoidable minimum of stylization, however, realism admits its impossibility and virtually abolishes itself. Taken in hand by the culture industry, it has become mass deception."[46] This rejection

---

46 Adorno, *Aesthetic Theory*, 249.

of realism essentially leaves the question of the form and style of autonomous art as an undefined abstraction open and unresolved.

Creating an alternative vision. According to Adorno, true art should also present future alternatives, not through specific, realistic representations but through changing consciousness such that people actively desire to transcend the current reality: "Art respects the masses by presenting itself to them as what they could be rather than by adapting itself to them in their degraded condition. ... That art stands as a reminder of what does not exist, promotes rage."[47] This is art's ideological role; the artworks convey their effect "not by haranguing but by the scarcely apprehensible transformation of consciousness."[48] Capitalist aesthetics, on the other hand, as John Berger pointed out has no vision of a different political future. Advertising or what he called "publicity images," "never speak[s] to the present. Often they refer to the past and always they speak of the future," but a future, he went on, that is "endlessly deferred." [49]

Adorno, however, does not make clear how consciousness is changed. Observe in the passage that follows his references to a "transformation" of empirical reality through the artwork:

> Thus truth content and social content are mediated, although art's truth content transcends the knowledge of reality as what exists. Art becomes social knowledge by grasping the essence, not by endlessly talking about it, illustrating it, or somehow imitating it. ... In art the object is the work produced by art, as much as containing elements of empirical reality as displacing, dissolving, and reconstructing

47 Adorno, *Aesthetic Theory*, 239-240.
48 Adorno, *Aesthetic Theory*, 243.
49 Berger, *Ways of Seeing*, 146.

them according to the work's own law. Only through such transformation, and not through an ever falsifying photography, does art give empirical reality its due, the epiphany of its shrouded essence and the merited shudder in the face of it as in the face of a monstrosity.[50]

It seems that his (justifiable) fear of co-optation led him to the opposite extreme, isolating autonomous art from having any active political impact. Reading Adorno, one is left with a sense of the overwhelming power of capitalist aesthetics and no real alternative resources to respond to its power. In the end Adorno can discourage the revolutionary artist. While his theory addresses some of the core weaknesses of postmodern aesthetic theory – the loss of meaning, the relationship of the autonomous artist to the social reality, the need to challenge capitalist aesthetics – his tepid conclusions provide no helpful way forward.

THE LEGACY OF POSTMODERNISM

IT IS TOO early to make a prognosis about whether postmodernism has a sufficiently different perspective from Modernism and how it defines art and its role in society. Like Modernism, postmodernism has no clearly discernible style, no identifiable political message or agenda, no readily accessible symbolic representation, and no narrative for dealing with the real world. It is dedicated to merely re-arranging the historical elements of art, in idealizing individual expression, and playing around with style.

Despite its shortcomings, critical postmodernism is firmly in place as a cultural phenomenon. It is less significant as a political force which raises the question of whether it has any revolutionary potential. In general, postmodern art has had little impact on politics. Its appeal has been to a limited audience – museums, galleries, private collectors, and academicians. Andy Warhol's soup

---

50 Adorno, *Aesthetic Theory*, 258-259.

cans inspire no revolutionary actions, reflected no political reality; minimalist painting only furrow eyebrows in puzzlement; and neo-Dada performance art is interesting but ephemeral. Postmodern art has no collective message, no focus – it celebrates only fragmentation. Walter Benjamin was concerned about whether art would eventually become irrelevant and lose its traditional role of illuminating and articulating the essence of cultures and peoples. He argued that the fragmentation of Modernism would eventually destroy the whole concept of authenticity in art. We can ask the same question of postmodernism.

CHAPTER 7

POSTMODERN ANARCHISM, POLITICS, AND AESTHETICS

A new spirit is rising. Like the streets of Watts we burn with revolution. ... We seek a total revolution, cultural, as well as social and political – LET THE STRUGGLE BEGIN.[1]

INTRODUCTION

AN EXAMINATION OF THE DISCOURSES OF TRADITIONAL AESthetics, modernist aesthetics, and the various threads of anarchist political aesthetics being pursued in the postmodern era may help identify new possibilities for a more effective challenge to the twenty-first century capitalist hegemony. It is out of the detritus of the postmodern world, after all, that a new society will emerge. The discussion here will set the stage for a deeper exploration in the concluding chapter where I discuss the elements of political aesthetics that advance the realization of a just and humane future.

---

1 Ron Hahne, *Black Mask and Up Against the Wall Motherfucker: The Incomplete Works of Ron Hahne, Ben Morea and the Black Mask Group* (London: Unpopular Books and Sabotage Editions, 1993), 7.

POSTMODERN ANARCHISM: A FRAMEWORK FOR CHANGE?

HISTORICALLY, THE CORE anarchist argument against all authority was an uncompromising critique of what Emma Goldman once called "power over." Over the course of the twentieth century, the system of power-over expanded beyond the traditional institutions of church and state to include the far more sinister structures of cultural control wielded by corporations, the mass media, technology, and sociological forces. The Situationist International called the whole system of control "the spectacle"; sixties radicals in the United States called it "the system"; and contemporary activists call it "globalization." Max Horkheimer and Theodor Adorno called one aspect of this hegemony of power the "culture industry." They all agreed on one thing: the over-arching phenomenon of the modern era has been the seamless merger of political power and cultural control in the service of capital.

Postmodern political realities presented contemporary anarchist culture with a dilemma. Historically, political theories – including anarchist political theories – were based on reasoned arguments that developed a coherent ideology grounded in reality. Postmodern thought took a different tack. Influenced by French poststructuralism and postmodernism, political analysis turned to redefining the political landscape. Postmodern theory based its arguments on a fragmented culture where the individual is feted as the primary source of knowledge and action, where there are calls for rejecting all ideologies, and where multitudes of discourses compete for attention. Armed with this analysis, how would postmodern anarchist politics address the challenges of a hegemonic power structure?

By the 1960's, individualist anarchist theory was on the ascendency in the United States and the various forms of social anarchism were relegated a back seat to the more libertarian political theories. Max Stirner's *The Ego and His Own* was re-issued and widely read in the 1960's and 1970's. Stirner's ideas resonated with the traditional

American values of individual freedom and the right to individual self-fulfillment. His philosophy was a perfect fit with the postmodern phenomenon, and some writers have even argued that his philosophy was the inspiration for postmodernism generally. Like postmodernism, individualist anarchism rejected the ideas of essences, symbols, structure, and formal ideology. In the resulting fragmentation of postmodern theory, anarchist theory shifted to celebrating individualist actions.

The ongoing interest in individualist anarchism in the United States reflected, in part, the experience of young activists who had grown up in a consumer society where the message of meeting individual wants and desires was paramount. They lived in a visual world and moved in a sea of consumer goods – an indulged generation, raised in an economic boom, nursed by the media. The emphasize on the individual self and the liberation of personal desire in the name of "freedom" are both qualities that are mirrored in the perfect consumer personality that exercises "choice" as freedom based on personal idiosyncrasies. The fascination with libertarian ideas in recent decades has further affirmed this individualist bent in American culture. In addition, the New Left activists – who tended to be young, white, and college educated – were less interested in the labor movement's focus on working class Marxist politics.

In the last quarter of the twentieth century anarchist theory evolved into "post-anarchism." Post-anarchism resonated with American individualism and the nihilism of postmodernism. According to political philosopher Benjamin Franks, post-anarchists are like postmodernists generally in many respects: they are relativists, and they insist on freedom from all institutional constraints, even those upon which they mutually agree.

The postanarchists who follow Stirner (and Nietzsche) reject universalism in both its realist and naturalist forms on three main grounds.

First, it would mean that external, universal standards would be shaping destinies, rather than individuals creating their own goals. Second, the application of universal principles promotes rather than eliminates hierarchies of power. Finally, there are no epistemic bases to universal rules, and thus the discovery and the promotion of such rules are, instead, the product of oppressive social powers.[2]

In 1985 Hakim Bey (Peter Wilson) revisited Stirner's radical egoism in his postmodern concept of ontological anarchy: all ideological purity should be abandoned and replaced with what he called "Type-3" anarchism. According to Bey, it was neither collectivist nor individualist, and it focused on the media, calling for the appropriation of popular entertainment and mass culture (including pornography) as vehicles for radical re-education. His "mystical anarchism" emphasized networking and direct action to create what he called "poetic terrorism."[3] The goals of anarchism were re-conceptualized. Instead of seeking to build a new political structure, Bey saw anarchism as a temporary guerilla force challenging the power structures in contemporary society – a politics of random acts of protest.

Bey was also skeptical of systematic political organization and argued that political activism should be built around his concept of a Temporary Autonomous Zone (TAZ). The TAZ was based on the idea of small groups organizing spontaneously to appropriate a space, create an action, and then disappear. According to Bey, the TAZ is "like an uprising which does not engage directly with the

---

2   Benjamin Franks, "Postanarchism and Meta-Ethics," *Anarchist Studies* 16, 2 (2008), 141.

3   Hakim Bey, *TAZ: The Temporary Autonomous Zone, Ontological Anarchy, Poetic Terrorism* (New York, NY: Autonomedia, 1985, 1991). http://www.hermetic.com/bey/taz_cont.html

state, a guerilla operation which liberates an area (of land, of time, of imagination) and then dissolves itself to re-form elsewhere/elsewhen, *before* the state can crush it."[4] His assumption was that through minimal, temporary political organization, the danger of institutionalizing political power structures could be contained; and the individual's freedom from oppression could be guaranteed.

For the most part, postmodern anarchists rejected long-held political arguments developed in the nineteenth century on the Marxist left. But, there were serious political consequences. As contemporary anarchist theorist Wolfi Landstreicher explained, at minimum, breaking with the communist/socialist left meant rejecting "a *political* perception of social struggle and an ideology ... that is placed above life and the individuals as a construct to be served." That rejection meant that organization and collectivism were viewed as repressive because they required "the subordination of the individual to the group."[5] In exchange for structured models of society and their collectively agreed-upon freedoms, individualist anarchism served up only the fragmented freedoms that random individual or roving groups of protesters could achieve. In *Social Anarchism or Lifestyle Anarchism: an Unbridgeable Chasm*, Murray Bookchin argued that a philosophy of individualism was the source of the shortcomings of contemporary individualist anarchist theory. What appeared to guarantee autonomy actually undermined autonomy.

> Left to his or her own self, the individual loses the indispensable social moorings that make for what an anarchist might be expected

---

4   Bey, *TAZ*.

5   Wolfi Landstreicher, "From Politics to Life: Ridding Anarchy of the Leftist Millstone," *Anarchy: A Journal of Desire Armed* (Fall/Winter 2002-2003), 49-51. http://www.theanarchistlibrary.org/HTML/ wolfi_landstreicher_from_politics_to_life_ridding_anarchy_of_ the_leftist_millstone.html

to prize in individuality: reflective powers, which derive in great part from discourse; the emotional equipment that nourishes rage against unfreedom; the sociality that motivates the desire for radical change; and the sense of responsibility that engenders social action.[6]

From Stirner's Union of Egoists to Hakim Bey's Temporary Autonomous Zones (TAZ), postmodern anarchists have offered only weak theories of social organization if at all; and most critics of postmodern anarchism focus on this weakness and the ineffectiveness of individual action to create meaningful political change. Stirner's Union of Egoists was a temporary association designed to enable individuals with mutual self-interests to achieve their goals – even at the expense of others. Even these informal unions were always on the verge of dissolution, Stirner noted, because "it will still contain enough of unfreedom and involuntariness. … still less do I obligate myself to the union for my future and pledge my soul to it."[7]

Professor John Armitage was critical of Bey's celebration of individual acts of protest: "Most of Bey's discussions of political action do not appear to anticipate class struggle at all. … Rather, they focus on the activities of individuals, or, at best, marginal groups." Further, Bey does not address the problem of state power: "Bey's attacks on the state are, in truth, attacks on *pictures* of the state. … This also explains why, for Bey, there is little point in 'confronting a 'power' which has lost all meaning and become sheer Simulation."[8] Armitage concluded that "All

6   Murray Bookchin, *Social Anarchism or Lifestyle Anarchism: An Unbridgeable Chasm* (Oakland and Edinburgh: AK Press, 1995).

7   Max Stirner, *The Ego and His Own: The Case of the Individual Against Authority,* Translated by Steven T. Byington (New York, NY: Dover, 1973), 308.

8   John Armitage, "Ontological Anarchy, the Temporary Autonomous Zone, and the Politics of Cyberculture: A Critique of Hakim Bey,"

Bey offers us, is 'poetic terrorism.' ... Indeed, his revolutionaries of everyday life, poetic terrorists if you will, are actually rather solitary figures. For they not only dance alone in the micro-spaces of globalitarian finance capital but commit acts of art sabotage in the name of nothing but an inner dialogue with themselves."[9] Because of the temporary nature of the TAZ, its political effectiveness is probably impossible to assess.

Where postmodern individualist anarchism is most vulnerable to criticism, however, is its lack of a clear analysis of power relations. Postmodern political philosopher Todd May argued that power relations in contemporary society are diffuse; and as a result, power can be effectively challenged through decentralized actions: "What I see as the essential link between anarchism and the poststructuralism of Lyotard, Deleuze, and especially Foucault, is the denial that there is some central hinge about which political change could or should revolve. ... Inasmuch as power is everywhere, the need for political reflection and critique is also everywhere."[10] His argument is consistent with the postmodern respect for multiple discourses and political realities. Recognizing diversity of visions and voices is a worthy and necessary goal – particularly in culturally and ethnically diverse contemporary societies. Nevertheless, unless some political effort is made to bring these voices together, this fragmented perspective also diffuses political discourse and elides the questions raised by the centralization of power in the hands of the state and capital. The political realities of hierarchy, of power-over, of oppression, and of exploitation have not gone away. They are manifested in real political

---

Angelaki: Journal of the Theoretical Humanities 4, 2 (1999), 120. Bey quoted from Hakim Bey, Millenium (New York, NY and Dublin: Autonomedia & Garden of Delight, 1996), 128.

9   Armitage, 121 and 122.

10 Todd May, "Poststructuralist Anarchism: An Interview with Todd May," Perspectives 4, 2 (2000). http://flag.blackened.net/ias/8may. htm

institutions; and they must be resisted politically, not as cultural manifestations. And, they will not be defeated by random individual acts of protest. A political theory that is based on a "political" principle of egoism seems to be a contradiction in terms. However much he or she may protest to the contrary, the individual protester does so only in isolation. The central question to be explored is: which power is most important to challenge; how much of it is centralized; and by whom is the power wielded? The limitations of a decentralized analysis of power are troubling because political activity often ceases at the edges of the boundaries between competing decentralized special interests. The power controlling our lives is centralized, and while it can have a decentralized and federated response, there must be some sort of collective agreement on where challenges must be directed.

Much is also made in the postmodern cultural studies movement of the role of anarchism in the cultural arena. During the last quarter of the twentieth century, the field of cultural studies concentrated its energies on studying mass culture and bemoaning its impact on contemporary life. Although cultural studies had its roots in the Europe with its history of socialist and class politics, in the United States, the shift to culture as the battleground for politics resulted in theorists turning away from analyzing political power in formal organizations – whether of the state or the corporation – to an analysis of the "soft" power of capitalist cultural artifacts. What was never articulated was the need for a deep analysis of the power structures behind the mass culture – an argument that Horkheimer and Adorno had developed early on. Contemporary philosopher Slavoj Žižek studied the role of cultural studies in the political arena and found their methodology wanting and their "politics" very thin at best:

> One again has to ask the old Benjaminian
> question: not how do they explicitly *relate to*

power, but how are they themselves *situated*
within the predominant power relations. ...
What if the field of Cultural Studies, far from
actually threatening today's global relations
of domination, fit their framework perfectly?
... Crucial here is the shift from English to
American Cultural Studies: even if we find
in both the same themes, notions, and so on,
the socio-ideological functioning is completely
different: we shift from an engagement with
real working-class culture [in England] to
academic radical chic [in the United States].[11]

There are other grounds unrelated to individualism
upon which one can critique postmodern anarchism.
Anarchist Jeff Shantz argued that post-anarchism was really a product of the academic world – where it "has tried
to meld anarchist theory with the esoteric philosophies of
post-structuralism."[12] He is concerned that the presence of
post-anarchist theorists in the academy leaves anarchism
ripe for vangardism. Anarchists, he argued, should be
extremely wary of adopting the position of an academic
vanguard: "Rather than tearing down the walls between
town and gown, head and hand, academic and amateur,
the move of anarchists into the academy may simply reproduce, reinforce, and even legitimize the political and
economic structures of the academy."[13]

Finally, in recent years some postmodern anarchist theorists have argued that the future of political activism lies
in creating virtual communities that use the power of the
internet to connect people and build community. People
taking up the ideas of Hakim Bey, for example, embraced

11 Slavoj Žižek, *Did Somebody Say Totalitarianism? Five Interventions in
the (Mis)Use of a Notion* (London, New York: Verso, 2001), 226.
12 Jeff Shantz, "Anarchists in the Academy: Concerns and Cautions,"
Social Anarchism 41 (2008-2008), 41.
13 Shantz, 39-40.

the cyberworld as an effective means of communicating and organizing. However, cultural studies professor Kevin Robins is critical of the efficacy of these virtual communities and the danger that they represent to democracy. According to Robins, real politics requires face to face, not virtual, interaction.[14] Virtual reality creates communities that are self-referencing and self-aggrandizing according to Robins: "Cyberspace, with its myriad of little consensual communities, is a place where you would go in order to find confirmation and endorsement of your identity. ... Encounters with others should not be about confirmation but about transformation."[15] Facebook is a classic example of how a conformational technology builds communities of consensus. The participants, however, continue to function as isolated units, not members of a true community.

In a real world of power relations, cyber communities are unlikely to muster an effective political response against the holders of real power, although they are extremely useful for sharing information, for mutual support, and for calling people to action. Even those abilities can be compromised, however, simply by the government pulling the plug on the communication networks. The likelihood that individuals will effectively challenge corporate power through the internet is magical thinking. In many ways the virtual culture is a classic creature of postmodern culture – it is fragmented, isolated, and individualistic.

Further, the technology of computers embodies the same strengths and shortcomings of other mass media platforms. Cyber communities are totally dependent upon a technological structure that corporate entities control. As Horkheimer and Adorno pointed out, technology is what maintains the power of control both over culture and politics: "Technical rationality today is the rationality of domination. ... The technology of the culture industry

---

14 Kevin Robins, "Against Virtual Community: for a politics of distance," *Angelaki: Journal of the Theoretical Humanities* 4, 2 (1999), 166.
15 Robins, 169.

confines itself to standardization and mass production and sacrifices what once distinguished the logic of the work from that of society."[16] While there may be the appearance of individual action and autonomy, the reality is one in which the technological process directs and channels the individual.

POSTMODERN ANARCHIST AESTHETICS

AFTER THE DECLINE in popularity of the social realist aesthetic, postmodern individual anarchist theory assumed a more important role in shaping anarchist aesthetics. The formal debate over anarchist aesthetics took place primarily in the academic postmodern cultural studies movement, but on the streets, anarchist artists evolved a vibrant anarchist aesthetic practice that was, by and large, indifferent to the academic theoretical discussions. Direct action for them meant performance art, posters, neighborhood murals, graffiti, and detournement of advertising images. These activities were driven by a desire to break down the split between art and life, and engage the viewer as active participant.

The theory

In recent years, post-anarchist critical theorists have turned for inspiration to the writings of French philosopher Jacques Rancière. Grasping Rancière's message is difficult, in part because he has essentially redefined the "political" in terms of what he calls "dissensus."[17] Rancière's "aesthetic revolution" must be considered in the context of his political philosophy. Both art and politics are social constructions; and in that sense,

---

16 Max Horkheimer and Theodor Adorno, "The Culture Industry: Enlightenment as Mass Deception," in *Dialectic of Enlightenment,* edited by Mieke Bal and Hent deVries, translated by Edmund Jephcott, 94-136 (Stanford: Stanford University Press, 2002), 95.

17 Jacques Rancière, *Dissensus: On Politics and Aesthetics,* ed. and trans. by Steven Corcoran (New York: Continuum, 2010), 139·

art can be said to incorporate political meaning: "Politics and art, like forms of knowledge, construct 'fictions', that is to say *material* rearrangements of signs and images, relationships between what is seen and what is said, between what is done and what can be done."[18] Rancière's aesthetic interventions are applicable to any situation. He argues, for example, that "if there exists a connection between art and politics, it should be cast in terms of dissensus, the very kernel of the aesthetic regime: artworks can produce effects of dissensus precisely because they neither give lessons nor have any destination."[19] Like the dadaists and early modernists, Rancière would like to see the whole separate category of aesthetics disappear and works of art emptied of pre-determined meaning. The whole category of art should be collapsed so as to be flexible enough to address multiple possibilities. He wants to deconstruct aesthetics as a specific category, and calls for "the ruin of any art defined as a set of systematisable practices with clear rules. ... the end, the ruin of the whole hierarchical conception of art." By breaking down the boundaries between the political and the social, he believes politics can be aesthetics. He further urged the expansion of the concept of art into new venues: "The aesthetic revolution is the idea that everything is material for art so that art is no longer governed by its subject, by what it speaks of: art can show and speak of everything in the same manner. ... It is the affirmation that poems are everywhere, that paintings are everywhere."[20] Because his postmodern philosophy and aesthetics are as murky as his favorite philosopher, Michael Foucault, pinning him down on how the

---

18 Jacques Rancière, *The Politics of Aesthetics*, trans. with an intro. by Gabriel Rockhill, with an afterward by Slavoj Žižek (New York: Continuum, 2005), 39.

19 Rancière, *Dissensus*, 140.

20 Jacques Rancière, "Politics and Aesthetics: an interview," trans. Forbes Morlock, with an intro. by Peter Hallward, *Angelaki: Journal of the Theoretical Humanities* 8, 2 (August 2003), 205.

transition from politics to aesthetics will happen is never adequately explained.

Rancière's politics as aesthetics does have some anarchist hallmarks: for example, he sees an important role for art as political direct action to create a "disruption" of the political status quo in order to change consciousness.

> I am trying to redefine what in art practices enables them to have a political role. ... Changing the fabric of sensibility means firstly the disruption of places and capacities. ... The political virtue of art takes effect when it blurs the borders separating it from non-art. ... And for me political action itself is an aesthetic activity to the extent that it makes us see as political, things not recognized as such, as when we are made to hear subjects left out of account, etc.[21]

Rancière's understanding of disruption, or what he calls dissensus, seems in many ways similar to Adorno's "shudder" and the Situationist International's idea of detournement, but with a broader application.

> [A]rtists are those whose strategies aim to change the frames, speeds and scales according to which we perceive the visible, and combine it with a specific invisible element and a specific meaning. Such strategies are intended to make the invisible visible, or to question the self-evidence of the visible; to rupture given relations between things and meanings and, inversely, to invent novel relationships between things and meanings that were previously unrelated.[22]

---

21 Todd May, Benjamin Noys and Saul Newman, "Democracy, Anarchism and Radical Politics Today: An Interview with Jacques Rancière," trans. John Lechte, *Anarchist Studies* 16, 2, 2008, 179.

22 Rancière, *Dissensus*, 141.

Aesthetics has a decided political function from this perspective, according to Sudeep Dasgupta: "This disturbing element must lead to the awareness that there is something wrong with the social order."[23] While Rancière goes on to caution that disruption in and of itself is not sufficient, he never suggests that the art should determine the outcome of what exactly should be done.

> As a matter of fact, political art cannot work in the simple form of a meaningful spectacle that would lead to an "awareness" of the state of the world. Suitable political art would ensure, at one and the same time, the production of a double effect: the readability of a political signification and a sensible or perceptual shock caused, conversely, by the uncanny, but that which resists signification.[24]

Rancière's primary objective seems to be to shift the perception of reality which could potentially bring about change, without defining just what those new realities might look like.

According to political theorist Saul Newman, Rancière has an important insight that might inform a revitalized anarchist aesthetic. Rancière is particularly interested in the relationship between art and politics in creating new communities of meaning: "Politics is ... about conflicts over what is visible and what is invisible, and art can therefore contribute to a reconfiguration of space and perception through which new political meanings may emerge."[25] Rancière's sense of "meaning," however, is equally elu-

23 Sudeep Dasgupta, "Art is Going Elsewhere, and Politics Has to Catch It: An Interview with Jacques Ranciére," *Krisis: Journal for Contemporary Philosophy* 1 (2008), 74.

24 Rancière, *The Politics of Aesthetics*, 63.

25 Saul Newman, "Editorial: Postanarchism," *Anarchist Studies* 16, 2 (2008), 104.

sive. Rancière seems to be suggesting that a disruptive art that enhances awareness of the social order will cause a reconfiguration of communities of meaning, a change in the narrative. But, Rancière does not sufficiently address the problems of fragmented meaning, of the absence of a political focus, and of the challenge of sustainability and comprehensibility linked to political action – all of which are also ongoing challenges to anarchism.

Despite his acceptance of some of Rancière's arguments, Newman remains critical of the post-anarchist movement because of its affinity with postmodernism's tendency toward fragmentation and relativism. He is particularly concerned about the lack of a defined meaning when post-anarchism rejected the dropped threads of 1970's semiotics analysis with its emphasis on "the role of images, symbols, and language in the construction of political identities and meanings." His criticism also highlights the differences with classical anarchist theory: "Unlike the classical anarchists who saw a rational coherence in social relations and a human essence at the base of social identities, ... [Rancière's] meanings and identities are inherently unstable and open to different and contingent articulations."[26] Rancière's philosophy is another manifestation of the postmodern fascination with fuzzy borders always changing, with relativism, and with a commitment to process over a product. In an afterward to Rancière's *Politics and Aesthetics*, Slavoj Žižek expressed concern about the limitations of Rancière's political philosophy – especially his de-coupling of Marxist economic theory from his narrow definition of politics.[27]

The shortcomings of postmodern anarchist aesthetics were also examined and found wanting in John Roberts's criticism. He concluded that postmodern radical art had abandoned any references to a collective political message.

---

26 Newman, 103.

27 Slavoj Žižek, "The Lesson of Rancière," in Rancière, *The Politics of Aesthetics*, 75-76.

In a review of a "Protest & Survive" art exhibition at London's Whitechapel Gallery, he observed that "the claims for the political in [the show], then, are remarkably consistent with the broader 'post-political' culture of the moment, in which both social-democratic traditions on the Left and extra-parliamentary socialisms are seen as equally irrelevant or defeated and as such unusable for the utopian imaginaries of art." In postmodern aesthetics, he argued, "*the political is assumed now to be either subsumed by the cultural or defeated by it at a more fundamental level.*"[28]

Roberts was scathingly critical of the art in the exhibition; it was art that reflected the inherent flaws of the postmodern individualist anarchist aesthetic. The art rejected representation; it was indifferent to the importance of an organizational analysis of politics; it did not offer any clearly defined collective agenda; and it was not grounded in a context of time, place, or meaning. What was left was the individual artist's self-celebration. A meaningful political art was set aside "in favor of a general enthusiasm for the return of art to 'life' and the artist's unbounded 'energy.' This return of 'art to life,' essentially, is the codification of a generation's antipathy to the administration of critique of representation and the institution."[29]

Before moving on to the final chapter, one additional theorist has challenged the relevance of postmodern art and politics in an even more radical fashion. Anarcho-primitivist John Zerzan argued that we should reject art entirely – a position first articulated by the Dada movement. He contended that art distances us from reality and disconnects us from the natural world. He is against the creation of symbols in general because they intervene in the actual apprehension of reality. "All art, as symbolization, is rooted in the creation of substitutes, surrogates

---

28 John Roberts, "Commentaries: Art, Politics and Provincialism," *Radical Philosophy* (March/April 2001). http://www.radicalphilosophy.com, Italics mine.

29 John Roberts, "Commentaries."

for something else; by its very nature, therefore, it is falsification."[30] As we saw with the dadaists, however, a nihilist rejection of art has absolutely no effect on the political reality in which political art seeks to act.

The practice

Direct political action in the arts expanded significantly in the latter half of the twentieth century. Radical aesthetics embraced in practice a variety of tactics and techniques, but generally adopted realism or surrealism as the dominant aesthetic in various artistic venues. The new art reflected the issues of day as the artists engaged with their communities to visualize and articulate the political desires of those communities.

In the 1960's, political imagery in the United States reflected the heady activism of Civil Rights protests, Anti-Vietnam War protests, and the women's movement. Some of these movements developed their own unique aesthetic statements, aligning theory with direct action. Black aesthetics, for example, reflected a range of political perspectives; a few were nationalistic, but the majority focused on raising awareness and encouraging activism. The starting point was often the historical experiences of oppression and the central role of race in fighting contemporary oppression. Black arts groups were established across the country, and black artists took on the role of advocates. Playwright and author LeRoi Jones, for example, wrote and directed plays embodying the concepts and principles of the Black Power Movement. The feminist movement, too, embraced a feminist analysis and expression of art. Women flocked to newly-established women's art galleries and national traveling exhibits like Judy Chicago's "Dinner Party." A new feminist art journal, *Helicon Nine*, highlighted women's art. But, the most widely-discussed

---

30 John Zerzan, "The Case against Art," in *Elements of Refusal*, by John Zerzan, 54-62 (Seattle: Left Bank Books, 1988) , 57. http://www. primitivism.com/case-art.htm

and iconic feminist direct action, a bra burning, never actually took place! Nevertheless, the "action" affirmed the power of performance art in political activism.

Much of this new art was also a celebratory art, creating participatory events filled with humor, fun and joyfulness—all with an underlying serious message. In the late 1960's, The Black Mask Group created a series of direct action art events, the most successful of which attracted wide attention. They sent out a news release in 1966 announcing that they were shutting down the Museum of Modern Art in New York. Police surrounded the building the next day, and one of the members of the group walked up to the door and taped a "Closed" sign on the front door to conclude the action! The Bread and Puppet Theatre created beautiful and graceful oversized puppets that were carried in home town parades and large political demonstrations across the country.

Throughout the second half of the century, community-based alternative theatre groups were established across the country. In August 1981, twenty "people's" theatres from across the country converged in St. Peter, Minnesota for "The Gathering" – a week of performances, parades, and workshops.[31] St. Peter's Cherry Creek Theatre sponsored the event that included performances by El Teatro de la Esperanza, Provisional Theatre, A Traveling Jewish Theatre, At the Foot of the Mountain, The Dakota Theatre Caravan, and The Illusion Theatre among many others.

Europe saw similar political unrest. Paris exploded in 1968 where students and workers united in spontaneous political actions. Inspired by the SI, students occupied the Sorbonne, workers occupied over one hundred factories, and a series of rolling strikes shut down the country for a while. The student movement manifesto, *On the Poverty of Student Life*, was co-created by the SI and the students

---

31 For more background on popular "people's" theatre see *We are Strong: A Guide to the Work of Popular Theatres across the Americas* (Mankato, MN: Institute for Cultural Policy Studies, 1983.

of Strasbourg. Revolutionary graffiti and political slogans were painted on the walls across France. Squatters in Germany occupied housing decorating the walls with colorful street art with political messages, and the Berlin Wall was covered with politically-charged graffiti. The neo-Marxist Autonomous movement spread from Italy across Europe, with active groups in France, Germany, The Netherlands, and Greece. Their militant and sometimes violent actions were the target of fierce government persecution. In Germany, groups that dressed in black and covered their faces to hide their identities earned the label, *der Schwarze Block* (the Black Bloc).

Beginning in the 1970's, environmentalists established Green parties in Switzerland, Britain, Belgium, and the movement made some parliamentary gains with their radical agenda. Green parties have since spread around the world. Greenpeace is a radical activist offshoot of the Green movement and to this day, continues to raise awareness worldwide about the environmental challenges facing the planet.[32] Throughout the 1980's the Greenham Commons Women's Peace Camp was established in England to blockade the Royal Air Force base and protest anti-Cruise missiles and nuclear power. On several occasions between 50,000 and 100,000 protesters encircled the base. All of this direct action activism was accompanied by visual representation.

Two-dimensional art played an important role in communicating these messages of political change. Radical magazines, graphic images, posters, and political protest performance actions appeared almost overnight. American publications such as *Black Rose, Anarchy: A Journal of Desire Armed*, and *Fifth Estate* featured vibrant and pointed

---

32 Founded in 1979, Earth First! is a more radical environmental network in the United States that is committed to anarchist direct action. The core belief of Earth First! is biocentrism – the belief that the earth comes first. They publish a journal that highlights issues and actions.

political art – most of it realistic or surrealistic. Poster
art was (and still is) a widely applied political art form in
Europe, hand-held placards were popular in the United
States,[33] and around the world graffiti continued to communicate political messages and political iconography.
Several visual artists will be highlighted here but they
are only representative of the hundreds or even thousands
of artists – many of them anonymous – who used their
talents and their passions to awaken people around the
world.[34] For example, in the 1960's and 1970's the graphic
work of Italian artist Flavio Costantini captured in styl-
ized detail violent historical incidents and confrontational
actions undertaken by anarchists at the turn of the twentieth century. Disillusioned with the Russian experience,
Costantini turned to portraying key historical moments
in the long history of anarchist protest. He was especially
drawn to the French anarchists.[35] His drawings are filled
with images of weapons held by both the anarchists and
the police. His subject matter included accounts of violent assassinations (*attendants*) by anarchists and anarchist
thieves like Ravachol (aka Sabot) who was well-known
for his terrorist bombings, murders, and thefts from the
rich. Hi work also portrayed violence by the government,
including images of guillotined anarchists and police violence against civilians.

In the 1980's British visual artist Gee Vaucher created
startling and shockingly graphic political art. Vaucher's
work is openly anarchistic, and she first came to broad attention through her designs of the album covers for the
punk band, Crass. Politics infuses all of her work, and she
works most often in realist or surrealist styles. One of her

---

33 In some cases, posters attached to sticks were banned by city of-
ficials out of fear they could be used as weapons.
34 For more examples, you might start with Josh MacPhee and Erik
Reuland's *Realizing the Impossible: Art against Authority*.
35 "Flavio Costantini," entry in Kate Sharpley Library, www.kate-
sharpleylibrary.net/t4b9k9

most iconic images is of the Statue of Liberty weeping. A powerful anti-war message is conveyed in "Onward Christian Soldiers" which portrays a dead soldier's body with a wooden cemetery cross planted in its chest. This work and others, borders on the grotesque, but there is no escaping the political message against death and destruction. One of her most grisly images is of a decaying arm and hand caught in a barbed wire fence. The title of the piece is simply, "Your Country Needs You." Her "Broken Gun" poster is obvious and politically transparent – Circle A symbols are repeated in rows across the entire poster. The poster "Oh America" features an evil Mickey Mouse contemplating a live mouse.[36]

Clifford Harper is another British artist and illustrator whose work has been produced in many, many anarchist journals. His imagery is bold and conveys political content. He has also produced comics art. In 1987 he wrote and illustrated a history of anarchist ideas, *Anarchy: A Graphic Guide*. James Koehnline's graphic imagery was featured in many radical journals and on book covers in the United States. His drawings and collages, along with Freddie Baer's powerful collages, will be discussed in greater detail in the next chapter.

In the spirit of the Situationist International (SI), Adbusters continued the assault on the culture of capitalism through the detournement of the realism of advertising aesthetics, arguing that their revolutionary aesthetic strategy would undermine capitalism. As post-anarchist theorist Lewis Call noted in support of the idea of detournement, "If power in the postmodern world is based largely upon illusion and the creative manipulation of reality, then revolutionaries have a clear and effective strategy available to them. They need only seize the engines of simulation,

---

36 Although this book is out of print, you can still acquire copies on the internet – for over $350 U.S. dollars. Gee Vaucher, *Crass Art and Other Pre Post-Modernist Monsters: A collection of work by Gee Vaucher* (AK Press, 1999).

puncture the veil of illusion, and replace the official discourse with a radical alternative narrative."[37] Adbusters adapted the idea of detournement and pioneered such political aesthetic action tactics of "adbusting" and "cultural jamming." In "Branding Anti-Consumerism," Anne Moore described the Adbusters tactics: "Methods range from the alteration of existing ads ('adbusting') to the organization of public-space reclamation parties; from the airing of TV 'subvertisements' to the performances of 'cultural interventions.'"[38]

Traditional anarchist graphic symbols such as the Wobbly black cat or the symbols of the black flag and the black rose persist in contemporary anarchist art; today the most ubiquitous anarchist symbols are the Circle A and the raised fist. These symbols are widely-reproduced on posters, protest signs, and spray painted on walls in every city in the world. The anarchist organization Food Not Bombs detourned the raised fist in their logo into a fist holding a carrot! A video produced by the Minnesota-based RNC Welcoming Committee detourned classic anarchist symbols in a satirical welcome to the 2008 Republican National Convention in Saint Paul, Minnesota. "We're Getting Ready" was widely circulated via the internet in the radical community as an invitation to exercise the constitutional right to organize and protest. The video used sophisticated editing techniques to produce an engaging and humorous piece: a masked female figure dressed in black throws a Molotov cocktail, which cuts in the next frame to the bottle igniting a charcoal grill on the other side of a garage; she hands off a set of bolt cutters to an

---

37 Lewis Call, "A is for Anarchy, V is for Vendetta: Images of Guy Fawkes and the Creation of Postmodern Anarchism," *Anarchist Studies* 16, 2 (2008), 163.

38 Anne Moore, "Branding Anti-Consumerism: The Capitalistic Nature of Anti-Corporate Activism," in *Realizing The Impossible: Art Against Authority*, Josh MacPhee and Erik Reuland, eds. (Oakland: AK Press, 2007), 286.

individual trimming hedges; and she throws a bowling ball in one frame, followed by a shot of the front door of a military recruiting station, followed by a shot of the bowling ball rolling down the sidewalk toward a set up of ten pins. Printed on the ball were the letters R.A.B.L. – a historical reference to a Twin Cities anarchist organization called the Revolutionary Anarchist Bowling League. The subtleties of the satire were lost on the authorities, however, who introduced the video in a trial of participants as evidence of an invitation to violence.[39]

THE CHALLENGES OF POSTMODERN ANARCHIST AESTHETICS

THE PROBLEM CONFRONTING postmodern anarchist aesthetics is the philosophy of postmodernism itself. Part of the difficulty lies in the very real limitations of the individualist approach to anarchist theory and practice which continues to shape contemporary post-anarchism. The combination of individual autonomy with individual political action was unlikely to have any real impact on centralized and entrenched power structures – even when individuals temporarily joined with others to take political action.

Getting beyond the theoretical, and somewhat overdrawn, tensions between social and individual anarchism is one challenge facing twenty-first century anarchism. In many ways the arguments on both "sides" have been overblown and over-simplified. This tension between the individual and society has long been debated in the anarchist community, and, is a perennial topic in political theory generally. Nevertheless, the different approaches bear careful scrutiny, especially as individualism is manifested in political discourse and action, and the resolution to this conundrum will require a more nuanced theoretical formulation.

In an effort to shift the balances of power and challenge

---

39 "We're Getting Ready" is available at several sites on the internet. Periodically it gets taken down because of copyright infringement concerning the music.

the hegemony of the spectacle and the corporate state, postmodern theory argued that power is decentralized and thus actions should also be decentralized. In the absence of coherence, political messages ended up as only fragments and relativistic posturing, rather than voices speaking together from the diverse communities. The emphasis on autonomous action in individualist anarchist theory – like the alienated rebellious individual artist in modernist theory – is further complicated by the incoherence and fragmentation of postmodern theory.

What did all of this mean for postmodern anarchist aesthetics? In an era characterized by philosophical and aesthetic fragmentation anarchist artists in the postmodern era largely ignored the formal academic philosophical debates where the "political" had retreated into the irrelevancies of cultural analysis and linguistic dissection. They struggled to reconcile the conflicting demands of individual artistic freedom of action and expression and political action with and for others. The good news was that they succeeded in making real connections with real communities, and in the process revitalized political art. The "mainstream" postmodern artists were relegated to the museums, irrelevance, or oblivion. For the most part, postmodern anarchist artists continued the traditions of earlier radical aesthetic movements: Dada's activism and outrage, surrealist visioning, performance art, detournment of advertising images, and public direct action events. They remained linked to their communities, in touch with political realities, articulating the hopes and dreams for change.

CHAPTER 8

SOCIAL ANARCHIST AESTHETICS IN AN AGE OF FRAGMENTATION

In my opinion art is a kind of anarchy. … It is a benevolent anarchy: it must be that and if it is true art, it is. It is benevolent in the sense of constructing something which is missing, and what it constructs may be merely criticism of things as they exist.1

THE DEVELOPMENT OF A VIABLE SOCIAL ANARCHIST AESTHETIC was sidetracked temporarily in the twentieth century when it was all but buried under the ideological and aesthetic rigidity of Socialist Realism, the manipulations of advertising, and the modernist and postmodernist digressions into alienation, chaos, and individualistic aesthetics. The creation of meaningful political art that addressed a larger, social vision was essentially marginalized and even considered suspect. In more recent years, political artists have taken on the challenge once again to reflect on current political realities and to shape an alternative political vision. The challenge is how to formulate a social anarchist aesthetic that moves beyond the limitations of previous

---

1   Tennessee Williams, "Something Wild," introduction to *27 Wagons Full of Cotton* (New Directions, 1949).

aesthetics and reclaims the original purpose of art as embodying meaning, to bring art and politics together to create a new reality.

ELEMENTS OF A SOCIAL ANARCHIST AESTHETICS

THE BASIC AESTHETIC elements of effective social anarchist art have been known since the mid-nineteenth century, according to Professor Jesse Cohn.

> The poetics called for by Proudhon, Bakunin, and Kropotkin (i.e., the social anarchists) called for a "social art" – and art that would 1.) reach broad working-class audiences without pandering or sacrificing complexity; 2.) charge static, abstract signs so that they *evoke* the concreteness and specificity of lived experiences; ... 3) not (only) reflect the world as it *is* but (also) participate in its *transformation;* and 4.) make visible, within the finite, real, present world, the infinite plurality of *possibilities* ... [and] tell the larger "truth" of what *can* and *should* exist, the truth of desire.[2]

Three additional elements are essential to provide the most effective means of communicating a political message: a return to the classical notion that the primary purpose of art is to articulate and to communicate cultural meaning; that the art must be grounded in real and identifiable communities, and that the artist must be actively engaged in articulating the visions and dreams of those communities; and finally, social anarchist art must actively work to overcome the fragmentation that capitalist aesthetics and postmodernist art created. These objectives can only be achieved if social anarchist art is designed around a cohesive alternative narrative – whether the story is told

---

2 Jesse Cohn, "The End of Communication? The End of Representation," *Fifth Estate* # 376, 42, 2 (2007), 41.

visually, musically, via written text, or through oral transmission. A coherent narrative can integrate the hopes and dreams of people and can be the framework on which a meaningful future can be built. It can merge art with politics, and it can bring heart and ideas together to realize the imaginings of the desire to be free.

Meaning

We all crave meaning. Cultural critic and philosopher Raymond Tallis calls this desire for meaning the "fourth hunger" which feeds the passions for life, which "arises from our curious condition of being animals. … Half-awakened, we are constantly engaged in making explicit sense of the world and of our fellow humans." Tallis goes on to explain that in our contemporary world we are distracted from fulfilling this basic human need for order and coherence:

> The commonest response to this sense that something is amiss is increasingly frenzied activity, usually involving consumption of goods, substances, entertainment and one another. … These, while excellent in themselves, do not palliate the fourth hunger: for a life more connected, for a more intense consciousness, for joyful experiences that are experienced with the solidity and intensity of the pain, starvation and terror from which we have been delivered.[3]

The modern preoccupation with immediate experience is reflected in a postmodern aesthetic that precludes our asking precisely what meaning the art conveys and what we should expect of art. Tallis described the distinction as the difference between art as idea and art as experience:

---

3   Raymond Tallis, "Art, humanity and the 'fourth hunger,'" *The Spiked Review of Books*, November 30, 2007. http://www.spiked-online.com/

"The idea has a clear *form* which the experience lacks."[4] Experience bereft of meaning, on the other hand, is fleeting and evanescent. The idea, in contrast, is based in experience but rises above and extends beyond experience. There must be a connection between the real and intended meaning. The idea interprets experience and places it in a known context of future anticipation and past memory. Something in our humanness, Tallis believes, wants to shape experience, to give it depth and meaning. Great art has always been symbolic of some greater reality by which we come to recognize a coherent meaning in our own lives. Through symbol-making, the complex knowledge of shared meaning is transmitted.

The modernist focus on the individual artist's internal vision reduced the breadth of meaning to a world of one. The challenge for social anarchist artists is to create alternative realities that re-connect us to one another and more effectively address that deep need for meaning, the fourth hunger. The challenge is to find a way of expressing and sharing the story of our collective meaning. Prior to the modern era, to imagine an art separate from the culture in which, and for which, it was created would have been impossible. Meaning is always a shared experience, produced between the artist and the viewer, the writer and the reader, musician and audience. Political art without reference to the symbolic representation of collective cultural and political ideals fails to do more than entertain or distract. Political art can fulfill the need for meaning by communicating the shortcomings of our current social reality, articulating our collective political desires, and transcending the current reality with visions of a different world.

The social nature of political art: context and community

In an essay on the role of the intellectual proletarian, Emma Goldman called for – and, indeed, expected – artists and other intellectuals to make common

---

4   Tallis.

cause with the people. To focus on one's own self-expression, one's own desires are not sufficient. The role of art is to be sensitive and responsive to changing realities, to proactively serve as an aid to action.[5] An artist can meet this challenge only if he or she is actively engaged in community. This expectation conflicted with a central premise of Modernism – the individual artist should remain outside of community, committed to self-expression, a heroic and alienated figure.

It is time to reassess the imbalance in our culture and our art between individual expression and responsiveness to the needs of society as a whole. This assessment does not have to mean self-repression or exercising self-restraint but an opportunity to expand and to open a new outlet for individual freedoms within a community of free people. Recently, Laurence Davis observed,

> a key attraction of anarchist communism is its emphasis on the equal and paramount value of both individualism and community, personal autonomy and social solidarity, individual freedom and responsibility to others, together with a history of theoretical argument and practical experimentation intended to demonstrate how and why a reconciliation between self and society might be approximated but never fully achieved.[6]

While the individual artist has a vital role to play in creative expression, for the social anarchist artist, individual creative autonomy is recast as individual-in-community-as-political-participant – an artist who engages and interacts with his/her world.

---

5   Emma Goldman, "Intellectual Proletarians," 176-185, In *Red Emma Speaks: Selected Writings and Speeches by Emma Goldman*, ed. Alix Kates Shulman, (New York, NY: Vintage Books, 1972).

6   Laurence Davis, "Social Anarchism or Lifestyle Anarchism: An Unhelpful Dichotomy," *Anarchist Studies* 18, 1 (2010), 76.

As philosophers of aesthetics have argued for millennia, art emerges from the richness of human interactions and lived experience, not the musings of the individual artist. In many traditional cultures, artists served as conduits rather than initiators of artistic expression. Traditional art, according to Walter Benjamin, had a social function, a certain "use value" in creating and maintaining community: "We know that the earliest art works originated in the service of a ritual – first the magical, then the religious kind. … In other words, the unique value of the 'authentic' work of art has its basis in ritual, *the location of its original use value*."[7] The artist is a political actor in a community of others. To be in community is to be in the real world, to be an active participant in a known context, a social and a political environment. Without this involvement, this immersion in an active political community revolutionary art cannot be authentic. The artist can decide to convey a political idea, but unless it resonates with the real lives of real people, its reach will be limited. According to David Bayles and Ted Orland:

> If art is about self, the widely accepted corollary is that making art is about self-expression. And it is – but that is not necessarily all it is. It may only be a passing feature of our times that validating the sense of who-you-are is held up as the major source of the need to make art. What gets lost in that interpretation is an older sense that art is something you do out in the world, or something you do about the world, or even something you do *for* the world. The need to make art may not stem solely from a need to express who you are, but

7   Walter Benjamin, "The Work of Art in the Age of Mechanical Reproduction," in *Illuminations*, translated by Harry Zohn, edited and introduced by Hannah Arendt, 217-251 (New York NY: Schocken Books, 1969), 223-224, Italics mine.

from a need to complete a relationship with something outside yourself. As a maker of art you are custodian of issues larger than self.[8]

In *What Is Art*, writer Lev Tolstoy argued that true art should go beyond representation – it should strengthen and inspire people to act, to develop their social relationships: "However poetical, realistic, effectful, or interesting a work may be, it is not a work of art if it does not evoke that feeling (quite distinct from all other feelings) of joy and of spiritual union with another (the author) and with others (those who are also infected by it)."[9] The primary task of the artist, according to Tolstoy, is to create art that "infects" people with the idea of the social:

> *The stronger the infection, the better is the art as art.* ... The degree of the infectiousness of art depends on three conditions: (1) on the greater or lesser individuality of feeling transmitted; (2) on the greater or lesser clearness with which the feeling is transmitted; (3) on the sincerity of the artist, i.e., on the greater or lesser force with which the artist himself feels the emotion he transmits.[10]

Thus, art should not merely reflect or portray social relationships but should inspire them, draw attention to the importance of them as a shared experience, and invite people to live in a real world with others and dream a new world for all. As Cohn has observed, "For anarchists, treating literature as 'autonomous' from the social means failing to think autonomy in social terms; ergo, questions

---

8   David Bayles and Ted Orland, *Art & Fear: Observations on the Perils (and Rewards) of Artmaking* (Santa Cruz, CA and Eugene, OR: The Image Continuum, 1993), 108.

9   Leo N. Tolstoy, *What Is Art?* (NY: Bobbs-Merrill, 1896, 1960), 139.

10 Tolstoy, *What is Art?*, 140.

of literature must always be situated in a wider social context with the aim of determining what kind of relationships the text offers to bring about between ourselves and one another, between ourselves and the world."[11] Social anarchist art is nourished only in the community, in a lived culture of words, images, and political action.

There is also an important interactive component in socially aware art. As silk screen artist Ricardo Morales observed, "Art, like language, is a means of communication. If I wish to communicate with you, not just talk at you, I need to know something about you. ... The more intimately I know you, your language, your way of seeing, the more able I am to choose words or images that will be meaningful in your life."[12]

Two examples in United States history highlight how art played a central role in inspiring, reflecting, and shaping political community. The outcomes were different, but art was at the heart of defining the national cultural direction. In the first example, the political and artistic culture of the 1930's coalesced around the real world experience of the economic crisis of the Great Depression. The Depression had affected all Americans, and there was a feeling of "we're in this together." In solidarity with others, artists emerged from and sought to articulate and to shape the experience, the visions, and the dreams of the community of individuals suffering want and deprivation. The artistic efforts of writers, painters, actors, and musicians emerged from specific communities – sometimes reflecting distinct regional communities, women's communities, ethnically diverse communities, workers communities. Artists from all progressive political backgrounds focused their

---

11 Jesse Cohn, "What is anarchist literary theory?" *Anarchist Studies* 15, 2 (2007), 117.

12 Ricardo Levins Morales, "The Importance of Being Artist," in *Reimaging America: The Arts of Social Change,* eds. Mark O'Brien and Craig Little (Gabriola Island, BC: New Society Publishers, 1990), 20.

efforts on the suffering around them. Socialists, anarchists, communists, pacifists, members of the John Reed clubs, unemployed councils, and labor unions worked within a variety of symbolic universes with the same goal of inspiring and uplifting the culture as a whole. Artists had a clear sense of shared mission, and the art reflected that deeper collective meaning.

In the "culture wars" of the 1980's, art was at the center of bitter and contentious ideological battles in the cultural arena. At stake was what it meant be an American and who would articulate the vision, who would tell the story. Tensions escalated over the artistic merits of voices and visions of diverse cultures that emerged to challenge the prevailing narrative of American culture. This struggle continues to this day. African-Americans, Hispanics, Native Americans, women, the GLBT community, and other groups demanded the right to define and to articulate their unique cultures and to introduce their own art, theatre, music, and literature into the dominant discourse. These voices were a direct political challenge to traditional mainstream culture.

The conservative right used the inflammatory rhetoric of a cultural "war" on "true" American values to frame the debate. These defenders of a highly selective traditional cultural "canon" made a concerted effort to challenge and to suppress the legitimacy of the diverse American cultures and their voices. Conservative books were written with a thinly-veiled sub-text of white supremacy warning of the destruction of traditional American society. The battles were fought largely over curriculum and content in education at all levels but most bitterly in university English departments. Courses entitled Women's Literature, The African American Voice, and Native American Studies were added to the curriculum as the battle lines firmed up between a canon of white, male writers and the new literature celebrating multicultural voices. Conservatives took the battle to the elementary level, flocking to school board meetings to challenge the inclusion of these alternative voices in school curricula.[13] Especially vitriolic debate characterized the political intensity of these battles. The tensions were even reflected at the federal level in the National Endowment for the Arts (NEA) and the National Endowment for the Humanities (NEH) over which Lynne Cheney presided. After leaving the office, she became an advocate for conservative values, challenging the new multicultural curriculum content and advocating that "traditional" standards be enshrined in the schools.

America's multicultural voices prevailed in the cultural battle, and the ideas of cultural diversity and inclusiveness were mainstreamed in the American education curriculum. For the first time, emerging communities reflecting a rich variety of social and cultural identities had a presence on the national stage, and their perspectives were heard. But, conservative commitments to a canonical aesthetic purity and control of message persist in American culture. As recently as 2010, in the throes of strong anti-immigration sentiments, the state of Arizona banned ethnic studies

---

13 See Alan Bloom, *The Closing of the American Mind: How Higher Education has Failed Democracy and Impoverished the Souls of Today's Students* (New York, NY: Simon & Schuster, 1987); Fred Whitehead, ed., *Culture Wars: Opposing Viewpoints* (San Diego, CA: Greenhaven Press), 1994. Much of this debate was spearheaded by Malcolm Lawrence, the founder of a group called Accuracy in Academia." Lawrence argued that the universities were run by communists and liberals, and he called for a consumer protection type of agency to overseen course content. He authored a "Parental Consent Letter" that urged schools to adopt rules requiring parental permission to include some 35 different issues in school curricula. His list included such topics as evolution, family income, sex attitudes, and even courses on world hunger. Federal legislation initiated by Senator Orin Hatch was adopted in1984 denying federal desegregation funds to local school districts that allowed "secular humanism" to be taught. Secular humanism was, thankfully, never defined; and the law faded into the background.

programs and even developed a list of banned books addressing ethnic diversity. Community is also about connection with and commitment to a particular place, a real and tangible world. Art critic Jed Perl emphasized the importance of place in creating a work of art. Perl, who is a critic of the lack of focus and context in postmodern aesthetics, observed: "Surely we are in a period when the sense of place as a sense of classical order is almost impossible to maintain. The fluid, the improvisational, the changeable, the ambiguous preoccupy most of the best artists right now."[14] In order to change the world, social anarchist art needs to reflect the reality of place and to appreciate the importance of place as a mechanism for change. Place is the essence of a social realism – a physical place, a shared social geography, a community of real people. Place is more than land or region or group identity, noted Perl: "A painting or a sculpture, whether abstract or representational, must always be a place – a unique locale, a little universe. The particularity of the place draws us in. We focus our attention, we linger, we explore."[15] It is also a political community of some meaningful whole, a world in which people belong. Place is where political inspiration begins, from which political action emerges, and where freedom is realized.

This recognition of the importance of diversity of context and experience provides a powerful antidote to the hegemony of capitalist aesthetics. At the same time, it is not fragmentation in the postmodern sense. Fragmentation is a breaking apart, a fracturing. Diversity is unity within difference. It is cohesion around a specific place, a community of similarities, an aspect of richness, of connection – fragmentation is without meaning and integrity.

The importance of place as social and political context has not been lost on capitalism and especially capitalist

---

14 Jed Perl, "Postcards from Nowhere," *The New Republic*, June 25, 2008. http://www.tnr.comPerl.

15 Perl.

aesthetics. As Ricardo Morales observed, while capitalism pollutes our visual environment, we are not without our own tools:

> The battle over meaning is everywhere reflected in billboards, radios, newspapers, workplace rules, video stores, zoning ordinances, television, and spray-painted walls. These public spaces are the arena in which society speaks to itself. They are shaped by and in turn help shape who we think we are. Whoever controls these spaces has tremendous power over the meaning of language – and the imagery of thought.[16]

Place in the capitalist world is not real but constructed and increasingly virtual. The construction of faux alternative realities is a key to the success of advertising. Worlds are created that are self-contained, coherent, and connect with a real heartfelt passion for belonging that, unfortunately, can never be realized in a meaningful way in the capitalist reality. As Max Horkheimer and Theodor Adorno pointed out long before the postmodern era, "The culture endlessly cheats its consumers out of what it endlessly promises."[17] Consumer products are placed against familiar backgrounds, and a variety of situations or lifestyles are created to highlight the product. This technique of careful and conscious product placement in a familiar setting is a subliminal way of perpetuating the command to go forth and consume. Capitalist-created "lifestyles" are social constructs in which we can imagine ourselves living and consuming. Those created worlds allow us to

---

16 Morales, 16.

17 Max Horkheimer and Theodor Adorno, "The Culture Industry: Enlightenment as Mass Deception," in *Dialectic of Enlightenment*, edited by Mieke Bal and Hent deVries, translated by Edmund Jephcott, 94-136 (Stanford: Stanford University Press, 2002), 111.

temporarily sidestep immediate realities and retreat into our own personal worlds of fantasy and desire. This desire for meaning that advertising preys upon is the desire for a living context, a community that brings coherence to our reality and that gives our experiences meaning. While capitalist aesthetics has mastered the importance of context, it is essentially an unreal context. In a brief essay critical of mass culture, "The Herd of Independent Minds," cultural analyst and art critic Harold Rosenberg drew an important distinction between *"common experiences* which are the substance of mass culture," and *"common situations* in which human beings find themselves." Rosenberg continued:

> The common situation is precisely what the common experience with its mass-culture texture conceals, *and is often intended to conceal.* ... To penetrate through the common experience to the actual situation from which all suffer requires a creative act – that is to say, an act that directly grasps the life of people during, say, a war, that grasps the war from the inside, so to speak, as a situation with a human being in it.[18]

Rosenberg's distinction is crucial to understanding the importance of recognizing how mass culture manipulates the public. To create effective political art, the political artist must seek to grasp insights from within the real situations that challenge the so-called common experiences and expose their falsity: "Only the individual can communicate experience, and only another individual can receive such a communication," Rosenberg concluded.[19]

Social anarchist art requires the conscious creation of a realizable free place, a place in which free people can

---

18 Harold Rosenberg, "The Herd of Independent Minds," in *Discovering the Present: Three Decades in Art, Culture, and Politics* (Chicago and London, The University of Chicago Press, 1973), 18-19.

19 Ibid., 27.

be at home. It must be a real place, in a geographic space, say, our own neighborhoods – the spaces in which we live and transform our everyday lives. The Situationist International technique of derive was designed specifically to identify and transform our relationship with our physical environment. If freedom is to be realized in a real future time, the path forward must begin in a real and present time and place. In addition, it must be perceived as potentially stable and permanent instead of temporary. Re-making place has to be a conscious artistic and political activity. Graffiti artists and muralists in particular are acutely aware of the power of images to control spatial reality. The practice of detourning billboards, creating new works of street art, or covering public wall spaces with murals and graffiti celebrating neighborhood life, all reflect this impulse to redefine meaning, to take control of public visual space, and to connect people to their lived environment.

An ongoing challenge facing social anarchist artists is integrating the diversity of our political culture with its rich variety of identity, linguistic, and ethnic communities into a broader political meta-narrative. Theatre director and designer Sal Salerno pointed out that the Industrial Workers of the World (IWW) faced a similar challenge in organizing the diverse immigrant populations arriving in the United States at the turn of the twentieth century. Salerno concluded that they were successful in creating "a common cultural sphere whereby the various ethnic groups could be united on the basis of shared sentiment."[20] By organizing workplace communities into what they called the One Big Union, the Wobblies were able to bring these different groups to a shared political awareness of their similar plights. In the contemporary world there will likely be new communities, new networks that will bring

---

20 Salvatore Salerno, *Red November Black November: Culture and Community in the Industrial Workers of the World* (Albany, NY: SUNY Press, 1989), 149.

people together in a meta-narrative to overcome fragmentation, while at the same time honoring and respecting their unique stories. To expand one's current world requires that the new world both accommodate and transform the known reality. At the same time, meta-narratives must maintain sensitivity to particular community representations in the artistic vision. Several of British artist Banksy's creations for the wall in Palestine, for example, were criticized as culturally insensitive. One of his images of a rat with a slingshot was destroyed because Palestinians were offended by his portrayal of fighters as rats.[21]

Minnesota photographer Wing Young Huie understood the importance of grounding his work in a real and diverse community. His University Avenue Project was an ambitious effort to capture and to portray the diversity of communities living along a major urban thoroughfare.[22] Between May and October of 2010, he displayed hundreds of photographs taken along a six-mile length of University Avenue which stretches from Saint Paul to Minneapolis in Minnesota. Multiple ethnic communities call University Avenue home; and over the life of project installations it was their diverse images that graced storefronts, walls, and bus shelters. He engaged the participation of his subjects by asking permission to take their photographs and then asking them if they wanted to comment on who they were, what they thought, what was important to them, or what race meant to them. Many of the photographs bear witness to their commitment to and engagement with the project. A young girl held up a sign that read, "My life can't be all about me"; a mother wrote, "I dream of my daughter's future"; a little girl wrote "I don't see myself as Asian but as a person (which she represented with a drawing of

---

21 William Parry, *Against the Wall: The Art of Resistance in Palestine* (Chicago: Lawrence Hill Books, 2011), 51.

22 Wing Young Huie, *The University Avenue Project: The Language of Urbanism: A Six-Mile Photographic Inquiry,* Vols. 1 and 2, Saint Paul, MN: Minnesota Historical Society, 2010.

a stick figure of a human being)." An older man held up a sign that said, "Race is an unfair tool by which to measure a person's character." Huie's conversations with the community continued over the course of the several months. He invited residents living along University Avenue to outdoor presentations of the photographs which were projected on the sides of buildings. Again, people were invited to discuss the images. In a televised interview Huie discussed the role of the independent artist, saying that he was honored that the project gave him an opportunity to "collaborate with everyone I photographed." In many ways his project was an excellent example of the situationist technique of derive, with Huie as the artist wandering through a neighborhood, seeking to create a holistic and reconstructed meaning out of the many fragments of rich life around him. The "place" of University Avenue has been enriched as a result of this work, and the art has created a venue for communication about matters of personal and political importance.

Political messages must be designed to articulate to and be understood in different cultural contexts. This is yet another way to bring people of diverse backgrounds into a shared community. Meaning is not abstract but grounded in specific communities and contexts. Graphic novelist Lynd Ward noted that honoring multiple contexts is especially important in graphic communication. He calls these contexts "communities of experience".[23]

> While it may be quite logical to count on a community of experience in a specific area – for example, we are all children and many of us are fathers and mothers – it is probably hazardous to expect that everyone will have a sufficiently similar background to ensure the easy recognition of every visual element encountered. Involvement in the narrative, of

---

23 Not to be confused with Rosenberg's concept discussed previously.

course, depends upon this immediate recognition. But then there is the further demand that a single image must convey not only what it literally is but must also give some understanding of what, by virtue of the associations and meanings the cultural matrix has given it, it symbolizes. It is to this duality of meaning that the best of pictorial narrative aspires. It must communicate on both levels.[24]

Creating a universally understandable context is a special challenge when trying to convey political messages. The messages must be sufficiently universal to bring easy recognition to most readers. In my own research I am continually searching for images without words where the image itself carries the message. The most effective images in the future, I believe, will be those that convey concepts and ideas across cultural borders, yet at the same time, resonate with individual cultural perspectives.

Social anarchist art must also be grounded in the historical context of people struggling to achieve their freedom. Understanding resistance across time further grounds the truth of resistance today. The awareness of shared contexts across time serves to reduce the sense of alienation and isolation. The inspiration for overcoming oppression depends upon bringing to life a lived sense of those freedoms.

The centrality of narrative

We need stories, as writer Boria Sax argues, because "without stories we would be overwhelmed by the vast number of things that seem to clamor for our attention."[25] The most powerful instrument for bringing

---

24 Lynd Ward, "On Madman's Drum," in Lynd Ward, *Six Novels in Woodcuts*, ed. Art Spiegelman (New York, NY: The Library of America, 2010), 790.

25 Boria Sax, "Storytelling and the 'Information Overload,'" *On the*

order out of chaos and fragmentation is the creation of a new story. In a recent review of a Museum of Modern Art retrospective on abstraction, art critic Peter Schjeldahl agreed: "We need stories. When they are banished within art [his criticism of abstraction], they re-form around and about it."[26] The fragmentation of the postmodern world cries out for new, meaningful narratives, stories that can make sense of our lives and of our times and that can counter the hyper-real narrative of capitalism. Narrative creates connectedness and shared meaning as we weave together the bits and pieces of our experiences, of the world around us, of our hopes and dreams. According to Raymond Tallis, "In practice, we are always trying to redeem our sense of being fragmented by means of the stories we recount about ourselves and each other and our world."[27]

The affective element is also an important aspect in political art, and should be incorporated into political art. The art should tell the story at many levels – cognitive as well as emotional. While ideas can inspire action, an emotional commitment is necessary for sustaining permanent change. Narrative engages the emotions; we are "caught up" in a story, following it to the end. As writer and editor Stevphen Shukaitis pointed out in *Imaginal Machines: Autonomy and Self-Organization in the Revolutions of Everyday Life*, "in order for political speech to cause affective resonance, conditions need to exist for the constituted audience to be able to identify with those who are expressing them, to possess a capacity to affect and be affected."[28]

A narrative provides coherence to art, the steps in a journey that is real and meaningful. A new context is

---

Horizon 14, 3 (Fall 2006), 147-151.

26 Peter Schjeldahl, "Shapes of Things: The Birth of the Abstract," *The New Yorker* (January 7, 2013), 68.

27 Tallis.

28 Stevphen Shukaitis, *"Imaginal Machines: Autonomy and Self-Organization in the Revolutions of Everyday Life* (London/NYC/Port Watson: Minor Compositions, 2009), 102.

created where both the artist and the viewer are partners in change, traveling to a new land, new economic practices, new beliefs, new politics and new dreams. There is an implicit sequential continuity to narrative work, a continuity that connects with the direct experience of the reader. The narrative also implies that the journey is not just random. Further, there is a conclusion to the journey, a closure that contains what used to be called "the moral of the story." The narrative offers a shared memory of feeling and experience, a re-collecting of knowledge, and a predictable process.

A social anarchist aesthetic is also concerned with the general ambiance or an attitude of wholeness and completeness that is expressed in the work of art. A work of art of any sort must be created and comprehended as a whole, and all aspects of the work need to be integrated. In the process of arranging the parts, there is always the need to understand and to express the whole, to see it emerge from the process itself and to result in a completion. Here is where postmodern art generally fails us. It refuses and even denies that there is a coherent context, a meaningful reality – even in the work of art itself.

Stability of context and clarity of vision are glaringly absent in consumer aesthetics. Advertising art is built on the premise that destabilization and an ever-changing social landscape sells more products. Rather than collective closure, there is only the individual experience of personal pleasure presumably shared by the rest of society. The "new" consumer product becomes the next achievable pleasure that at the same time remains out of reach. Several critics have argued that postmodern art mirrors only the fragmentation of the reality that capitalist aesthetics creates, pulling us from one perspective to another. According to anarchist activist and educator Cindy Milstein, "Contemporary artwork that portrays fragmentation serves only to mimic rather than to decry our societal 'breaking apart,' precisely because the damage has already been done. So, here comes one task for art: to depict resistance not as fragmentation per se ... but to illustrate how social acquiescence to it has become a valued commodity."[29] Coherence and stability must anchor the worldview underlying the artistic vision. It is not just a matter of holding a mirror up to the broken world; the artist must find a way to show how those fragments can be reassembled into a new vision.

The fragmentation of experience and resistance to organization and structure everywhere characterizes postmodern reality. Echoing Errico Malatesta, Cohn observed, "Fragmentation ... is simply the secret of authority's success."[30] It has even generated its own pseudophilosophy – deconstructionism. Contemporary avant-garde artists revel in new ideas and constant change and disruption. But these disruptions do not necessarily lead to substantive political and cultural change and may, in fact, only be passing fancies, new fashions in the ongoing marketplace. Harold Rosenberg described in detail the pitfalls confronting the avant-garde in a capitalist society:

> In all its qualities – ephemeralness, shock, exoticism, competitiveness – avant-garde art is haunted by fashion, the chief resources of which are also novelty and attention-getting. ... But in entering the world of fashion the avant-garde finds itself in a trap. Fashion injects vanguard creations with a transience different from the epochal span that each avant-garde expects its revelations to define.[31]

29 Cindy Milstein, "Reappropriate the Imagination!" in *Realizing The Impossible: Art Against Authority*, eds., Josh MacPhee and Erik Reuland (Oakland, CA: AK Press, 2007), 302.

30 Jesse Cohn, "NeMe: Anarchism, Representation, and Culture." January 16, 2006. http://www.neme.org/main/310/anarchism-representation-and-culture

31 Rosenberg, "The Avant-Garde," in *Discovering the Present*, 85-86.

Rosenberg concludes, "In sum, avant-garde today means a flurry of fashion, whether in painting, sex, or insurrectionary politics."[32] In many ways the avant-garde as an effective political force has been corrupted and bankrupted. The challenge for the social anarchist artist is to find those irrecuperable elements of real contexts and real narratives that will persist beyond the ephemeral and temporary. Postmodernism with its deconstructionist tools created fragments; but, as poet Jude Nutter observed, there is always potential in those fragments: "fragments are the story, without them there can be no story."[33] A transformative art weaves these fragments together and in the process mends the culture. Social anarchist art must tell a story that creates a new social reality out of the fragments of the old. Stories are grounded in a social reality; they assume a dialogue between a narrator and an audience; they come to a conclusion and have meaning. Storytelling is also a very effective way of communicating the complex visions and messages of political change. According to Sax,

> The toughness and flexibility of storytelling make narrative especially important in periods of transition, particularly at the origin of new religions, ideologies, institutions, or technologies. Storytelling is especially effective because it has a sensuality that places it especially close to experience. Tales evoke sights, smells and sounds, while philosophies and precepts usually do not. For another thing, storytelling has great flexibility. Narratives can more easily be adjusted to different eras and circumstances than can rules or ideologies.[34]

32 Rosenberg, "The Avant-Garde," 86.
33 Jude Nutter, "Untitled," *I Wish I Had a Heart Like Yours, Walt Whitman* (Notre Dame, IN: University of Notre Dame Press, 2009), 8.
34 Sax.

The link between a visual narrative and political reality will become increasingly important as our society moves away from a print to a visual culture. Although vision is our most powerful sense, our visual reality is a constant sea of movement; and a narrative is the best means by which we can bring order to the visual chaos. Graphic novels, comic books, and political cartoons and posters have proven especially effective in sharing political messages.[35] Lynd Ward's graphic novels portraying the economic and political realities of the Great Depression were extremely popular. He described the graphic novel as a visual experience where "communication of what *is* and what *is happening* is accomplished entirely or predominantly in visual terms."[36] Ward's artistry reflected the two central aspects of narrative art: communication and representation. An effective visual narrative can be easily "read," the meaning quickly grasped. In his introduction to a collection of Ward's novels, Art Spiegelman noted, "It can be contended that a balance between formal qualities in visual expression and concern with having something to say has resulted in some of the greatest visual statements of the past."[37] He observed that "wordless novels are *filled* with language; it just resides in the reader's head rather than on the page."[38]

Comics are also grounded in strong narrative messages. In *Understanding Comics: The Invisible Art*, comics artist Scott McCloud outlines some of the characteristic techniques of visual narratives. Comics are a "sequential" art

---

35 See David A. Berona, *Wordless Books: The Original Graphic Novels* (New York, NY: Abrams, 2008). For an especially fine collection of wordless novels see Lynd Ward, *Six Novels in Woodcuts*, ed. Art Spiegelman (New York, NY: Library of America, 2010).

36 Lynd Ward, "On God's Man," in Lynd Ward, *Six Novels in Woodcuts*, 781.

37 Art Spiegelman, "Reading Pictures: A Few Thousand Words on Six Books without Any," Introduction to Lynd Ward, *Six Novels in Woodcuts*. Quoting Lynd Ward, xi.

38 Art Spiegelman, "Reading Pictures," xvi.

that calls for "reading" a visual story line, combining words and images to tell stories: "In comics at its best, words and pictures are like partners in a dance and each one takes turns leading."[39] Comics also require more significant participation by viewer/readers than other art forms. Finally, McCloud makes a case for the power of comics to engage all of the senses, not just the visual, through the techniques of line, shape and color to produce emotional responses. Well-crafted narratives are easily remembered and emotionally satisfying, integrating sight and feeling.

A narrative can serve as a guide to attend to certain elements in the visual experience more seriously, to "capture" (a word I use with some caution) our attention and focus our thinking. Political art assumes a speaker, a vocabulary, and a narrative (whether visual or literary) that are common to the audience and are integral to creating a new, coherent meaning. As author Robert Wilson observed, "Narratives intersect and diverge, combine and recombine. Understanding one narrative may require the creation of another. Most fundamentally, narrative is *how* we understand. Narrative is how we understand the universe; and it is, most obviously, how we understand ourselves."[40]

THE SOCIAL ANARCHIST ARTIST AND THE AVANT-GARDE

HENRI DE SAINT-SIMON coined the term "avant-garde" in the early nineteenth century when it was used to describe military leadership.[41] Subsequently the definition was expanded to express leadership generally (a vanguard) and to express the idea of challenging the status quo in the arts by breaking through existing aesthetic conventions.

---

39 Scott McCloud, *Understanding Comics: The Invisible Art* (Northampton, MA: Tundra Publishing Ltd., 1993), 156.

40 Robert Charles Wilson, *Blind Lake* (New York, NY: Tom Doherty, 2003), 261.

41 David Graeber, "The Twilight of Vanguardism," in *Realizing The Impossible: Art Against Authority*, eds. Josh MacPhee and Erik Reuland (Oakland, CA: AK Press, 2007), 251.

Avant-garde artists were artists who positioned themselves outside of and against the traditional techniques,
forms, or content, while simultaneously advocating a new
approach to art. In this meaning, any art movement that
breaks with the past and creates new trends or new fashions is avant-garde.

Another sense of the term combines political and aesthetic meanings: artists are messengers of change and cultural
advancement. An avant-garde artist is meant to be disruptive, to challenge the status quo, to jolt us out of our current
reality, to get us to stop and think. The idea of an avant-
garde was especially attractive to those artists who nurtured
the role of an alienated outsider critical of the mainstream
– a role that they shared with anarchists. Throughout history a core premise of aesthetics has been the assumption
that art – and by extension the artist – has some kind of
intrinsic power to influence people. What the origin of that
power is and what to do with that power are both a political
and an aesthetic question. However, arts activist, poet, and
playwright Alice Loveless warned artists:

> This is something most artists truly believe,
> that they are exceptional people with so much
> to teach others. They believe they have power
> and education and want to share it.
>
> My truth has shown me that it is best to
> come to this work naked – stripped of your
> sense of power and exceptionalism. Come un-
> derstanding that you do not possess anything
> that does not already exist in the community.
> Come understanding that if you are lucky,
> they will teach you something. Come know-
> ing that your job is to ensure that the commu-
> nity recognizes it does not need you – that the
> work is in their hands and that it is their work,
> not yours.[42]

---

42 Alice Lovelace, "come to this work naked …," in *Wild Caught Stories*.

The social anarchist artist has to consciously and actively reject a leadership role and avoid being seduced by the idea that art has power that the individual can wield. There are serious criticisms of the idea of an avant-garde. According to author Michael Scrivener, the communist anarchist Peter Kropotkin was an early critic of the idea of an avant-garde art: "Nietzsche, the aesthetes, the symbolists, the new anarchists in France sympathetic with the avant-garde, were all labeled by Kropotkin as bourgeois individualists, self-indulgent, and irresponsible."[43] Kropotkin argued instead for an unalienated art, an art that would reflect a utopian end to political and aesthetic struggle. Scrivener disagreed, however, and went on to argue that the idea of an avant-garde will likely persist since there really can be no unalienated future art because art will always undertake new directions. While most theorists accept that the artist must maintain a critical perspective, the extent of their alienation from the social reality, however, is still at issue, particularly for the political artist. There is no guarantee, for example, that avant-garde artists are committed to radical politics, or that radical artists are elitist in that sense of avant-garde.

More recently, anarchist David Graeber explored the relationship between the avant-garde and anarchism in a positive light. The fact that anarchist ideas strongly influenced nineteenth and twentieth century avant-garde artists especially impressed him: "The number of nineteenth century artists with anarchist sympathies is quite staggering," he observed, and they "defined themselves, like anarchists, by a certain form of practice rather than after

---

5, If community engaged art making is transformational, what are the moral and ethical dimensions of the work? (Center for the Study of Art and Community, Bainbridge Island, WA, November 16, 2008). www.artandcommunity.com

43 Michael Scrivener, "The Anarchist Aesthetic," *Black Rose* 1, 1 (1979), 15.

some heroic founder."[44] Graeber sees this anarchist "form of practice" as a fusion of artist and anarchist politics.

Seeking new paths to freedom requires critiquing existing realities. One of the key characteristics of anarchism is its emphasis on the necessity of analyzing and critiquing from "outside" the current reality. This critical stance allows the anarchist artist to be open to new perspectives. Like Theodor Adorno and Frederic Jameson, Graeber argued that the social anarchist artist must maintain a critical perspective about both his or her art and the social reality in which that art is created. He asked himself why, across time, artists were drawn to revolutionary politics and concluded, "It seems to me the answer must have something to do with alienation."[45] But, this alienation does not mean withdrawal; it means up-close critical engagement with the current political reality as part of the process of creating new visions. Adopting a critical stance is a conscious effort to remain immersed in empirical reality but alert to the latent elements of potentiality in the culture that will lead to a better world.

Artists need to assess their own motivations and they need to fully understand the implications of those motivations in the political sphere. Kenyan poet and playwright Ngugi Wa Thiong'o argued that artists consciously have to align their art with a political agenda. This alignment requires a serious commitment to engagement with the real world and to a careful analysis and illumination of the political environment. He suggested that artists who seek to undertake political art consider the following questions:

1. Will the artist choose the angle of vision of the possessing classes? Or will he choose the angle of vision of the dispossessed?

2. Is the artist operating in a situation in which he is continually being harassed by

---

44 Graeber, 252, 253.
45 Graeber, 253.

the state, or continually under the threat
of harassment?

3. Is he operating within a social structure
    that inhibits all social systems?[46]

The first question requires the artist to make a choice
that will influence subsequent responses. The answer to
the second question speaks to the artist's role as critic and
affirms the awareness that political art is potentially a dangerous undertaking, requiring a serious commitment. The
role of critic is never a neutral one. The third question challenges the artist to understand the nature of oppression
and what limitations must be overcome in the process of
creating alternative social systems and alternative visions.

Maintaining a critical stance is especially important if
the artist is to avoid succumbing to a vision of the artist as
a wielder of power. Graeber concluded that artists might
be able to avoid the seductions of power by constantly re-
assessing political agendas so that they do not fall victim
to co-optation or compromise.[47] A critical stance – including self criticism – plays an important role in keeping art
and the artist free, continually open to making new adjust-
ments to the political environment, open to confronting
new forms of oppression, and continually moving ahead
with alternative visions.

CONFRONTING POWER: THE ROLE OF SOCIAL ANARCHIST AESTHETICS

A CENTRAL THEME in political art is power – who has it,
who doesn't have it, how it operates in our communities,
how it affects us personally, how it must be overcome.

---

46 Ngugi Wa Thiong'o, "Freedom of the Artist: People's Artists versus
    People's Rulers," *Art on the Line, Essays by Artists about the Point Where
    Their Art & Activism Intersect*, ed. Jack Hirschman (Williamantic,
    CN: Curbstone Press, 2002), 207-208.

47 Graeber, 253.

An aesthetic grounded in community will be especially concerned about communal relatedness in the context of political power relations, about defining and expressing a culture of political resistance, and about nourishing a hunger for freedom and an alternative world. Art that does not directly challenge oppressive power structures is not sufficiently political. However, just being "against" is not sufficient either – critical art must undermine and transform the balance of power in the culture. Power always operates in a particular time and place. The social anarchist artist has a special responsibility to portray place as a nexus of power relations. Marxist aesthetician Adolpho Vásquez in his essay "Truly Popular Art" argued that art should always be consciously political and ideological. Further, art could not be true art unless it was tendentious.[48] Art must always challenge, always express a specific point of view, expose the power operating against people, and influence a challenge to that power. What drives its purpose is the desire for freedom, however latent that desire may appear to be in the culture. The existing power context must be illuminated and be dialectically situated in opposition to a new alternative context, one free of domination and exploitation.

As Pat Kane observed, artistic efforts that challenge dominant messages are especially dangerous: "The need to persuade, seduce and command attention – in short, the arts of rhetoric – have always been suspected by the powerful. ... Those who want their authority to be based on a stable interpretation of reality will be suspicious of those who mess that up, who allow style and substance to intermingle."[49] Art is uniquely positioned to shape powerful political messages, Kane believes, because

---

48 Adolpho Sánchez Vázquez, *Art and Society: Essays in Marxist Aesthetics* (New York, NY and London: Monthly Review Press, 1973).

49 Pat Kane, "Review of *The Economics of Attention* by Richard A. Lanham," *The Independent*, July 14, 2006.

artists are the ultimate "economists of attention," who think with the most sophistication about grabbing their chunk of our mind-share. They want us both to look through their artworks to the reality behind, and look at their artworks to enjoy the artifice of communication. ... [T]hat forces us to dwell on our tricky relationship with reality and its representation.[50]

The analysis and critique of all types of power relations should be transparent in a social anarchist aesthetic. By deconstructing the effects of power in whatever guise it is manifested, a progressive aesthetic celebrates and empowers people. Empowerment is at the heart of anarchist politics and art. An art of empowerment is essential to help move people toward greater freedom and greater control over their lives. The artist must confront and challenge the power relations by embedding alternative acts of resistance in the work of art. The analysis and critique of power relations should be sufficiently broad and complex to illuminate how power influences our lives and how people can realize their own power.

The more active artists become in political communities, the more the experience of working with others will shape their vision. One of the major shortcomings of Socialist Realism, according to John Roberts, was that the art was often alienated from political activities going on around it and from real empowering activities underway: "There is never a moment's recognition that people are already engaged in practices in the world which are critical and transformative."[51] Cindy Milstein challenged artists to portray power as it operates in everyday life:

---

50 Kane.

51 John Roberts, "Commentaries: Art, Politics and Provincialism," *Radical Philosophy* (March/April 2001). http://www.radicalphiloso-phy.com

"Contemporary art should, instead, scrutinize and expose present-day mechanisms of power: how the mundane as well as the lovely – the bus to work, the toothpaste tube, or the nice new neighbor – are made into objects of anxiety-as-control."[52] She called for an "art-as-dialogue, working together to both critique and reconstruct our lived public places."[53]

In *Surplus Powerlessness*, Michael Lerner argued that building community through political involvement is one of the most effective means of overcoming powerlessness. [54] As a society the ethics of the marketplace have shaped us by separating us from meaningful community, lulling us into passivity, and molding us into isolated individual selves. In place of meaningful political and economic communities, some Americans have retreated into various substitute communities such as the family, consumer lifestyles, and religions. Many of these communities reinforce isolation and passivity if they remain apolitical. Just by being engaged in politics, Lerner believes, people can build community and become empowered together: "Politics is a kind of community production – and the product that is being produced is the future. ... [P]eople begin to act as though what is going to happen in history is not independent of what they do. They can play a decisive role in the outcomes."[55] By recognizing and honoring transformative activities as they are happening, the community is further empowered.

Challenging the power of the state

Post-anarchism's emphasis on culture as the battleground for political engagement has obscured

---

52 Milstein, 303.

53 Milstein, 306.

54 Michael Lerner, *Surplus Powerlessness: The Psychodynamics of Everyday Life ... and the Psychology of Individual and Social Transformation* (Oakland, CA: The Institute for Labor and Mental Health, 1986), 253.

55 Lerner, 230.

the importance of the traditional anarchist challenge to the state and state power. How social anarchist art portrays the state therefore, is crucial to refocusing critical attention to the systemic and organizational oppression that the state practices.

James Koehnline's political images include many powerful messages about the role of government in our lives.[56] Koehnline's work is an example of political art that is relatively easy to "read." In some political art, artists build political messages into the title. Linking the title to the image can work, and the viewer may have an "aha" experience. But in the case of Koehnline's work, the symbols portrayed convey the principle message; and the title merely reinforces or exaggerates the message. "Seizure and Forfeiture," for example, is a detournement of the iconic "Uncle Sam Wants You" recruitment poster. The title reads, "I want yours, I seize, You forfeit." "Skull and Bones," which also graced the Spring 2004 cover of *Fifth Estate* magazine, includes images of George W. Bush and John Kerry, both members of the Yale society of the same name. Both men, as representatives of the state, represent death. In "Bunker," George W. Bush is portrayed peeking out fearfully from behind a pyramid, looking at the Department of Homeland's color coding of security levels. In the background are skulls and crossbones, missiles, and corporate logos. Bush appears again in "Out of the Burning Bush," a reflection on 9/11. The pyramid is a common symbol in Koehnline's work. He has effectively appropriated the pyramid image from the back of the Great Seal of the United States. This same image is portrayed on the back of the dollar bill. The "eye of providence" appears in political imagery of both the left and the right carrying connotations of spying. Its meaning seems to vary from context to context, but seems to imply

---

56 James Koehnline. See www.koehnline.com for background information on the artist, and www.james119.deviantart.com/gallery to view the body of his work.

surveillance, the power structures that rule the world, and various conspiracy theories about the Illuminati or the mafia. In Koehline's work it is often linked to corporate and governmental power.

The absence of government images can also convey powerful political messages by offering an alternative narrative about state power to the one the state projects. In "'We Will Continue:' Street Art in Oaxaca," writer John Gibler contrasts revolutionary stenciled graffiti art posted on walls throughout Oaxaca with official communication by the state through mainstream media. Official media carries apolitical message – reality shows and local innocuous news; the revolutionaries portray another reality on the streets – graffiti images of Molotov cocktails, raised fists, and timely political messages. "[Y]ou walk out into the street and watch the walls as you walk and the walls tell you that the police assassinate, that 22 murders of activists in your town remain in impunity, and that people keep organizing, people rise up, people fight back."[57] The graffiti is quickly painted over; but its effectiveness remains like an afterimage. And just as quickly the political messages are replaced.

Challenging capitalism

A crucial challenge is how to portray and to undermine the hegemony of global corporate capitalism. Critiquing that world and then creating transformative visions of that world should be a primary goal of the social anarchist artist. Behind the curtain of capitalist aesthetics are also real people and real institutions – first and foremost the transnational corporation. Exposing the corporate power behind the imagery is a formidable challenge. Simply countering corporate messages in provocative or satirical ways does not get to the hard realities of who makes the decisions and how global capitalist power

---

57 John Gibler, "'We Will Continue': Street Art in Oaxaca," *Fifth Estate* 380 (Spring 2009), 36.

is wielded. An artistic assault on global capitalism must have a global "face" reflecting the international and interlocking nature of corporate capitalism's reach.

There are many examples of efforts to portray the power of global corporations. In many of his political works, Koehnline effectively portrays the linkages between the state and corporate power. "Burning the Midnight Oil" combines ecological and political messages, highlighting the interlocking relationships between fire and destruction, oil, the United States Capital building, and a highway. In "New World Order," corporate logos and names grace a huge matrix extending to infinity. "Empire of the Dead" is a landscape of corporate logos. "Pandora's New Box" portrays contemporary horrors in a skull and crossbones landscape where corporate logos cover the sides of Koehnline's pyramid of power. To the left of the pyramid, familiar symbols warning of danger erupt from the top of the pyramid.

One persistent image in the radical culture is the world-controlling octopus. The 2003 award-winning Swedish film, *Surplus: Terrorized into being Consumers*, is another powerful example of how to educate people about the complexity of global capitalism.[58] The film does an excellent job of linking the inanity of the consumer culture with destruction of the planet, the oppression of workers in the developing world, the corporate mentality, the collusion of governments, and radical black bloc activism. Another, older film – the futuristic silent film *Metropolis* – can also serve as an example of effective use of imagery to convey strong political messages about the corporate agenda.[59]

---

58 *Surplus: Terrorized into being Consumers*, a film by Erik Gandini, ed. Johan Söderberg. Produced by ATMO for Swedish Television. 2003, 52 minutes. Available in English, French, Spanish, Portugese, Italian, and Swedish. Winner of the Silver Wolf Award, IDFA Amsterdam, 2003. The film is available on YouTube in sections.

59 *Metropolis*, directed by Fritz Lang, Germany, 1927. Restored 2002, with original music score. Available on DVD with subtitles in

The film is set in the year 2026 and is a powerful graphic message about the exploitation of labor. Unfortunately, the love story narrative line doesn't play well in today's political culture. Nevertheless, the film is worth studying for the power of its imagery.

Despite several prominent clashes with the world's economic leaders, beginning in Seattle in 1999, the anarchist-inspired global anti-corporate movement has made little headway in educating people to the magnitude and danger of the power of corporations shaping their lives. Relying on access to the mainstream media to communicate an alternative vision is by and large a losing cause. After a decade of activism, mainstream television media coverage of political protest activities is still largely limited to endless loops of windows being smashed by masked individuals dressed in black. The protesters' behavior is never examined or explained. The 2011 protests across Europe, for example, did not adequately portray the economics behind the austerity measures and how they led to the protests. The underlying political narrative is purposely ignored. The continual reproduction of black bloc images by the mass media has served only to discredit anti-globalization and anti-corporate actions, to obscure the message, and to close off communication with people who might otherwise be sympathetic.

The Occupy Wall Street movement has opened up the possibility of changing the narrative that the mainstream media portrays. To overlook the presence of protesters in the home territory of corporate power – Wall Street – is difficult. The anarchist political message was conveyed to the majority of the American people in ways that had immediate relevance to them: protesters set up living room furniture in the lobbies of large banks, created an alternative social and political structure in a small park down the street from the world's largest investment firms, occupied foreclosed homes, and designed protest posters drawing

English, French, and Spanish. Kino Video, NY.

sharp distinctions between the wealthy one percent and the ninety-nine percent of people excluded from wealth. Nevertheless, the media is not interested in communicating what the Occupy Wall Street protesters are doing internal to their community, what issues they are discussing, how they are involving others – especially their work in hurricane Sandy relief. The TV cameras only appear when direct confrontation with the state is likely to occur.

To overcome the dominance of mainstream media communication, political artists have successfully exploited alternative media for sharing political messages – creating networks on the internets, YouTube films, full length documentaries, live streaming, and comic books, Facebook pages, among others. Two dimensional graphic artworks can be especially effective in communicating political messages, and posters are successfully communicate political messages: they can be reproduced and shared easily as posters or via the internets, on T-shirts, or posted in a public space.

Challenging advertising art

Advertising is global capitalism's primary representational tool; it is powerful, and it works. The challenge for the social anarchist artist is to break through this unreality. Advertising doesn't challenge anything; it doesn't expose the nature of exploitation, doesn't raise questions about existing economic and power relations. It reinforces passivity, assuring people that the status quo is okay and that no change is necessary. It doesn't inspire political action or an understanding of our connections with one another. It can reflect nostalgically on real or imagined times gone by, it can fantasize about a capitalist future reality, but it can never empower or make that reality happen.

Co-optation is always a threat to art in a market economy. Powerful memes are recuperated quickly, and their message is tied to expanded consumption. Even political art runs the risk of becoming just another object for endless reproduction and mass consumption. Capitalism profits from art in several ways: by standardizing it, appropriating it to sell the "new", and mass marketing it as just another object to be consumed. Once art becomes a commodity and no longer has a higher purpose, it loses any real value as "art" in the sense that we are proposing here – it has been captured and put to the service of corporate power.

Capitalist aesthetics thrives on standardization. Political art, on the other hand, celebrates complexity; and complexity challenges the mind-numbing repetitiveness of modern advertising. To challenge standardization, social anarchist realism must communicate that the world around us has multiple realities and that another world is possible. Successful social anarchist art will avoid the tyranny of standardization and, instead, recognize and celebrate a multiplicity of human perspectives.

Creating political memes that are not recuperable is also an especially effective technique. There are many examples that have remained free of corporate cooptation: The raised fist, the recent image of the policeman pepperspraying student protesters, the Guy Fawkes mask, the Abu Ghraib hood – all have so far remained in the radical domain. These are effective because they are perceived to be a break with the current situation and because they have embedded within them criticism as well as the potential for alternatives to the status quo.

The Situationist International understood the vast reach of global capitalism which they named the "spectacle", and they felt that global capitalism must be challenged in its own territory, its most visible face – advertising art. If capitalist imagery is deconstructed, they argued, a visible rupture opens up the possibility for new symbolic imagery. The SI, and their aesthetic heirs, Adbusters, developed many excellent theoretical tools to challenge advertising art; those tools must be accessible to everyone to effectively undermine the structures of advertising power. Information and reflection alone are not sufficient. Activists must put into practice the insights of the SI and create an action agenda.

Advertising is perceived by everyone to be manipulation. People aren't sure why or how, but they know that they are being "worked on". People are also generally aware of propaganda, although they connect it with politics. They do not consciously label advertising as propaganda. Nevertheless, the advertising industry is acutely aware of how to use propaganda techniques effectively. Propaganda is not a new phenomenon in human communication. Beginning with Plato's warnings about the manipulative powers of the skilled rhetorician, questions about control of message have been central to all political discourse. Should the political artist use these propaganda techniques to communicate a message of social change and political action? Can the artist persuade without manipulating? It would be naïve to assume that social anarchist artists would forego using these techniques. So the answer is a qualified yes. The techniques can be used, but with some careful consideration and reflection on the artist's intentions and the social significance of the outcomes. For propaganda to be really effective, however, it must resonate deeply with the hopes and dreams of the community. It cannot be imposed from above.

Some propaganda techniques can be used without manipulating the audience. The techniques themselves are neutral. They can be used to coerce or to empower. So how does the political artist make a distinction between persuasion and propaganda? First, more attention could be paid by political activists to educate the general public about how these techniques work. The technique of detournement effectively educates people to the truth behind advertising, exposing how advertising first embeds reality in artificial constructs then twists the meaning. Second, since these techniques will be used to consciously convey radical messages, the artist has a heavy responsibility to ensure that the techniques used have clearly defined and transparent outcomes. A heavy dose of self-criticism is essential, with a careful examination of personal motivations and perspectives.

Finally, grounding both the techniques and the outcomes in realism can also mitigate some of these concerns. The primary role of political art is to reflect the reality of people lives and transform their reality into a vision of a better future. True political art will also be more transparent if it reflects the real social aspirations (rather than product consumption desires) that inspired the art in the first place.

NOURISHING THE IMAGINATIVE: A BRIDGE TO THE POSSIBLE

AS THEODOR ADORNO observed, it is the dialectic between the real in which we are grounded and the possible to which we aspire that creates the tension of great art. The biggest challenge for social anarchist artists is bringing the real and the possible together. The possible, of course, is always latent in the real. The challenge to art is to awaken that potential, to visualize, and to vitalize it. Social anarchist art is about representing life, according to Cohn: "By 'life,' we mean not only the actual but also the plural *potentials* which are dormant within it. … There is no potential which does not emerge from some concrete actuality; conversely, there is no actuality which does not harbor[sic] multiple potentialities."[60] The new world must be a realizable world, not abstract or idealized.

The social anarchist artist must take on the additional task of representing the potential for change itself. As Kenneth Heilman and Russel Donda reminded us, all people have a capacity for change: "It is an individual's ability to diverge from what is familiar and move beyond the known into a new understanding which is the essence

---

60 Cohn, "What is anarchist literary theory?" 124.

of creativity, and that which gives rise to advancement."[61] People who believe they can change are more likely to act on that belief. Social anarchist art can actualize this ability to change our worldview by building a bridge to an alternative that incorporates an ongoing process for change in an arena of political action. Cohn observed that

> a key function of radical art is to facilitate this shift of perspective by making the status quo order of things look odd, counter-intuitive, nonsensical, bizarre (to "defamiliarize" it, as the Russian critics put it), while representing the radically new in familiar, recognizable, and comprehensible terms, rendering it intuitive and plausible, reducing the anxiety intrinsic to all social change.[62]

Only change that begins in a real world context and moves the viewer to a realizable future will empower people to act on their hopes and dreams. To change, people must imagine new ways of doing and being and believe they can make the transition. Portraying the process of realizing goals by portraying *how* to change will create a new world, will make the future achievable, not merely futuristic fantasy. The future must be linked with the present, but portray a different path forward.

Nourishing the power of the imagination is another important tool for inspiring political change. This was the essence of the surrealist idea. The free play of imagination is a necessary prerequisite and is critical to the creation of political art. Artist Elizam Escobar argued for prioritizing a more political imagination:

---

61 Kenneth M. Heilman, and Russel S. Donda, "Neuroscience and Fundamentalism," *Tikkun*, July 2009. http://www.tikkun.org/magazine/tik0709/frontpage/neuroscience

62 Cohn, "End of Communication," 40.

> If art is to become a force for social change,
> it must take its strength from the *politics of art,*
> art's own way of affecting both the world and
> the political directly. The politics of art will
> happen only if the power of the imagination
> is able to create a symbolic relationship be-
> tween those who participate, the artwork and
> the concrete world, always understanding the
> work of art's sovereignty (or relative autono-
> my) in relation to concrete reality.[63]

Imagination in the political sphere cannot be limited
to the private, personal dreams of the artist. This was the
weakness of Surrealism – where the individual private
imagination became the source of inspiration. Imagination
must be social; and it is the task of the social anarchist
artist to articulate the social imagination of the people, by
bringing their individual dreams into a larger social context.

To date, social anarchist art has been most effective
in its critical mode – challenging contemporary political
reality. However, social anarchist art is far less effective
portraying what a future anarchist world might look like
and feel like. A plethora of images describe the horrors
of war, the excesses of corporate capitalism, of starving
children, of the banality of consumption, of destruction
of the environment. While these images are poignant and
stir up emotions of compassion, sorrow, anger, frustration,
and even terror, they freeze the viewer and the subject in
time and space, inhibiting the possibilities for change in
the future. Imagination is a process, not an outcome. And
it must be linked intimately with action. It is a process of
imaging a future, of imaging a new way of seeing, and then

---

63 Elizam Escobar, "Art of Liberation: A Vision of Freedom", in *Art
on the Line, Essays by Artists about the Point Where Their Art & Activism
Intersect,* ed. Jack Hirschman (Williamantic, CN: Curbstone Press,
2002), 248-249.

making that world real. Artists can help by imagining a world without capitalism, a world where wealth is shared, a world where people live in harmony with nature. Socialist Realism succeeded to some extent in bridging the real with the possible with its portrayal of happy workers caught up in the collective dream of technological and industrial advancement. In the same way, Norman Rockwell portrayed the myth of the bounty of American society. Both styles foundered on a lack of imagination, a stifling of the potential for change. Instead, they were designed to conform to a pre-determined worldview that merely reinforced the capitalist dream.

The answers, in part, can be found in the portrayal of successful alternative political and economic models – both historical examples, and contemporary practices. There are endless examples of successful alternative models of living and working. Some of my favorites include the 2000 Watt Society, a workable contemporary model for cutting energy consumption and living in balance with the environment;[64] credit unions that offer owner/members an alternative to banks; food cooperatives, the Mondragon Cooperatives in Spain that model a successful economic network; among many others.

Two contemporary anarchist artists who have succeeded in creating effective future imagery are James Koehnline and Freddie Baer. By employing the technique of collage, both artists have effectively combined criticism of contemporary reality with visions of alternatives. Their collages challenge contemporary political reality by portraying its disintegration and then creating new visions from the broken fragments. Collage is a popular technique with many modern artists, but a collage often ends up as merely a pastiche of cuteness, a collection of meaningless

---

64 Eberhard Jochem, *Steps towards a Sustainable Development: a white-book for Re3D of energy-efficient technologies* (Novatlantis, March 2004). (The 2000 Watt Society). www.novatlantis.ch/fileadmin/downloads/2000watt/Weissbuch.pdf

fragments pasted together. A truly effective collage brings different meanings together in a dialectic gestalt to create a new, integrated meaning.

Freddie Baer's collages are especially effective in contrasting the death of contemporary civilization and imagining a new world. She brings the old and the new into dialectical interaction and the postmodernist fragmented narrative is re-integrated. She portrays the contemporary world as a sterile technological, mechanistic environment of controls, clocks, and organization. To counter this vision and to open up the possibility for a different reality, she appropriates into her collages images of the natural environment, social life, interaction – all representing a culture of life and vitality, suggesting growth and expansion. Baer makes effective use of historical images – memes and moods that are familiar and comfortable. Some of her images are reminiscent of, if not direct appropriations of classical Greek sculptural art, nineteenth century graphic art, organic images of Art Nouveau, as well as clippings from contemporary newspapers. The titles of her works carry political messages as well: an image of a woman warrior striding down a nineteenth century boulevard bearing flowers in both hands is entitled, "Don't Fuck with Mother Nature." In others, the humble and the personal is shown in stark contrast to a large and menacing machine – a Japanese woman goes about her business serving tea and playing a musical instrument while in the background gigantic gears seem to be ready to chew her up. Baer sums up elements of her aesthetic style in the introduction to *Ecstatic Incisions: The Collages of Freddie Baer*:

> A more coherent theory needs to be developed that takes into account past history and current events, a theory that won't become stagnant and dogma[tic] but can grow and incorporate the changes taking place in our world and respond to current events. This

theory needs to be self-critical and self-examining. Anarchists should also examine their own motives, need to change. Dysfunctional by living in this society, by which methods can individuals heal themselves, becoming more whole and complete beings? How can we change the world and ourselves simultaneously?[65]

James Koehnline's collage, "Creating Anarchy," was created as a frontispiece for Ron Sakolsky's book by the same name. Dominating the top half of the image is a large Circle A anarchist symbol, with the foundations of the letter "A" emerging out of the rubble below it. The bottom half of the collage is a chaos of destruction. Images include the infamous meme of the Abu Ghraib hooded prisoner; Koehnline's trademark all-seeing eye covered with corporate logos; and in the lower right hand corner, the head of George W. Bush. In the lower right hand corner is the following label: "A Service of U.S. Freedom and Democracy, Inc. Have a Nice Day!" What is most striking about the central image is the sense of hope and power emerging from the horrors of contemporary American culture.

Social anarchist art must also overcome the capitalist hold on the imagination. People are captive to the powerful images of the advertising industry, which shape contemporary reality. We all see ourselves through the filtered lens of the image-driven consumer culture. Max Cafard pointed out that advertisers understand the great power of the imagination:

> The one successful aspiration of May '68 was: *"L'imagination au pouvoir!"* – "Power to the imagination!" ... For the imagination is indeed in power today. Though, sad to say, it is not the one that the visionaries of '68 hoped for.

---

65 Freddie (Friederike) Baer, *Ecstatic Incisions: The Collages of Freddie Baer* (Oakland, CA: AK Press, 1992), 10.

Instead, it is the consumptionist imaginary
that dominates contemporary culture. ... [W]
e inhabit a world ... in which we take *their* desires for *our* realities.[66]

Without question, advertising art is clever and engaging; but, in truth, it can never be imaginative; it feeds on
individual wants and desires, not collective hopes and
dreams grounded in freedom. The standardization that
capitalist culture and advertising aesthetics demands results in a general leveling of all taste and discrimination,
such that we become intolerant of any unique or different interpretation of social reality. Capitalism is always
the same movie; only the product placements change. A
group-think mentality as opposed to a true collective mentality emerges as the cultural norm, and our growth both
as individuals and societies is constricted. We become dependent, child-like, and easily manipulated. This impov-
erishment of the imaginative sense stifles future creativity
and destroys future potentials.

We must also re-think the role of technology in shaping
our visions and its affect on the imagination in the making
and transmission of art. In *To Hell with Culture*, anarchist
critic Herbert Read argued that the industrial mechanical
process had a profound influence on a central component
of aesthetics – the human need for imaginative thinking:
"There exists in the whole process of industrialization and
technological invention a tendency to destroy sensuous
perception and imaginative experience, the very facul-
ties upon which our scientific knowledge of the nature of
things finally depends. In short, technology (and the automatism that goes with it) tends to destroy human sensibility.[67]

---

66 Max Cafard, *The Surre(gion)alist Manifesto and Other Writings* (Baton
   Rouge: Exquisite Corpse, 2003), 18.
67 Herbert Read, "The Great Debate," in *To Hell with Culture* (New
   York, NY: Schocken Books, 1970), 183.

Walter Benjamin's insights into the role of reproducible art in shaping the modern era are also relevant here. The mass media are the fulfillment of a technological, centralized system of control that is set on an infinite, automated loop of re-runs of dead dreams. Reinforcing Benjamin's distinction between reproducible art and classic art, contemporary art critic Arthur Danto agreed that something essential about art was lost in modernist aesthetics because of the new technologies. He believes, for example, that "most of the images we see are photographs, and their effect can be dulling if not desensitizing."[68] Traditional handcrafted art, on the other hand, captures some of the essence of the aura: "The mystery of painting, almost forgotten since the Counter-Reformation, lies in its power to generate a kind of illusion that has less to do with pictorial perception than it does with feeling."[69]

Newly-imagined worlds are often portrayed as utopias. Historically, utopia implied an idealized space that was separate in time, distance, and experience. Most utopian narratives take us out of the world around us and place us abruptly elsewhere, often far into the future. However much we might enjoy the "escape" from our current realities, we must be cautious about these utopian ideal worlds, especially wary of whose dreams are being presented. Some utopias are future-oriented; some keep us locked into realities that are harmful. Some utopias are so distant that they are deemed unachievable. There are all sorts of utopias as Cafard pointed out, but not all of them are what they seem, and some are dystopias:

> The highest aspirations of the imagination are called utopia. But utopia is just as much the enemy of the imagination, and is our own Nemesis. We live in the shadow of a terrifying

68 Arthur C. Danto, "The Body in Pain," *The Nation*, November 27, 2006, 24.

69 Danto, "The Body," 24.

utopia. And we must search the shadows for those other utopias that have been eclipsed. … The dominant utopia is the utopia of Progress, of the conquest of nature, of the rationalization of society. It is a utopia of infinite powers of production and infinite desires for consumption.[70]

We need an art of the *possible* that brings a sustainable utopia within reach and nourishes the belief that we really can change the world. Art can bring a realistic utopia close to us, writer Robert Fulford concluded, "The arts also let us live, imaginatively, within the world where they are produced. They give us an alternative human narrative – and perhaps that's their most generous gift to us. … Art give us, as well, the opportunity to look at everything around us in a slightly different light. It changes our perspective."[71] An achievable utopia is not fixed in some future time and place but keeps alive always the potential of advancing from where we are to where we want to be. The artist's biggest challenge will be creating visions of a sustainable future. Art can imagine such a world, one that will be rich and fulfilling.

ART AS ACTION: A "DYNAMIC REALISM"

BEYOND SIMPLY CHALLENGING the status quo, a social anarchist aesthetic must create new contexts that are exciting, desirable, and challenging. These contexts must move the spectator/participant to action. Contexts are not just settings; they are active environments that inspire action. Further, a social anarchist art does not just have a distant goal of inspiring political action but assumes that the observer and the artist are both active participants in taking action; it must directly *act* for change. The real becomes

---

70 Cafard, 24.

71 Robert Fulford, "My church: the mind's 'theatre of simultaneous possibilities,'" *National Post*, December 22, 2007, n.p..

the actual, shaping the future. Cohn uses the adjective "dynamic" to describe a social anarchist aesthetic that would capture art as action in the same way that anarchist political theory insists upon direct action. Cohn's call for dynamic forms of representation will challenge artists to rethink realism and precisely what is represented. Representation must be grounded in the real world – a realism that portrays

> *non*-reifying, *non*-alienating *forms* of representation – *dynamic* forms, … an alternative *model* of representation that is *dynamic*, which does not seek to escape the world of multiplicity and motion but embraces these phenomena as the essence of living. A social anarchist aesthetic, in short, does not simply map the ideal onto the real, or take the ideal for the real; rather, it discovers the ideal within the real, as a moment of reality.[72]

Social anarchist art must engage people to *act*. According to Scrivener, the call for an engaged art has been a part of anarchist theory since the nineteenth century. Proudhon, he pointed out, was "antagonistic to the avant-garde and encouraged instead an *engagé* art, one closely aligned to the aspirations of the social movement."[73] At the same time, social anarchist art must also appeal on a personal level: "An event becomes real when the pictures become personal."[74] Can people put themselves into the picture? Can people see themselves as active participants? Does the message resonate with them personally and with people like them? Without a personal connection, people will not become

---

72 Cohn, "NeMe: Anarchism, Representation, and Culture."

73 Scrivener, 16.

74 CBS-TV news report on Neda, 6/22/09, the young Iranian woman killed during political protests whose image became an icon for resistance.

engaged politically.

Political art must also be public, not private; it should assume the existence of, and create for, an audience of many, not one. The message has to be taken to where people see and hear it. Historically, political artists turned to pasting posters on fences and walls of buildings to communicate political ideas; murals were, and are, a permanent example of the same outreach effort. Corporate advertising and the state have appropriated the public space in the current cultural reality, and radical political art is essentially banned from the television and print mass media. Nevertheless, radical artists continue to find new ways of reaching wider audiences. So far the internets are a relatively accessible medium, but the sheer volume of information available and the limitations of customer choice by the one-to-communication channels drown out meaningful organization of political communication. According to Alisa Solomon, contemporary political performance art that merges the roles of artist and activist is another important public outreach technique. Activities like "Reclaim the Streets, Art and Revolution, and Bill Talen's creation, the Reverend Billy of the Church of Stop Shopping," Solomon noted, certainly get the attention of small audiences and "dissolve the distinction between being artists and activists."[75] The technique of detournement is yet another tried and true way to undermine the images of the dominant political and economic culture by transforming them. But, all of these actions must take place in a public setting.

Street art and graffiti are prevalent everywhere, but, for the most part their content is not political. While the walls of European cities are replete with many visual statements about struggle and revolution, political graffiti is less visible in the United States. American graffiti could realize its political potential if it developed a narrative beyond merely marking gang territory or defacing property just for the

---

75 Alisa Solomon, "Art Makes a Difference," *The Nation*, November 8, 2004, 32.

hell of it. The power of graffiti is that it is local; its artists live in geographic and political time and they claim visual territory. Some of the best graffiti addresses local or neighborhood issues. In recent years, the eye-catching images that the mysterious English artist Banksy created, has inspired political graffiti around the world. Many of his stencils are overtly political – for example, the grim image of a young girl hugging a bomb. Some of the stencils are comments on cultural elements such as the "Cash Machine and Girl" which portrays a young girl being grabbed by a huge mechanical arm emerging from an ATM. "TV Out of the Window" is an image of just that – a television set being thrown out of a window.[76] Unfortunately, his work has become quite marketable (and, thus, recuperable). In some cases, even the surfaces themselves have been removed to museum or to gallery settings.

The Occupy Wall Street (OWS) movement, along with its spinoffs – Occupy the Environment, Bank Transfer Day, Occupy Our Homes, Strike Debt, Occupy Sandy Relief (in response to the East Coast hurricane) and local Occupy efforts in hundreds of cities and towns worldwide – provides excellent examples of effective direct political action. The revolutionary movements in the Middle East (the Arab Spring) and the worldwide Occupy Movement burst on the political scene in 2011, and were accompanied by an explosion of political art and graffiti. The Arab Spring and *Adbusters* magazine inspired the Occupy Wall Street movement. The meme of Occupy Wall Street was the right vision at the right time. *Adbusters'* editor and co-founder Kalle Lasn credited the Situationist International as the inspiration for OWS. Activism returned again to the streets and the dream of 1968 was revised on American soil:

> We are not just inspired by what happened
> in the Arab Spring recently, we are students

---

76 Martin Bull, Banksy: *A Collection of Graffiti Locations and Photographs in London, England*, Vols. 1 and 2, Oakland, CA: PM Press, 2011·

of the Situationist movement. Those are the people who gave birth to what many people think was the first global revolution back in 1968. … The idea that if you have a very powerful meme – a very powerful idea – and the moment is ripe, then that is enough to ignite a revolution.[77]

The word "occupy" is an active verb; it urges movement and involvement and action, and it also has a powerful political message – taking back stolen spaces, whether they be public squares or homes scheduled for foreclosure. The OWS meme bundled political agendas: the imperative to confront corporate power, to occupy economic space; to occupy geographic space with sit-ins, and to occupy visual space. Combining idea and action, the OWS movement operated on many levels, integrating criticism, creating an environment of empowerment, and modeling direct democracy decision-making in the general assemblies. The OWS idea/action expanded horizontally, involving growing numbers of individuals.

Since the beginning of the Occupy movement in the fall of 2011, the sharing of political imagery has exploded across the internets. The limitations on the length of posts in these media encourage the sharing of images instead. One of the most delightful images is the Occupy Wall Street poster of the ballerina *en pointe* on the back of the Wall Street bull, capturing in one image the idea of protest and celebration. The movement has created its own graphic arts center, Occuprint, where artists are encouraged to share their ideas.[78] Alternative media platforms have also become more sophisticated and served to share

77 Kalle Lasn, quoted in Ken Knabb, "The Situationists and the Occupation Movements (1868/2011.˝ www.counterpunch. org/2011/11/08/the-situationists-and-the-occupation-movements-19682011/

78 www.occuprint.org

the imagery of activism even when the mainstream press ignored the OWS.

In the United States, the OWS messages of protest, change, and revolution often took the form of handmade signs rather than taking over public spaces with wall art. The handmade signs conveyed a greater sense of immediacy and personal commitments but required mass media to convey the messages to the larger world. The handmade signs were very effective as Ken Knabb pointed out.

> [T]here is a rich mix of joy and humor, insight and irony, poetry and poignancy, camaraderie and community. Like the graffiti, the signs are of course only a modest, visible expression of the movement, but they tend to express its nature, what is really going on in the participants' hearts and minds, better than any official declarations or political programs.[79]

Art critic Barry Schwabsky was also impressed with the vibrancy of the Occupy signage, pointing out that these signs circulated in multiple contexts: at the site of protest and passed from person to person on the internets: "The content of a protest sign is not just a message that lives and dies as part of an event but also the half-life a sign gains by being photographed and then posted online. It's 'guerrilla semiotics.'"[80] Walter Benjamin would certainly appreciate the power of reproductions to inspire revolution!

CONCLUSION: ART AND FREEDOM

SOCIAL ANARCHIST ART will be built on actualizing the idea of freedom – not by having some abstract goal but by bringing people in touch with ways of living freedom in the present and the future, what Kai Barrow called

---

79 Ken Knabb, "The Situationists and the Occupation Movements."

80 Barry Schwabsky, "Signs of Protest: occupy's Guerilla Semiotics." *The Nation* (December 14, 2011). www.thenation.com

"art beyond the aesthetic and as a process of libratory engagement."[81] Social anarchist art must break open the reality of oppression and allow freedom to express itself, to help people get in touch with their repressed desires for freedom. Freedom is also about joy and igniting the imagination. Zenos Frudakis's sculpture, "Freedom", is a powerful visual metaphor of people breaking free and celebrating their freedom.[82] The sculpture is a wall embedded with faces and four human figures in various stages of emergence from the wall, moving from left to right. The fourth figure is free of the wall standing in a frozen moment of absolute joy.

There are inherent dangers in the free expression of the desires for freedom as we shift to a visual culture. In the fragmentation of the postmodern era, the critical skills of visual literacy have also been blunted. Mark McGinnis noted: "Looking and thinking no longer seem related, since looking so often is accompanied by oral explanations or an onslaught of images that drowns out thought. Looking has become a passive experience in which information is given, instead of being an active experience that requires thought."[83] The challenge for the radical artist is how to break through this passivity to re-energize a dialogue with the world, to help people see new ways to re-engage with the world through political action, and to change that world. This is the essence of cooperation and engagement. True freedom will require critical thinking, active participation, and political activism, and learning to see the world in new ways.

If social anarchist art does have an overarching goal,

81 Kai Barrow, "Liberatory Art and Authentic Collaboration," *New Formulation: An Anti-Authoritarian Review of Books* 2, 2 (Winter-Spring 2004), 46-passim. http://www.newformulation.org/contents.htm

82 The sculpture is on public display in Philadelphia, Pennsylvania.

83 Mark McGinnis, "An Overdose of Television Has Deadened the Visual Imagination of Our Students," *The Chronicle of Higher Education*, February 20, 1991.

it is to overcome the collective self-delusion of capitalist society. We live in a visual world dominated by a false reality, a contemporary Potemkin village. We are distracted by the glittering generalities of capitalist aesthetics, confused by relativistic postmodern aesthetic "experiences," and overcome by the mind-numbing weight of economic oppression. We must crack open the rotten egg of contemporary society to reveal the horrors of our contemporary world and to seek in its place new visions, new ideological representations of the beauty of freedom in order to realize the freedom of the beautiful.

Our art has been stolen from us; its creative energy destroyed and commodified; its artistic qualities compromised. Aesthetics is daily sacrificed to the standardization of the machine, to the profit motive, and to the need for mindless consumption of objects. True art is, at its finest, revolutionary, especially when it serves the politics of freedom and a realizable future. Aesthetics is ultimately politics. Where engaged art flourishes, freedom is realized. The key to our collective freedom lies in developing these revolutionary aesthetic sensibilities.

BIBLIOGRAPHY

Aaron, Daniel. *Writers on the Left Episodes in American Literary Communism*. New York, NY: Octagon, 1974.

Achten, Udo, Matthias Reichelt, and Reinhard Schultz in zusammenarbeit mit Kai Reschke. *Mein Vaterland ist International: Internationale Illustrierte Geschichte des 1. Mail 1886 bis Heute*. Berlin (West): Neue Gesellschaft für Bildende Kunst in Zusammenarteit mit den Ruhrfestspielen Recklinghausen, 1986.

Adams, Don and Arlene Goldbard. "Reflections on Cultural Democracy." Mimeo. Ca. 1980.

Adbusters America: Journal of the Mental Environment. See also http://www.adbusters.org/

Adorno, Theodor W. *Aesthetic Theory*. Edited by Gretel Adorno and Rolf Tiedemann. Translated with a translator's introduction by Robert Hullot-Kentor. Minneapolis: University of Minnesota Press: 1997.

Ahrens, Gale. "Dreaming, Playing, & Breaking Up the Existing Order," In *Surrealist Subversions: Rants, Writings and Images by the Surrealist Movement in the United States*, edited by Ron Sakolsky, 251. New York, NY: Autonomedia, 2002.

Ajayi, Omofolabo. "From His Symbol to Her Icon: An Analysis of the Presentation of Women in African Contemporary Literary Works." *The American Journal of Semiotics* 8, 3 (1991): 31–52.

Alegría, Claribel. "From the Bridge." In *Poetry Like Bread: Poets of the Political Imagination*, edited by Martin Espada, 33-39. Willimantic, CT: Curbstone Press, 1994.

Anonymous. "*Anarchism: left for dead amid the carnage.*" Review of *Anarchist Modernism* by Alan Antliff. January 16, 2003. http://www.notbored.org/antliff.html

_____. "Whatever happened to the Situationists?" Review of *Public Secrets* by Ken Knabb and *What is Situationism? A Reader*, edited by Stewart Home. *Aufheben 7* (Autumn 1998). http://www.libcom.org

_____. "Section A. The Last *Avant-gardes*: Situationists." http://www.angelfire.com/art/corei/SI/SIseca.htm;

288 Neala Schleuning

"Section B. "Methods of Situationists." http://www.
angelfire.com/art/corei/SI/SIsecb.htm and "Section C.
Situationists' Notion of Urban Space." http://www.angel-
fire.com/ar/corei/SI/SIsecc.htm

_____. "Drifting with the Situationist International."
Anarchy: A Journal of Desire Armed 29 (1991): 20–21.

_____. *Education and Art in Soviet Russia – in Light of Official
Decrees and Documents.* Forward by Max Eastman. New
York, NY: Socialist Publication Society, 1918.

_____. "1976: End of the 'American Way of Life.'" *Arsenal/
Surrealist Subversion* 3 (1976). In *Surrealist Subversions:
Rants, Writings and Images by the Surrealist Movement in the
United States,* edited by Ron Sakolsky, 472-474. New York,
NY: Autonomedia, 2002.

Ansatzpunkte kritischer Kunst heute. Berlin (West): Bonner
Kunstverein and Neue Gesellschaft für Bildende Kunst,
1984.

Antliff, Allan. *Anarchist Modernism: Art, Politics, and the First
American Avant-Garde.* Chicago and London: The University
of Chicago Press, 2001.

_____. *An Anthology of Anarchist Culture.* Winnipeg:
Arbeiter Ring Publishing, 2001.

_____. "Anarchist Modernism Revisited: A Reply to
Patrick Frank." *Anarchy: A Journal of Desire Armed* (2002-
2003): 62-63.

_____. "Carl Zigrosser and the Modern School:
Nietzsche, Art, and Anarchism." *Archives of American Art
Journal* 13, no 4 (1994): 16-18.

_____. "Open form and the abstract imperative: Herbert
Read and contemporary anarchist art." *Anarchist Studies*
16, no 1 (2008): 6-19.

_____. *Anarchy and Art: From the Paris Commune to the Fall
of the Berlin Wall.* Vancouver: Arsenal Pulp Press, 2008.

Antliff, Mark. "Fascism, Modernism, and Modernity." *The Art
Bulletin* 84, 1 (March 2002): 148-169.

_____. "Anarchy and Culture: The Aesthetic Politics
of Modernism." Book Review. *Modernism/Modernity* 6, 1
(1999): 167-69.

Aristotle, *Nicomachean Ethics*, 1106:10. In *Philosophies of Art and
Beauty: Selected Readings in Aesthetics from Plato to Heidegger,*
edited by Albert Hofstadter and Richard Kuhns, 93-94.
New York, NY: Modern Library, 1964.

Aristotle, *Poetics*, Part IV, http://classics.mit.edu//Aristotle/po-
etics.html

Armitage, John. "Ontological Anarchy, the Temporary Autonomous Zone, and the Politics of Cyberculture: A Critique of Hakim Bey." *Angelaki: Journal of the Theoretical Humanities* 4, 2 (1999): 115-128.

Baer, Freddie (Friederike). *Ecstatic Incisions: The Collages of Freddie Baer.* Oakland, CA: AK Press, 1992.

Ball, Hugo. "Dada Manifesto," 1916. En.wikipedia.org/wiki/Hugo_Ball

Barrow, Kai. "Liberatory Art and Authentic Collaboration." *The New Formulation: An Anti-Authoritarian Review of Books* 2, 2 (Winter-Spring 2004), 46-passim. http://www.newformulation.org/contents.htm

Baudrillard, Jean. "The Implosion of Meaning in the Media and the Implosion of the Social in the Masses." In *Questioning Technology: A Critical Anthology,* edited and introduced by John Zerzan and Alice Carnes, 158-162. London: Freedom Press, 1988.

Bayles, David and Ted Orland. *Art & Fear: Observations on the Perils (and Rewards) of Artmaking.* Santa Cruz, CA and Eugene, OR: The Image Continuum, 1993.

The Beehive Design Collective. www.beehivecollective.org

Benhabib, Seyla. "Feminism and the Question of Postmodernism." In *The New Social Theory Reader,* edited by Steven Seidman and Jeffrey C. Alexander, 156-165. New York, NY: Routledge, 2001.

Bell, Daniel. "Modernism Mummified." *American Quarterly* 39, 1 (1987): 122-132.

Benjamin, Walter. *Surrealism: The Last Snapshot of the European Intelligentsia.* 1929. http://www.generation-online.org/c/fcsurrealism.htm

_____. "The Work of Art in the Age of Mechanical Reproduction." In *Illuminations,* translated by Harry Zohn, edited and introduced by Hannah Arendt, 217-251. New York NY: Schocken Books, 1969.

Berger, Harry Jr. "Naive Consciousness and Culture Change: An Essay in Historical Structuralism." *Midwest Modern Language Association Bulletin* 6, 1 (Spring 1973): 1–44.

Berger, John. *Ways of Seeing.* London: British Broadcasting System and Penguin Books, 1972.

Berliner Kultureplätze 1: Theaterspielen nach Feierabend. Berlin (West): Neue Gesellschaft für Bildende Kunst, n.d.

Berliner Kultureplätze 2: In Selbstverwaltung. Berlin (West): Neue Gesellschaft für Bildende Kunst, n.d.

Berliner Kultureplätze 3: Frauen, Autonomie Kreativitat, Subkultur.

Berlin (West): Neue Gesellschaft für Bildende Kunst, n.d.
*Berliner Mauerbilder: Fotografien und einleitender Essay Hermann
Waldenburg.* Berlin: Nicolaische Verglagsbuchhandlung,
1990.

Berman, Morris. *The Twilight of American Culture: Ideas of
Creativity in Western Culture.* New York, NY: W.W. Norton,
2000.

Bernays, Edward L. "The Engineering of Consent." *The Annals
of the American Academy of Political and Social Science* 250
(1947): 113-120.

——————. *Propaganda.* New York, NY: Horace
Liveright, 1928.

Berona, David A. *Wordless Books: The Original Graphic Novels.*
New York, NY: Abrams, 2008.

Berube, Michael. *Public Access: Literary Theory and American
Cultural Politics.* London: Verso, 1994.

Bey, Hakim. *TAZ: The Temporary Autonomous Zone, Ontological
Anarchy, Poetic Terrorism.* New York: Autonomedia, 1985,
1991. http://www.hermetic.com/bey/taz_cont.html

——————. *Millenium.* New York, NY and Dublin:
Autonomedia & Garden of Delight, 1996.

——————. *Immediatism.* Edinburgh: AK, 1994.

Birkerts, Sven. *The Gutenberg Elegies: The Fate of Reading in an
Electronic Age.* New York, NY: Fawcett Columbine, 1994.

Black, Bob. "The Realization and Supression of Situationism."
http://www.library.nothingness.org

Blonsky, Marshall, ed. *On Signs.* Baltimore: Johns Hopkins
University Press, 1985.

Bluestein, Gene. *The Voice of the Folk.* Boston: University of
Massachusetts Press, 1972.

Bookchin, Murray. *Social Anarchism or Lifestyle Anarchism: An
Unbridgeable Chasm.* Oakland and Edinburgh: AK Press,
1995.

Bread and Puppet: Stories of Struggle and Faith from Central America.
Burlington, VT: Green Valley Film and Art, 1985.

Breton, Andre. *Manifestoes of Surrealism.* Translated by Richard
Seaver and Helen R. Lane. Ann Arbor: U of Michigan
Press, 1969.

——————. *What is Surrealism?* Lecture at the meeting of the
Belgian Surrealists, Brussels, June 1, 1934. http://www.
surrealist.com

——————. *What is Surrealism? Selected Writings.* Franklin
Rosemount, Ed., Translated by Samuel Beckett and others
and introduced by Franklin Rosemount. New York, NY:

Monad, Pathfinder Press, 1978. See "Visit with Trotsky" and "After Dada."

Breton, Andre and Leon Trotsky. *Manifesto: Towards a Free Revolutionary Art*. 1938. http://www.generation-online.org/fcsurrealism1.htm

Brodner, Steve, ed. *Artists against the War*. Introduced by Steve Brodner. Nevada City, CA: Underwood Books, 2010.

Brown, Stephen and Anthony Patterson, Eds. *Imagining Marketing: Art, Aesthetics and the Avant-Garde*. London and New York: Routledge, 2000.

Bruckner, D.J.R., Seymour Chwaste and Steven Heller. *Art against War: 400 Years of Protest in Art*. New York, NY: Abbbeville Press Publishers, 1984.

Buhle, Paul and Nicole Schulman, eds. *Wobblies! A Graphic History of the Industrial Workers of the World*. London and New York, NY: Verso, 2005.

Buhle, Paul and Mike Alewitz. *Insurgent Images: The Agitprop Murals of Mike Alewitz*. New York, NY: Monthly Review Press, 2002.

Bull, Martin. *Banksy: A Collection of Graffiti Locations and Photographs in London, England*, Vols. 1 and 2. Oakland, CA: PM Press, 2011.

Burger, Peter. *Theory of the Avant-Garde*. Minneapolis: University of Minnesota Press, 1984.

Cafard, Max. *The Surre(gion)alist Manifesto and Other Writings*. Baton Rouge: Exquisite Corpse, 2003.

Cahill, Holger. "American Resources in the Arts." In *Art for the Millions: Essays from the 1930s by Artists and Administrators of the WPA Federal Art Project*, edited by Francis V. O'Connor, 33-44. Boston: New York Graphic Society, 1975.

"Call for an American Writers' Congress." *New Masses*, January 22, 1935: 20.

Call, Lewis. "A is for Anarchy, V is for Vendetta: Images of Guy Fawkes and the Creation of Postmodern Anarchism." *Anarchist Studies* 16, 2 (2008): 154-172.

"Calling All Comrades! The Long-lost Propaganda Posters that Rallied the Soviets against Hitler." *Foreign Policy* (August 19, 2011). www.foreignpolicy.com

Camus, Albert. *The Rebel*. Translated by Anthony Bower. Harmondsworthy, Middlesex: Penguin, 1973.

Canjuers, Pierre and Guy Debord. "Preliminaries toward Defining a Unitary Revolutionary Program." In *Situationist International Anthology*, edited and translated by Ken Knabb, 305-309. Berkeley: Bureau of Public Secrets, 1981.

Cardenal, Ernesto. "The Peasant Women from Cuá," In *Poetry like Bread: Poets of the Political Imagination*, edited by Martin Espada, 87-89. Willimantic, CT: Curbstone Press, 1994.

Castillo, Otto René. "Let's Go Country" In *Poetry like Bread: Poets of the Political Imagination*, edited by Martin Espada, 99-105. Willimantic, CT: Curbstone Press, 1994.

Caudwell, Christopher. *Studies and Further Studies in a Dying Culture*. New York, NY and London: Monthly Review Press, 1937, 1971.

_____. *Illusion and Reality*. New York, NY: International Publishers, 1937, 1977.

Close, Glen S. "Literature and politics in early twentieth-century Argentina: The anarchist modernism of Roberto Arlt." *Anarchist Studies* 12, 2 (2004): 124-146.

Cohn, Jesse. "What is Postanarchism 'Post'"? Review of *From Bakunin to Lacan: Anti-Authoritarianism and the Dislocation of Power*, by Saul Newman. 2002. http://www.infoshop.org/library/Cohn:_What_is_Postanarchism_%22Post%22

_____. "NeMe: Anarchism, Representation, and Culture." January 16, 2006. http://www.neme.org/main/310/anarchism-representation-and-culture

_____. "What is anarchist literary theory?" *Anarchist Studies* 15, 2 (2007): 115-131.

_____. "The End of Communication? The End of Representation." *Fifth Estate* 376, 42, 2 (2007): 40-44.

Cohn, Jesse and Shawn Wilbur. "What's Wrong with Postanarchism?" April 29, 2010. http://theanarchistlibrary.org

Community Media Workshop Newstip. "Chicago Muralists Heralded." October 20, 2005. http://www.newstips.org

Copland, Aaron. *Music and Imagination*. Cambridge: Harvard University Press, 1953.

Cortesini, Sergio. "Depicting National Identities in New Deal America and Fascist Italy: Government Sponsored Murals." In *Kunst und Propaganda: Im Streit der Nationen 1930-1945*, edited by Hans Jörg, Hans und Nikola Doll. Berlin: Deutsches Historisches Museum, 2007: 36-47.

Cortez, Carlos, ed. *Viva Posada! A Salute to the Great Printmaker of the Mexican Revolution*. Chicago: Charles H. Kerr, 2002.

Costantini, Flavio. *The Art of Anarchy*. London: Cienfuegos Press, 1975.

Crain, Caleb. "Twilight of the Books: What will life be like if people stop reading?" *The New Yorker*, December 24 & 31, 2007, 134-139.

Crawford, John. "Philips' Political Odyssey through Literature and Life." *The New York Smith* 1, 2 (1977): 42 passim.

Craven, David. *Abstract Expressionism as Cultural Critique.* Cambridge: Cambridge U Press, 1999.

Danto, Arthur C. "When Seeing Was Believing." Review of *The Reformation of the Image* by Joseph Leo Koerner. *The Nation*, March 7, 2005: 32-34.

_____. "The Body in Pain." *The Nation,* November 27, 2006, 23-26.

D'Ambrisio, Paul S. *Ralph Fasanella's America.* Cooperstown, NY: Fenimore Art Museum, 2001.

Dasgupta, Sudeep. "Art is Going Elsewhere, and Politics Has to Catch It: An Interview with Jacques Rancière." *Krisis: Journal for Contemporary Philosophy* 1, 2008: 70-76.

Dauvé, Gilles (Jean Barrot). *Critique of the Situationist International.* Translated by Louis Michaelson *Red-eye* 1, 1979. Reprinted twice: as a pamphlet retitled "What is Situationism ?" London: Unpopular Books, (1987) and in the anthology *What is Situationism ? A Reader*, edited by Stewart Home. London: AK Press, 1996.

Davis, Laurence. "Social Anarchism or Lifestyle Anarchism: An Unhelpful Dichotomy." *Anarchist Studies* 18, 1, 2010: 62-82.

Debord, Guy. *The Society of the Spectacle.* Detroit: Black and Red, 1983.

_____. *Comments on* The Society of the Spectacle. Sheffield: Pirate Press, 1991.

_____. "For a Revolutionary Judgment of Art." 1961. Reprint from the *Situationist International Anthology*, edited and translated by Ken Knabb, 310-313. Berkeley, CA: Bureau of Public Secrets, 1981.

_____. "Report on the Construction of Situations and on the International Situationist Tendency's Conditions of Organisation and Action." 1957. In *Situationist International Anthology*, edited and translated by Ken Knabb, 17-25. Berkeley, CA: Bureau of Public Secrets, 1981.

_____. "Theory of the *dérive.*" 1958. In *Situationist International Anthology*, edited and translated by Ken Knabb, 50-64. Berkeley: Bureau of Public Secrets, 1981.

Debord, Guy and Gil J. Wolman. "Methods of *Détournement.*" 1956. In *Situationist International Anthology*, edited and translated by Ken Knabb, 8-13. Berkeley: Bureau of Public Secrets, 1981.

de Cleyre, Voltairine. "The Dominant Idea." In *Anarchy: An*

Anthology of Emma Goldman's Mother Earth, edited and with commentary by Peter Glassgold, 185-195. Washington, DC: Counterpoint, 2001.

Denning, Michael. *The Cultural Front: The Laboring of American Culture in the Twentieth Century.* London and others: Verso, 1996.

Dewey, Donald. "Drawing Russia." *Russian Life.* September/October 2006: 444-49.

Dewey, John. *Art as Experience.* New York, NY: Minton, Balch, 1958.

Diederich, Reiner and Richard Grubling. "Under die Schere mit den Geiern!": *Politische Fotomontage in der Bundesrepublik und Westberlin.* Berlin: Elefanten Press Galerie, 1977.

Drawing the Line: The Protest Poster in America. San Francisco: Pomegranate Artbooks, 1994.

Drucker, Johanna. *Theorizing Modernism: Visual Art and the Critical Tradition.* New York, NY: Columbia University Press, 1994.

Eagleton, Terry. "Future Fetishists and Artists Who Don't Paint: How the Revolutionary Aims of the Avant-garde Led to the 'Sick Joke' of postmodernism." Review of *100 Artists' Manifestos: From the Futurists to the Stuckists,* edited by Alex Danchev. *The Times Literary Supplement.* March 23, 2011. http://entertainment.timesonline.co.uk/tol/arts_and_entertainment/the_tls/article7173276.ece

Eastman, Max. *Venture.* New York, NY: A. & C. Boni, 1927.

Egbert, Donald Drew. *Socialism and American Art: In the Light of European Utopianism, Marxism, and Anarchism.* Princeton, NJ: Princeton University Press, 1967.

Eisenstein, Sergei. *The Film Sense,* edited and translated by Jay Leyda. New York, NY: Harcourt, Brace and World, 1975.

Eksteins, Modris. *Rites of Spring: The Great War and the Birth of the Modern Age.* New York, NY and others: Doubleday, 1989.

──────────. "Drowned in *Eau de Vie.*" Review of *Modernism: The Lure of Heresy from Baudelaire to Beckett and Beyond,* by Peter Gay, *London Review of Books.* http://www.Lrb.co.uk/v30/n04

Ellsberg, Robert, ed. *Fritz Eichenberg: Works of Mercy.* Maryknoll, NY: Orbis Books, 1993.

Endlich: Postrevolutionäre Kunst im IV. Reich. Berlin (West): Neue Gesellschaft für Bildende Kunst, 1990.

Englische Arbeiterkunst. Berlin (West): Neue Gesellschaft für Bildende Kunst, 1977.

Escobar, Elizam. "Art of Liberation: A Vision of Freedom." In *Art on the Line, Essays by Artists about the Point Where Their Art & Activism Intersect*, edited by Jack Hirschman. Williamantic, CN: Curbstone Press, 2002.

Espada, Martin, ed. *Poetry Like Bread: Poets of the Political Imagination*. Willimantic, CT: Curbstone Press, 1994.

Espada, Martin. "Federico's Ghost." In *Poetry Like Bread: Poets of the Political Imagination*, edited by Martin Espada, 130-132. Willimantic, CT: Curbstone Press, 1994.

Exit through the Gift Shop: A Banksy Film. Directed by Banksy. Music by Geoff Barrow. 2010.

Family, Nation, Tribe, Community, Shift: Zeitgenössische Künstlerische Konkzepte im Hause der Kulturen der Welt. Berlin (West): Neue Gesellschaft für Bildende Kunst, 1996.

Farr, Roger. "The 'Insurrectionary Wilderness of the I:' Phyllis Webb's Anarchist Poetics." *West Coast Line* 45 (2005): 63-76.

_____. "The Intimacies of Noise: A Reply to Jesse Cohn." *Fifth Estate* #376, 42, 2 (2007): 44-45.

_____. "Anarchist Poetics." *Fifth Estate* 373 (2006): 34-38.

Felshin, Nina, ed. *But is it Art? The Spirit of Art as Activism*. Seattle: Bay Press, 1995.

Fischer, Ernst. *The Necessity of Art*. Translated by Anna Bostock. London: James Curry Ltd., 1990.

"Flavio Costantini." Entry in Kate Sharpley Library. www.katesharpleylibrary.net/t4b9k9

Fleming, Jim and Peter Lamborn Wilson, eds. *SEMIOTEXT [E] USA*. New York, NY: Autonomedia, 1987.

Foley, Barbara. "Art or Propaganda?" In *Radical Representations: Politics and Form in U.S. Proletarian Fiction, 1929-1941*, by Barbara Foley, 129-169. Durham and London: Duke University Press, 1993.

_____. "The Continuing Relevance of Proletarian Literature in a Time of 'Endless War.'" *Fortune City*. March 2003. http://www.victorian.fortunecity.com

Ford, Simon. *The Situationist International: A User's Guide*. London: Black Dog Publishing, 2005.

Four B[u]y Four. *A No Record Deal and Other Exercises in Crass Commercialism*. San Francisco: Pressure Drop Press, n.d.

Franks, Benjamin. "Postanarchism and Meta-Ethics." *Anarchist Studies* 16, 2 (2008): 135-153.

Frase, Brigitte. "Do artists know best?" Review of *Proust was a Neuroscientist*, by Jonah Lehrer, Minneapolis *Star Tribune*, December 16, 2007, F13.

Freeman, Joseph. "Discussions and Proceedings." In *American Writers' Congress*, edited by Henry Hart, 165-192. New York, NY: International Publishers, 1935.

Fulford, Robert. "My church: the mind's 'theatre of simultaneous possibilities.'" *National Post*, December 22, 2007. http://www.robertfulford.com/2007-12-22-arts.html

Gabrik, Suzi. "The Nature of Beauty in Contemporary Art." *New Renaissance* 8, 1 (1998). www.ru.org/81gablik.html

_____. *The Reenchantment of Art*. NY and London: Thames & Hudson, 1992.

_____. *Has Modernism Failed?* NY and London: Thames & Hudson, 1984.

Galeano, Eduardo. *Upside Down: A Primer for the Looking-Glass World*. Translated by Mark Fried. New York, NY: Henry Holt, 2000.

Gamman, Lorraine and Margaret Marshment, eds. *The Female Gaze: Women as Viewers of Popular Culture*. Seattle: The Real Comet Press, 1989.

Gayle, Addison, Jr., Ed. *The Black Aesthetic*. Garden City: Doubleday, 1972.

Geras, Norman. "Essence and Appearance: Aspects of Fetishism in Marx's Capital." *New Left Review* 65 (1971): 69–85.

Gibler, John. "'We Will Continue': Street Art in Oaxaca" *Fifth Estate* 380 (Spring 2009): 36-37.

Gilman-Opalsky, Richard. *Spectacular Capitalism: Guy Debord and the Practice of Radical Philosophy*. NY and London: Minor Compositions/Autonomedia, 2011.

Glassgold, Peter, ed. *Anarchy: An Anthology of Emma Goldman's Mother Earth*. Washington, DC: Counterpoint, 2001.

Glavin, Michael. "Power, Subjectivity, Resistance: Three Works on Postmodern Anarchism." Review of *Postmodern Anarchism*, by Lewis Call; *The Political Philosophy of Poststructuralist Anarchism*, by Todd May; and *From Bakunin to Lacan: Anti-Authoritarianism and the Dislocation of Power*, by Saul Newman. *The New Formulation: An Anti-Authoritarian Review of Books* 2, 2 (2004): 1-6.

Glenn, David. "The Tease of Memory: Psychologists are dusting off 19th-centruy explanations of déjà vu. Have we been here before?" *The Chronicle of Higher Education*, July 23, 2004, A12.

Goldman, Emma. "An Unpublished Letter," *Freedom* 1 (1919): 4-7.

_____. *Living My Life*. 2 vols. 1931; rpt. New York,

NY: Dover, 1970.

_____. "Intellectual Proletarians." In *Red Emma Speaks: Selected Writings and Speeches by Emma Goldman*, edited by Alix Kates Shulman, 176-185. New York, NY: Vintage Books, 1972.

Gofman, John W. *An Irreverent, Illustrated View of Nuclear Power.* San Francisco: Committee for Nuclear Responsibility, 1979.

Gorman, John. *Banner Bright: An Illustrated History of Trade Union Banners.* Essex: Scorpion Publishing Ltd., 1986.

Graeber, David. "The Twilight of Vanguardism." In *Realizing The Impossible: Art Against Authority*, edited by Josh Macphee and Erik Reuland, 250-253. Oakland: AK Press, 2007.

Graham, John, ed. *"Yours for the Revolution:" The Appeal to Reason, 1895-1922.* Lincoln, NB and London: University of Nebraska Press, 1990.

Greenberg, Clement. "Avant-Garde and Kitsch." *Partisan Review* 6, 5 (1939): 34-49. http://www.sharecom.ca/greenberg/kitsch.html

_____. "Avant Garde Attitudes." The John Power Lecture in Contemporary Art. University of Sydney, May 17, 1968. Power Institute of Fine Arts, University of Sydney, 1969. http://www.sharecom.ca/greenberg/kitsch. html

_____. "Modern and Postmodern." William Dobell Memorial Lecture, Sydney, Australia, October 31, 1979. *Arts* 54, 6 (February 1980). http://www.sharecom. ca/greenberg/

Greenwald, Dara and Josh Macphee in association with Exit Art. *Signs of Change: Social Movement Cultures 1960s to Now.* Oakland and New York: AK Press and Exit Art, 2010.

Grindon, Gavin. "Carnival against capital: a comparison of Bakhtin, Vaneigem and Bey." *Anarchist Studies* 12, 2 (2004): 147-161.

_____. "Surrealism, Dada, and the Refusal of Work: Autonomy, Activism, and Social Participation in the Radical Avant-Garde." *Oxford Art Journal* 34, 2 (2011): 79-96.

Grosz/Heartfield: The Artist as Social Critic. Minneapolis, MN: University Gallery University of Minnesota, 1980.

Groys, Boris. "Stalinism as Aesthetic Phenomenon." In *Textura: Russian Essays on Visual Culture*, edited and translated by Alla Efimova and Lev Manovich, forward by

Stephen Bann,115-126. Chicago and London: University of Chicago Press, 1993.

Hahne, Ron. *Black Mask and Up Against the Wall Motherfucker: The Incomplete Works of Ron Hahne, Ben Morea and the Black Mask Group.* London: Unpopular Books and Sabotage Editions, 1993.

Harper, Clifford. *Anarchy: A Graphic Guide.* London: Camden Press, 1987.

Harrington, Austin. "New German Aesthetic Theory: Martin Seel's art of diremption." *Radical Philosophy* 109 (September/October, 2001). http://www.radicalphilosophy.com

Hart, Henry, ed. *American Writers' Congress.* New York, NY: International Publishers, 1935.

Haug, Wolfgang Fritz. *Critique of Commodity Aesthetics: Appearance, Sexuality and Advertising in Capitalist Society.* Translated by Robert Bock. Minneapolis: University of Minnesota Press, 1986.

Haywood, Bill (attributed). In *Venture*, by Max Eastman, 27. New York, NY: A.&C. Boni, 1927.

Hebdige, Dick. *Hiding in the Light: On Images and Things.* New York, NY: Routledge, 1988.

Hegel, George Wilhelm Friederich. "The Philosophy of Fine Art" Introduction, I and II. In *Philosophies of Art and Beauty: Selected Readings in Aesthetics from Plato to Heidegger*, edited by Albert Hofstadter and Richard Kuhns, 382-395. New York, NY: Modern Library, 1964.

Heilman, Kenneth M. and Russel S. Donda. "Neuroscience and Fundamentalism." *Tikkun.* July 2009. http://www.tikkun.org/magazine/tik0709/frontpage/neuroscience

Henri, Robert. *The Art Spirit.* Margaret A. Ryerson, compiler. New York, NY: J.B. Lippincott Co., 1960.

Heresies: A Feminist Publication on Art and Politics. 27 issues. 1977-1993.

Hess, Stephen and Sandy Northrup. *Drawn and Quartered: The History of American Political Cartoons.* Montgomery, AL: Elliott and Clark Publishers, 1996.

Hewitt, Andrew. *Fascist Modernism: Aesthetics, Politics, and the Avant-Garde.* Stanford, CA: Stanford University Press, 1993.

Hicks, Granville, Joseph North, Paul Peters, Isidor Schneider and Alan Calmer, eds. *Proletarian Literature in the United States*, with a critical introduction by Joseph Freeman. New York, NY: International Publishers, 1935.

Hirschman, Jack, ed. *Art on the Line, Essays by Artists about the*

Point Where Their Art & Activism Intersect. Williamantic, CN: Curbstone Press, 2002.

Hoberman, J. "Pop and Circumstance." Review of Gijs van Hensbergen, *Guernica: the Biography of a Twentieth Century Icon. The Nation,* December 13, 2004, 22-26.

_____. "Class Acts." Review of Alan Wald, *Trinity of Passional: The Literary Left and the Antifascist Crusade. The Nation,* October 8, 2007, 30 passim.

Hobsbawm, Eric. "Man and Woman in Socialist Iconography." *History Workshop Journal* 6 (Autumn 1978): 121-138.

Hofstadter, Albert and Richard Kuhns, eds. *Philosophies of Art and Beauty: Selected Readings in Aesthetics from Plato to Heidegger.* New York, NY: Modern Library, 1964.

Holbrook, Stewart H. *Dreamers of the American Dream.* New York, NY: Doubleday, 1957.

Holz, Keith. "Homogenous Nazi Art? A Bold Reading from 1994." Book Review. Eric Michaud. *The Cult of Art in Nazi Germany.* Stanford: Stanford University Press, 2004. www.h-net.org/reviews/showrev.php?id=10682

Hong, Nhat. *The Anarchist Beast: The Anti-Anarchist Crusade in Periodical Literature (1884-1906).* Minneapolis: Soil of Liberty, n.d. Rpt. with an introduction by CAL Press. Berkeley: CAL Press, 2011.

Horkheimer, Max and Theodor Adorno. "The Culture Industry: Enlightenment as Mass Deception." In *Dialectic of Enlightenment,* edited by Mieke Bal and Hent deVries, translated by Edmund Jephcott, 94-136. Stanford: Stanford University Press, 2002.

Howe, Irving. *Politics and the Novel.* New York, NY: Avon, 1957, 1967.

Huck, Gary and Mike Konopacki. *Mad in U.S.A.: The Labor Cartoons of Gary Huck and Mike Konopacki.* Chicago: Charles H. Kerr, 1993.

_____. *Bye! American: The Labor Cartoons of Gary Huck and Mike Konopacki.* Chicago: Charles H. Kerr, 1987.

Huie, Wing Young. *The University Avenue Project: The Language of Urbanism: A Six-Mile Photographic Inquiry,* Vols. 1 and 2. Saint Paul, MN: Minnesota Historical Society, 2010.

Hyde, Lewis. *The Gift: Imagination and the Erotic Life of Property.* New York, NY: Vintage, 1983

Internationale Situationniste #1 (June 1958). "Preliminary Problems in Constructing a Situation." In *Situationist International Anthology,* edited and translated by Ken

Knabb, 43-44. Berkeley: Bureau of Public Secrets, 1981.

Internationale Situationniste #3 (December 1959). *"Détournement* as Negation and Prelude." In *Situationist International Anthology,* edited and translated by Ken Knabb, 55. Berkeley: Bureau of Public Secrets, 1981.

International Situationniste #6 (August 1961). "Elementary Program of the Bureau of Unitary Urbanism," In *Situationist International Anthology,* edited and translated by Ken Knabb, 65-67. Berkeley: Bureau of Public Secrets, 1981.

Internationale Situationniste #6 (August 1961). "Instructions for Taking Up Arms." In *Situationist International Anthology,* edited and translated by Ken Knabb, 63-64. Berkeley: Bureau of Public Secrets, 1981.

Internationale Situationniste #8 (January 1963). "Ideologies, Classes and the Domination of Nature." In *Situationist International Anthology,* edited and translated by Ken Knabb, 101-108. Berkeley: Bureau of Public Secrets, 1981.

Internationale Situationniste #9 (August 1964). "Questionnaire." In *Situationist International Anthology,* edited and translated by Ken Knabb, 138-142. Berkeley: Bureau of Public Secrets, 1981.

Internationale Situationniste #12 (September 1969), "The Beginning of an Era." In *Situationist International Anthology,* edited and translated by Ken Knabb, 225-256. Berkeley: Bureau of Public Secrets, 1981.

Jacobs, Karrie and Steven Heller. *Angry Graphics: Protest Posters of the Reagan/Bush Era.* Salt Lake City: Peregrine Smith Books, 1992.

Jameson, Frederic. "Postmodernism, or the Cultural Logic of Late Capitalism." *New Left Review* 146, 4 (July-August, 1984): 53–93.

Jenkins, Iredell. *Art and the Human Enterprise.* Cambridge, MA: Harvard University Press, 1958.

Jhally, Sut. *The Codes of Advertising: Fetishism and the Political Economy of Meaning in the Consumer Society.* New York, NY: St. Martin's Press, 1987.

Jörg, Hans und Nikola Doll, eds. *Kunst und Propaganda: Im Streit der Nationen 1930-1945.* Berlin: Deutsches Historisches Museum, 2007.

Kahn, Douglas and Diane Neumaier, eds. *Cultures in Contention.* Seattle: The Real Comet Press, 1985.

Kane, Pat. "Review of *The Economics of Attention* by Richard A.

Lanham." *The Independent*, July 14, 2006.

Kappeler, Susanne. *The Pornography of Representation*. Minneapolis: University of Minnesota Press, 1986.

Kaufman, Alan, ed. *The Outlaw Bible of American Poetry*. New York, NY: Thunder's Mouth Press, 1999.

Kearney, Richard. *The Wake of Imagination: Ideas of Creativity in Western Culture*. Hutchinson, London, Minneapolis: University of Minnesota Press, (1988), Routledge, London and New York (2004).

Kelley, R. Gordon. "Literature and the Historian." *American Quarterly* XXVI, 2 (May, 1974): 153-170.

Kelley, Robin D. G. "Freedom Now Sweet: Surrealism and the Black World." In *Surrealist Subversions: Rants, Writings and Images by the Surrealist Movement in the United States*, edited by Ron Sakolsky, 134-150. New York, NY: Autonomedia, 2002.

Khatchadourian, Raffi. "In the Picture: An Artist's Global Experiment to Help People Be Seen." *The New Yorker* (November 28, 2011): 56-63.

King, David. *Red Star over Russia: A Visual History of the Soviet Union from 1917 to the Death of Stalin*. London: Tate Publishing, 2009.

Kipnis, Laura. *Ecstasy Unlimited: On Sex, Capital, Gender, and Aesthetics*. Minneapolis and London: University of Minnesota Press, 1993

Kirsch, Adam. "The Philosopher Stoned." *The New Yorker*. August 21, 2006: 79-84.

Knabb, Ken. "The Situationists and the Occupation Movements (1868/2011). *Counterpunch* (November 8, 2011). www.counterpunch.org/2011/11/08/the-situationists-and-the-occupation-movements-1968/2011

_____. *Public Secrets*. Berkeley: Bureau of Public Secrets, 1997.

Knabb, Ken, ed. and trans. *Situationist International Anthology*. Berkeley: Bureau of Public Secrets, 1981.

Koehnline, James. See www.koehnline.com for background information on the artist, and www.james119.deviantart.com/gallery to view the body of his work.

Kozol, Wendy. "Questions of Looking," Review of Susan Buck-Morss, *The Dialectics of Seeing: Walter Benjamin and the Arcades Project*. *American Quarterly* 46, 2 (June 1994): 276–289.

Kuhns, Richard. *Structure of Experience: Essays on the Affinity between Philosophy and Literature*. New York, NY: Harper &

Row, 1970.

Kultureplätz: Materialien zur dezentralen Kulturarbeit. Berlin (West): Neue Gesellschaft für Bildende Kunst, 1985.

Kunst aus der Revolution: Sowjuetische Kunst während der Phase der Kollektivierung under Industrialisierung 1927-1933. Berlin (West): Neue Gesellschaft für Bildende Kunst in Zusammenarbeit mit der Staatliche Tretjakov-Galerie Moskau, USSR, 1877.

"Kunst in die Produktion!" Sowjetische Kunst während der Phase der Kollektivierung under Industrialisierung 1927-1933. Berlin (West): Neue Gesellschaft für Bildende Kunst, 1977.

Künstler auf Einer Geschichtsdeponie. Berlin (West): Neue Gesellschaft für Bildende Kunst and Gesellschaft zur Rettung der Stadtgeschichte, 1988.

Kunststück Farbe: Ein Experiment in Stadt und Landschaft. Berlin (West): Neue Gesellschaft für Bildende Kunst, 1988.

Kwon, Miwon. *One Place after Another: Site-Specific Art and Locational Identity.* Cambridge, MA: Massachusetts Institution of Technology, 2002.

Lamantia, Philip. "Poetic Matters: A Critique of the 'New American Poetics.'" In *Surrealist Subversions: Rants, Writings and Images by the Surrealist Movement in the United States,* edited by Ron Sakolsky, 283-290. New York, NY: Autonomedia, 2002,

Lamantia, Philip and Nancy Joyce Peters, "The Future of Surrealism." In *Surrealist Subversions: Rants, Writings and Images by the Surrealist Movement in the United States,* edited by Ron Sakolsky, 230-231. New York, NY: Autonomedia, 2002.

Landstreicher, Wolfi. "From Politics to Life: Ridding Anarchy of the Leftist Millstone." *Anarchy: A Journal of Desire Armed* (Fall/Winter 2002-2003): 47-51.

Lanoux, Armand. *Paris in the Twenties.* New York, NY: Golden Griffin Books/Essential Encyclopedia Arts, Inc., 1960.

Lasn, Kalle. *Design Anarchy.* Vancouver, BC: Adbusters Media Foundation, 2006.

_____. *Meme Wars: The Creative Destruction of Neoclassical Economics.* New York, NY: Seven Stories Press, 2012.

Larson, Gary O. *The Reluctant Patron: The United States Government and the Arts, 1943-1965.* Philadelphia: University of Pennsylvania Press, 1983.

Lears, Jackson. "Keeping It Real." Review of Martin Jay, *Songs of Experience: Modern American and European Variations on a Universal Theme. The Nation* (June 12, 2006): 23-30.

_____. "Uneasy Courtship: Modern Art and Modern Advertising." *American Quarterly* 39, 1 (1987): 133-154.

Lee, Anthony W. *Painting on the Left: Diego Rivera, Radical Politics, and San Francisco's Public Murals.* Berkeley and others: University of California Press, 1999.

Lee, Alfred McClung and Elizabeth Briant Lee, eds. *The Fine Art of Propaganda: A Study of Father Coughlin's Speeches.* New York, NY: Harcourt Brace & Co., 1939

Lenin, Vladimir I. *On Literature and Art.* Moscow: Progress Publishers, 1967.

Lerner, Michael. *Surplus Powerlessness: The Psychodynamics of Everyday Life ... and the Psychology of Individual and Social Transformation.* Oakland, CA: The Institute for Labor and Mental Health, 1986.

Le Sueur, Meridel. *Journals.* n.d.

Letse Avant-garde kunst 1910-1935. Deventer: Bergkerk Kunst, 1991.

Levy, Rob. "The Politics of Language in Social Movements of the Information Age." In *Design Anarchy,* by Kalle Lasn, n.p. Vancouver, BC: Adbusters Media Foundation, 2006, n.p.

Lewis, Beth Irwin. *Grosz/Heartfield: The Artist as Social Critic (Germany in the Twenties).* Teaneck, NJ: Holmes & Meier Publishers, 1984.

Lippard, Lucy R., ed. *From the Center: Feminist Essays on Women's Art.* New York, NY: E.P. Dutton & Co., 1976.

Litvinov, Victor, ed. *The Posters of Glasnost and Perestroika.* Introductions by Alexander Yegorov and Victor Litvonov. London and Others: Penguin Books, 1989.

Lorde, Geraldine Audre. *Sister Outsider: Essays and Speeches.* New York, NY: Crossing Press, 1984.

Lovelace, Alice. "come to this work naked ...," in *Wild Caught Stories,* Vol. 5, If community engaged art making is transformational, what are the moral and ethical dimensions of the work? Bainbridge Island, WA: Center for the Study of Art and Community. November 16, 2008. www.artandcommunity.com

MacBean, James Roy. *Film and Revolution.* Bloomington and London: Indiana University Press, 1975.

MacPhee, Josh, Ed. *Celebrate People's History: The Poster Book of Resistance and Revolution.* Forward by Rebecca Solnit. New York, NY: Feminist Press, 2010.

_____. *Paper Politics: Socially Engaged Printmaking Today.* Oakland, CA: PM Press, 2009.

MacPhee, Josh and Alec Dunn, Eds. *Signal: 01*. Oakland, CA: PM Press, 2010.

MacPhee, Josh and Erik Reuland, eds. *Realizing the Impossible: Art against Authority*. Oakland and Edinburgh: AK Press, 2007.

Maquet, Jacques. "Objects as Instruments, Objects as Signs." In *History from Things: Essays on Material Culture*, edited by Steven Lubar and W. David Kingery. Washington and London: Smithsonian Institution Press, 1993, 30-40.

Marx, Karl and Friedrich Engels. *The German Ideology*. Moscow: Progress Publishers, 1964.

Mason, Tim. "The Domestication of Female Socialist Icons: A Note in Reply to Eric Hobsbawm." *History Workshop: A Journal of Socialist Historians* 7 (Spring 1979): 170–175.

May, Todd. *The Political Philosophy of Poststructuralist Anarchism*. University Park PA: University of Pennsylvania Press, 1994.

_____. "Poststructuralist Anarchism: An Interview with Todd May." *Perspectives* 4, 2, 2000. http://flag.blackened. net/ias/8may.htm

May, Todd, Benjamin Noys and Saul Newman. "Democracy, Anarchism and Radical Politics Today: An Interview with Jacques Rancière." Translated by John Lechte. *Anarchist Studies* 16, 2, 2008: 173-185.

McCloud, Scott. *Understanding Comics: The Invisible Art*. Northampton, MA: Tundra Publishing Ltd., 1993.

McGinnis, Mark. "An Overdose of Television Has Deadened the Visual Imagination of Our Students." *The Chronicle of Higher Education*, February 20, 1991.

McKinzie, Richard D. *The New Deal for Artists*. Princeton University Press, 1973.

McLay, Farquhar. *Art and Anarchism*. Glasgow: Autonomy Press, n.d.

Menand, Louis. "Dwight Macdonald's War on Midcult." *The New Yorker* (September 5, 2011): 72-78.

_____. "Unpopular Front: American art and the Cold War." *The New Yorker*, October 17, 2005: 173-179.

_____. "Culture Club: The short, happy life of the American highbrow." *The New Yorker*, October 15, 2001: 202-210.

Metropolis, directed by Fritz Lang, Germany, 1927. Restored 2002, with original music score. Available on DVD with subtitles in English, French, and Spanish. Kino Video, NY.

Milstein, Cindy. "Reappropriate the Imagination!" In *Realizing the Impossible: Art Against Authority*, edited by Josh Macphee and Erik Reuland, 297-307. Oakland and Edinburgh: AK Press, 2007.

Mitzman, Arthur. "Anarchism, Expressionism, and Psychoanalysis." *New German Critique* 10, Winter, 1977: 77-104.

Mirza, Munira. "Is modern art a left-wing conspiracy?" *Spiked*, November 22, 2007. http://www.spiked-online.com

Moore, Anne Elizabeth. "Branding Anti-Consumerism: The Capitalistic Nature of Anti-Corporate Activism." In *Realizing The Impossible: Art Against Authority*, edited by Josh Macphee and Erik Reuland, 285-295. Oakland: AK Press, 2007.

Moore, John. "The Insubordination of Words: Poetry, Insurgency and the Situationists." *Anarchist Studies* 10, 2 (November 2002): 145-164.

Morales, Ricardo Levins. "The Importance of Being Artist." In *Reimaging America: The Arts of Social Change*, edited by Mark O'Brien and Craig Little, 16-24. New York: New Society Publishers, 1990.

_____. See Ricardo Levins Morales work at www.rlmarts.com

Morris, Brian. "Reflections on the 'New Anarchism.'" *Social Anarchism* 42 (2008-2009): 36-50.

Morrison, Theodore. *Chautauqua: A Center for Education, Religion, and the Arts in America*. Chicago and London: University of Chicago Press, 1974.

Mumford, Lewis. *Art and Technics*. New York, NY: Columbia University Press, 1952.

_____. *The Pentagon of Power*. New York, NY: Harcourt, Brace, Jovanovich, 1970.

Munton, Alan. "Anarchism, Modernism and Cultural Theory: The Ousting of Raymond Williams. *Key Words* 4 (2003). http://www.arasite.org/amwilliams.html

Murdoch, Iris. *The Black Prince*. London: Penguin, 1975

_____. *The Sovereignty of Good*. New York, NY: Schocken, 1971.

Nagel, Alexander. *Berlin West: Ein Fotobilderbuch*. Berlin: Galerie für creative Fotografie, 1977.

Nelson, Bruce C. *Beyond the Martyrs: A Social History of Chicago's Anarchists, 1870-1900*. New Brunswick NJ: Rutgers University Press, 1988.

Nelson, Cary. *Revolutionary Memory: Recovering the Poetry of the*

American Left. New York, NY and Others: Routledge, 2001.

Nematollahy, Ali. "Proudhon, from aesthetics to politics." *Anarchist Studies* 13, 1 (2005), 47-60.

Neruda, Pablo. *A Call for the Destruction of Nixon and Praise for the Chilean Revolution.* Translated byTeresa Anderson. Cambridge, MA: West End Press, 1980.

_____. *Let the Rail Splitter Awake and Other Poems.* New York, NY: International Publishers, 1988.

Nettlau, Max. "Anarchism: Communist or Individualist? – Both." In *Anarchy: An Anthology of Emma Goldman's* Mother Earth, edited and with commentary by Peter Glassgold, 79-83. Washington, DC: Counterpoint, 2001.

Newman, Saul. "Editorial: Postanarchism." *Anarchist Studies* 16, 2 (2008): 101-106.

NO! art. Berlin (West): Neue Gesellschaft für Bildende Kunst, 1995.

North, Joseph, ed. *New Masses: An Anthology of the Rebel Thirties.* New York, NY: International Publishers, 1969.

Nur eine Woge: Drehbuch und Materialien zum Film. Berlin (West): Neue Gesellschaft für Bildende Kunst, 1977.

Nutter, Jude. "Untitled." In *I Wish I Had a Heart Like Yours, Walt Whitman,* by Jude Nutter, 8-10. Notre Dame, IN: University of Notre Dame Press, 2009.

O'Connor, Francis. V, ed. *Art for the Millions: Essays from the 1930s by Artists and Administrators of the WPA Federal Art Project.* Boston: New York Graphic Society, 1975.

www.occuprint.org Posters of the Occupy movement.

O'Neill, William L., ed. *Echoes of Revolt: The Masses 1911-1917.* Chicago: Ivan R. Dee, Inc., 1989.

Ostreicher, Richard. "From Artisan to Consumer: Images of Workers 1840-1920." *Journal of American Culture* 4 (Spring 1984): 47-64.

Palante, Georges. *La Sensibilite individualiste (The Anarchist Sensibility).* Paris: Folle Avoine, 1909. Also known as "Anarchism and Individualism." Translated by Mitch Abidor. www.marxists.org/archive/palante/1909/individualism.htm and www.theanarchistlibrary.org

Panofsky, Erwin. *Meaning in the Visual Arts.* Garden City, New York, NY: Doubleday/Anchor, 1955.

Parry, Albert. *Garrets and Pretenders: A History of Bohemianism in America.* New York, NY: Dover, 1960.

Parry, William. *Against The Wall: The Art of Resistance in Palestine.* Chicago: Lawrence Hill Books, 2011.

Patke, Rajeev S. "Walter Benjamin, Surrealism and Photography." Paper presented at Workshop on 'Literature as Revolt in Twentieth Century Europe', 17 August 1998, The University of Haifa, Israel (6th ISSEI Conference). http://www.sunwalked.wordpress.com/2009/12/17/interesting-paper-on-walter-benjamin-surrealism-and-photography-by-rajeev-s-patke

Pellis, Richard H. *Radical Visions and American Dreams: Culture and Social Thought in the Depression Years.* New York, NY: Harper & Row, 1973.

Perl, Jed. "Postcards from Nowhere." *The New Republic.* June 25, 2008. www.tnr.com

_____. "Cash and Carry Aesthetics." *The Baffler* 20 (2012).

Petrovich, Dushko. "A painter's call for 'a practical avant-garde.'" *The Boston Globe*, March 4, 2007. http://www.bostonglobe.com

Peters, Louis F. *Kunst en Revolt: het politieke plakkaat en de opstand van de franse studenten.* Westfriesland: Hoorn, 1969.

Phillips, William and Philip Rahv. "Recent Problems in Revolutionary Literature." In *The Anxious Years*, edited by Louis Filler, 338-344. New York, NY: G.P. Putnam's Sons, 1963.

Pinter, Harold. "Art, Truth and Politics." Speech upon receipt of Nobel Prize. December 8, 2005. http://books.guardian.co.uk/news/articles/0,6109,1661516,.00.html

Plagens, Peter. "Who's Art Is It Anyway?" *The Nation*, October 30, 2006: 27-32.

Plato. In *Philosophies of Art and Beauty: Selected Readings in Aesthetics from Plato to Heidegger*, edited by Albert Hofstadter and Richards Kuhns. New York, NY: Modern Library, 1964. See the following dialogues: *Ion*, 53-57; *Phaedrus*, 57-67; *Symposium*, 68-77.

_____. *The Republic.* In *The Collected Dialogues*, edited by Edith Hamilton and Huntington Cairns. Princeton, NJ: Princeton University Press, 1973. http://www.classics.mit.edu/Plato/republich.html

Plotinus, *Ennead I*, Sixth Tractate, "Beauty." In *Philosophies of Art and Beauty: Selected Readings in Aesthetics from Plato to Heidegger*, edited by Albert Hofstadter and Richards Kuhns, 141-150. New York, NY: Modern Library, 1964.

Pohl, Francis. "Rockwell Kent and the Vermont Marble Workers' Strike." *Archives of American Art Journal* 29, 3 and 4 ((1989): 58.

Pope, Amanda and Tchavdar Georgiev. *The Desert of Forbidden*

Art. DVD, 80 minutes. www.desertofforbiddenart.com

"Poststructuralist Anarchism: An Interview with Todd May." *Perspectives on Anarchist Theory* 4, 2 (Fall, 2000). http://flag. blackened.net/ias/8may.htm

Proudhon, Pierre. *Du Principe de l'art et de sa destination sociale*. Paris: Garnier Frères, 1865.

_____. *La Pornocratie, ou les femmes dans les temps moderns*. Paris: A Lacroix, 1875.

Proyect, L. "Trotskyism and the Abstract Expressionists." n.d. http://www.columbia.edu/~lnp3/mydocs/culture/guilbaut. htm .

Rancière, Jacques. *On the Shores of Politics*. London: Verso, 1995.

_____. "Politics and Aesthetics: an interview." Translated by Forbes Morlock with an introduction by Peter Hallward. *Angelaki: Journal of the Theoretical Humanities* 8, 2, August 2003: 191-211.

_____. *The Politics of Aesthetics: The Distribution of the Sensible*. Translated with an introduction by Gabriel Rockhill, with an afterward by Slavoj Žižek. New York, NY: Continuum, 2004, 2005.

_____. *Dissensus: On Politics and Aesthetics*. Edited and Translated by Steven Corcoran. New York, NY: Continuum, 2010, 2011.

Randall, Margaret. "Immigration Law." In *Poetry like Bread: Poets of the Political Imagination*, edited by Martin Espada, 182. Willimantic, CT: Curbstone Press, 1994.

Read, Herbert. "The Great Debate." In *To Hell with Culture: and Other Essays on Art and Society*, by Herbert Read, 178-185. New York, NY: Schocken Books, 1970.

_____. *Education through Art*. New York, NY: Pantheon, 1956.

Richter, Hans. *Dada: Art and Anti-Art*. London and New York, NY: Thames and Hudson, 1965, 1997.

Rideout, Walter B. *The Radical Novel in the United States 1900-1954*. New York, NY: Hill and Wang, 1956.

Roberts, John. "Commentaries: Art, Politics and Provincialism." *Radical Philosophy*. March/April 2001. http://www.radicalphilosophy.com

_____. "After Adorno: Art, Autonomy, and Critique." Paper delivered at apexart, London. March 8, 2000. http://www.apexart.org/residency/roberts.htm

_____. "Oh, I love trash..." Review of *gargantua: manufactured mass culture* by Julian Stallabrass. London: Verso,

Variant Magazine 1 (n.d., mid-1980s). http://www.variant. randomstate.org/1texts/John_Roberts.html

Robins, Kevin. "Against Virtual Community: for a politics of distance." *Angelaki: Journal of the Theoretical Humanities* 4, 2 (1999): 163-170.

Roediger, Dave and Franklin Rosemont, eds. *Haymarket Scrapbook*. Chicago: Charles H. Kerr, 1986.

Rosemont, Franklin. *Jacques Vaché and the Roots of Surrealism*. Chicago: Charles H. Kerr Publishing Company, 2008.

_____. *Revolution in the Service of the Marvelous*. Chicago: Charles H. Kerr Publishing Company, 2004.

_____. "Introduction: Andre Breton and the First Principles of Surrealism." In *What is Surrealism? Selected Writings*. Franklin Rosemount, Ed., Translated by Samuel Beckett and others and introduced by Franklin Rosemount. New York, NY: Monad, Pathfinder Press, 1978.

Rosemont, Franklin, Ed. *Arsenal: Surrealist Subversion*. Chicago: Black Swan Press, 1989.

Rosemont, Franklin, Penelope Rosemont and Paul Garon, eds. "Introduction." *The Forecast is Hot! Tracts and Other Collective Declarations of the Surrealist Movement in the United States 1966-1976*,. Chicago: Black Swan Press, 1997.

Rosemont, Penelope. *Dreams & Everyday Life: André Breton, Surrealism, Rebel Worker; sds and the Seven Cities of Cibola*. Chicago: Charles H. Kerr Publishing Company, 2008.

Rosenberg, Harold. *Discovering the Present: Three Decades in Art, Culture, and Politics*. Chicago and London: The University of Chicago Press, 1973. See especially "The Herd of Independent Minds," "Spectators and Recruiters," "The Avant-Garde," and "Virtuosos of Boredom."

_____. Harold Rosenberg, "The American Action Painters," Art News 1/8, Dec. 1952. http://www.pooter. net/intermedia/readings/06.html

_____. *De-definition of Art*. Chicago: University of Chicago Press, 1983.

Rosenfeld, Kathryn. "Who the Hell Wants to be Reasonable?" *Social Anarchism* 37 (2004-2005): 44-52.

_____. "This Is Not an Essay on Political Art." *In These Times*, September 15, 2003. http://www.inthesetimes. com/article/this_is_not_an_essay_on_political_art/

Rubin, William S. *Dada and Surrealist Art*. New York: Harry N. Abrams, 1985.

Rucker, Rudy, Peter Lamborn Wilson, and Robert Anton

Wilson, Eds. *SEMIOTEXT[E] SF*. New York, NY: Autonomedia, 1989.

Rupp, Leila J. *Mobilizing Women for War: German and American Propaganda 1939–1945*. Princeton, NJ: Princeton University Press, 1978.

Sakolsky, Ron. "Introduction – "Surrealist Subversion in Chicago: The Forecast is Hotter than Ever!" In *Surrealist Subversions: Rants, Writings and Images by the Surrealist Movement in the United States*, edited by Ron Sakolsky, 23-110. New York, NY: Autonomedia, 2002.

_____. "The Surrealist Adventure and the Poetry of Direction Action: Passionate Encounters between the Chicago Surrealist Group, the Wobblies and Earth First!" *The Journal of Aesthetics & Protest* 8 (2011). www.joaap.org/issue8/Sakolsky_surrealists.htm

Salerno, Salvatore. *Red November Black November: Culture and Community in the Industrial Workers of the World*. Albany, NY: SUNY Press, 1989.

Salzman, Jack, ed. *Years of Protest: A Collection of American Writings of the 1930's*. New York, NY: Pegasus, 1967.

Salt of the Earth. Screenplay by Michael Wilson, Commentary by Deborah Silverton Rosenfelt. Old Westbury, NY: The Feminist Press. 1953, 1978.

Saunders, Frances Stonor. "Modern Art was a CIA 'Weapon.'" *Independent* (22 October 1995). www.independent.co.uk/news/world/modern-art-was-cia-weapon-1578808.html#

Sax, Boria. "Storytelling and the 'Information Overload.'" *On the Horizon* 14, 3 (Fall 2006): 165-170.

Schleuning, Neala J. Political Poster Collection. University of Delaware Library. http://www.lib.udel.edu/spec/findaids/graphics/findaids/schleun2.htm

Schjeldahl, Peter. "The Painting on the Wall: Diego Rivera in New York." *The New Yorker* (November 28, 2011): 84-85.

_____. "Young at Heart: Dada at MOMA." *The New Yorker* (June 26, 2006): 84-85.

_____. "Big Bang: Abstract Expressionism on full show at MOMA," *The New Yorker* (October 18, 2010): 94-95.

_____. "Shapes of Things: The Birth of the Abstract," *The New Yorker* (January 7, 2013), 68-70.

Schmid, Siegfried. "Storytelling and the 'Information Overload.'" *On the Horizon*. 2006.

Scholes, Robert. "In the Brothel of Modernism: Picasso and Joyce." *The American Journal of Semiotics* 8, 1/2 (1991):

5–25.

Schwabsky, Barry. "Signs of Protest: Occupy's Guerilla Semiotics. *The Nation* (December 14, 2011). www.the-nation.com

Schwartz, Stephen. "Bad Poet, Bad Man." *The Weekly Standard* 9, 43 (July 26, 2004).

Scrivener, Michael. "The Anarchist Aesthetic." *Black Rose* 1, 1 (1979): 7-21.

Sebeok, Thomas A. "Fetish." *The American Journal of Semiotics* 6, 4 (1989): 51–65.

Seven Voices: Seven Latin American Writers Talk to Rita Guibert. Translated by Frances Partridge, Introduction by Emir Rodríquez Monegal. New York, NY: Knopf, 1973.

Shantz, Jeff. "Anarchists in the Academy: Concerns and Cautions." *Social Anarchism* 41 (2008-2008): 36-42.

Shattuck, Roger. "The D-S Expedition: Part I." *The New York Review of Books* 18, 9 (May 18, 1972). http://www.nybooks. com/articles/archives/

Shivani, Anis. "Where Does Collaboration with Fascist Aesthetics Begin and End?" www.bu.edu/agni/essays/on-line/2004/shivani-fascist.html

Short, Robert S. "The Politics of Surrealism, 1920-1936." *Journal of Contemporary History* 1, 2 (1966): 3-25.

Shover, Michele J. "Roles and Images of Women in World War I Propaganda." *Politics and Society* 5, 4 (1975): 469–489.

Shukaitis, Stevphen. *Imaginal Machines: Autonomy and Self-Organization in the Revolutions of Everyday Life.* London/ NYC/Port Watson: Minor Compositions, 2009.

Shulman, Alix Kates, ed. *Red Emma Speaks: Selected Writings and Speeches by Emma Goldman.* New York, NY: Vintage Books, 1972.

Situationalist International. "Watts 1965: The Decline and Fall of the Spectacle-Commodity Economy." *Anarchy: A Journal of Desire Armed* 34 (Fall 1992): 49 passim.

Solomon, Alisa. "Art Makes a Difference." *The Nation* (November 8, 2004): 28-32.

Sontag, Susan. *On Photography.* New York: Farrar, Straus and Giroux, 1977.

_____. "Fascinating Fascism." Review of *The Last of the Nuba* by Leni Reifenthal and *SS Regalia* by Jack Pia. *The New York Review of Books*, February 6, 1975. www.nybooks. com/articles/archives/1975/feb/06/fascinating-fascism/

Spiegelman, Art. "Reading Pictures: A Few Thousand Words on Six Books without Any." Introduction to Ward, Lynd.

Six Novels in Woodcuts. Edited by Art Spiegelman. New York, NY: The Library of America, 2010.

Spiegelman, Art and Francois Mouly, eds. *Read Yourself Raw.* New York, NY: Pantheon Books, 1987.

Stencil in Athens. TOIXO   , Vol. 2, 2008.

Strauss, David Levi. *Between Dog and Wolf: Essays on Art and Politics in the Twilight of the Millenium.* Brooklyn, NY: Autonomedia, 1999.

Stirner, Max. *The Ego and His Own: The Case of the Individual Against Authority.* Translated by Steven T. Byington. New York, NY: Dover, 1973.

Surplus: Terrorized into being Consumers. Directed by Erik Gandini, edited by Johan Söderberg. Produced by ATMO for Swedish Television. 2003, 52 minutes. Available in English, French, Spanish, Portugese, Italian, and Swedish. Winner of the Silver Wolf Award, IDFA Amsterdam, 2003. The film is available on YouTube in sections.

Swados, Harvey, ed. *The American Writer and the Great Depression.* New York, NY: Bobbs-Merrill, 1966.

Sypher, Eileen. "Toward a Theory of the Lyric: George Lukacs and Christopher Caudwell." *Praxis* VI, 3 (1977): 173-182.

Tabaka, Maija. *Bilder 1962-1978.* Berlin (West): Neue Gesellschaft für Bildende Kunst künstlerhaus bethanien in zusammenarbeit mit verband der künstler der udssr verband der künstler der lettischen ssr, 1979.

Tallis, Raymond. "Art, humanity and the 'fourth hunger.'" *The Spiked Review of Books.* November 30, 2007. http://www.spiked-online.com/

Tate, Allan to Malcolm Cowley, Correspondence December 1930-December 1934. In Daniel Aaron, *Writers on the Left: Episodes in American Literary Communism.* New York, NY: Octagon, 1974.

Taylor, Charles. "Ill Will." Review of *Leni Rifenstahl: A Life* by Jurgen Trimborn and *Leni: The Life and Work of Leni Riefenstahl* by Steven Bach, *The Nation,* May 7, 2007, 44-49.

The Lord's Prayer. With Drawings by Mary Elizabeth Given. New York, NY: The Vanguard Press, 1931.

Taylor, NAJ. "The Falling Man: 9/11's Private Moments." *Al Jazeera* (September 2011). www.aljazeera.com/indepth/opinion/2011/09/201191014423515812.html

Thiong'o, Ngugi Wa. "Freedom of the Artist: People's Artists versus People's Rulers." In *Art on the Line, Essays by Artists about the Point Where Their Art & Activism Intersect,* edited by Jack Hirschman, 203-221. Williamantic, CN: Curbstone

Press, 2002.

Tisa, John, ed. *The Palette and the Flame: Posters of the Spanish Civil War.* New York, NY: International Publishers, 1979.

Tobocman, Seth. *You Don't have to Fuck People Over to Survive.* San Francisco: Pressure Drop Press, 1990.

Tolstoy, Leo N. *What Is Art?* New York, NY: Bobbs-Merrill, 1896, 1960.

Tolstoy, Vladimir, Irina Bibikova, and Catherine Cooke. *Street Art of the Revolution: Festivals and Celebrations in Russia 1918-1933.* London: The Vendome Press, 1990-.

To Street Art. A. TOIXO , Vol 1, 2007.

Tse-Tung, Mao. *Talks at the Yenan Forum on Literature and Art.* Peking: Foreign Language Press, 1967.

Unbeachtete Produktionsformen. Berlin (West): Neue Gesellschaft für Bildende Kunst, 1982.

Unleash. "There are Ills the only Cure for which is Literature." *Fifth Estate* 373 (Fall 2006): 13.

Vaneigem, Raoul. *The Revolution of Everyday Life.* Translated by Donald Nicholson-Smith. London: Left Bank Books and Rebel Press, 1994.

——————— (Jules-François Dupuis). *A Cavalier History of Surrealism.* Translated by Donald Nicholson-Smith. Edinburgh and Others: AK Press, 1977, 1999.

Varnedoe, Kirk. "A Shared Culture of Private Visions." *The Chronicle of Higher Education* 53, 15, December 1, 2006, B23.

Vaucher, Gee. *Crass Art and Other Pre Post-Modernist Monsters: A collection of work by Gee Vaucher* . New York and Others: AK Press, 1999.

Vázquez, Adolpho Sánchez. *Art and Society: Essays in Marxist Aesthetics.* New York, NY and London: Monthly Review Press, 1973.

Viklund, Andreas. "Adorno, Barthes, and Benjamin." March 28, 2007. http://andyw.wordpress.com/2007/03/28/ador-no-barthes-and-benjamin/

Vollbild: Eine Kunst-Ausstellung über Leben and Sterben. Zusammengestellt von Frank Wagner. Berlin (West): Neue Gesellschaft für Bildende Kunst, 1988.

Von Blum, Paul. *The Critical Vision: A History of Social and Political Art in the U.S.* Boston: South End Press, 1982.

Walsh, David. "Gustave Moreau: An exhibit at the Metropolitan Museum of Art, New York City (June 1-August 22). *World Socialist Web Site*, July 14, 1999. http://www.wsws.org/articles/1999/jul1999/mor1-j14_prn.shtml

Ward, Lynd. *Gods' Man: A Novel in Woodcuts.* Mineola, NY:

Dover Publications, 1929, 1957.

_____. "On God's Man." In Lynd Ward, *Six Novels in Woodcuts*, edited and introduced by Art Spiegelman, 777-791. New York, NY: The Library of America, 2010.

_____. *Six Novels in Woodcuts*, edited and introduced by Art Spiegelman. New York, NY: The Library of America, 2010.

_____. "On Madman's Drum." In Lynd Ward, *Six Novels in Woodcuts*, edited and introduced by Art Spiegelman, 787-791. New York, NY: The Library of America, 2010.

Ward, Tom. "The Situationists Reconsidered." In *Cultures in Contention*, edited by Douglas Kahn and Diane Neumaier, 145-165. Seattle: The Real Comet Press, 1985.

Watson, Patrick. *Fasanella's City: The paintings of Ralph Fasanella, with the store of his life and art*. New York, NY: Alfred A. Knopf, 1973.

We Are Strong: A Guide to the Work of Popular Theatres Across the Americas. Mankato, MN: Institute for Cultural Policy Studies, 1983.

Weir, David. *Anarchy and Culture: the Aesthetic Politics of Modernism*. Amherst: University of Massachusetts Press, 1997.

White, Stephen. *The Bolshevik Poster*. New Haven and London: Yale University Press, 1988.

Whitehead, Fred. *Against Canons*. Kansas City, KS: John Brown Press, 1992.

_____. "Our Hidden Heritage of People's Culture: Summary Report of a Conference." Kansas City, KS, 1985.

Whitehead, Fred, Ed. *Culture Wars: Opposing Viewpoints*. San Diego: Greenhaven Press, 1994.

Williams, Tennessee. "Something Wild." Introduction to *27 Wagons Full of Cotton*. New York, NY: New Directions, 1949.

Wilson, Robert Charles. *Blind Lake*, New York, NY: Tom Doherty, 2003.

Wind, Edgar. *Art and Anarchy*. New York, NY: Random House, 1969.

Winner, Langdon. "Mythinformation." In *Questioning Technology: A Critical Anthology*, edited and introduced by John Zerzan and Alice Carnes, 163-170. London: Freedom Press, 1988.

Witt, Rebecca. "Poststructuralist Anarchism: An Interview with Todd May." *Perspectives on Anarchist Theory* 4, 2 (Fall 2000). http://flag.blackened.net/ias/8may.htm

Wolin, Richard. "A Metaphysical Materialist." *The Nation* (October 16, 2006): 30-35.

Zabala, Horacio. "The Image of Duplication." *Leonardo* 25, 1 (1992): 47-50.

Zeitlian, Hraztan, editor/designer. *Semiotext [E] Architecture.* New York, NY: Columbia University/Autonomedia, 1992.

Zerzan, John. "The Case against Art." In *Elements of Refusal,* by John Zerzan, 54-62. Seattle: Left Bank Books, 1988. http://www.primitivism.com/case-art.htm

_____. *Twilight of the Machines.* Port Townsend, WA: Feral House, 2008. whttp://www.feralhouse.com

Zinovich, Jordan, ed. *Canadas.* New York, NY and Canada: Semiotext(e)/marginal editions, 1994.

Žižek, Slavoj. *Did Somebody Say Totalitarianism? Five Interventions in the (Mis) Use of a Notion.* London, New York: Verso, 2001.

_____. "The Lesson of Rancière." In *The Politics of Aesthetics,* by Jacques Rancière, translated with an introduction by Gabriel Rockhill, with an afterward by Slavoj Žižek, 69-79. New York: Continuum, 2005.

Zwischenspiele: Junge Künstler and Künstlerinnen aus der Deutschen Demokratischen Republik. Berlin (West): Neue Gesellschaft für Bildende Kunst, 1989.

INDEX

Hewitt, Andrew, 45, 47
Harper, Clifford, 229
Horkheimer, Max, 143, 155, 190, 197, 204, 210, 216, 218, 244.
    See also culture industry.
Hüelsenbeck, Carl, 77
Huie, Wing Young, 247-248

Imagination, 20, 87, 88, 90, 112, 154, 197, 270-278
Individualism, 118, 131, 172, 178-180, 213, and Modernism, 62-65
Individualist anarchism, 29, 48, 55, 64, 65, 210, 211, 213, 224, 231
Industrial Workers of the World (IWW), 6, 56, 57, 61, 99, 120, 246

Jameson, Fredric, 189, 190, 194, 197, 200, 201, 202, 258
Jhally, Sut, 158-160

Knabb, Ken, 283
Koehnline, James, 229, 263-264, 265, 273, 275
Kropotkin, Peter, 34, 56, 234, 257

Lamantia, Philip, 100; and Nancy Joyce Peters, 95
Landstreicher, Wolfi, 213
Lange, Dorothea, 3, 128
Lasn, Kalle, 164n, 165n, 173n, 181n, 282
Lears, Jackson, 14, 40, 51-53, 54
Lettrism, 19, 27, 178, 183, 188

McCarthy Era, 122, 123; Hollywood 10, 122, 139

Marinetti, Filippo, 46
Marxism, 29, 40, 76, 87, 88, 91, 93, 94, 99, 102, 112, 118, 145,
    155, 171, 176, 213, 223; and aesthetics, 44, 66, 156. See also
    Socialist Realism
Marx, Karl, 34, 37, 58, 156. See also Fetishization of the com-
    modity
Mass communication media, 18, 21, 22, 27, 32, 35, 97, 147, 182,
    190, 191, 197, 198, 1299, 202, 203, 218, 267, 277
May, Todd, 215, 221n

MINOR COMPOSITIONS

As well as a multitude to come…

Lightning Source UK Ltd.
Milton Keynes UK
UKOW04f2303300114

225616UK00002B/21/P